Governance, Citizenship and the New European Football Championships

Over the past decade, European football has seen tremendous changes impacting upon its international framework as well as local traditions and national institutions. Processes of Europeanization in the fields of economy and politics provided the background for transformations of the production and consumption of football on a transnational scale. In the course of such rearrangements, football tournaments like the UEFA Championship or the European Champions League turned into mega-events and media spectacles attracting ever-growing audiences. The experience of participating in these events offers some of the very few occasions for the display and embodiment of identities within a European context.

This volume takes the 2008 EUROs hosted by Austria and Switzerland as a case study to analyze the political and cultural significance of the tournament from a multidisciplinary angle. What are the special features and spatial arrangements of a UEFA-esque Europe, in comparison to alternative possibilities of a Europe? Situating the sport tournament between interpretations of collective European ritual and European spectacle, the key research question will ask what kind of Europe was represented in the cultural, political and economic manifestations of the 2008 EUROs.

This book was published as a special issue of *Soccer & Society.*

Wolfram Manzenreiter is associated with the Department of East Asian Studies, University of Vienna, where he teaches modern Japanese society. His research is mostly concerned with issues of sports, popular culture, media, and labor in a globalizing world.

Georg Spitaler has widely published on sports, popular culture and the politics of nationalism. He is a university assistant at the Department of Political Science, University of Vienna, as well as an editorial board member of Austria's leading football magazine, *Ballesterer.*

Governance, Citizenship and the New European Football Championships

The European Spectacle

Edited by
Wolfram Manzenreiter and Georg Spitaler

Routledge
Taylor & Francis Group
LONDON AND NEW YORK

First published 2012
by Routledge
2 Park Square, Milton Park, Abingdon, Oxon, OX14 4RN

Simultaneously published in the USA and Canada
by Routledge
711 Third Avenue, New York, NY 10017

Routledge is an imprint of the Taylor & Francis Group, an informa business

First issued in paperback 2013

This book is a reproduction of *Soccer & Society*, vol.11, issue 6. The Publisher requests to those authors who may be citing this book to state, also, the bibliographical details of the special issue on which the book was based.

British Library Cataloguing in Publication Data
A catalogue record for this book is available from the British Library

ISBN13: 978-0-415-55106-9 (hbk)
ISBN13: 978-0-415-84874-9 (pbk)

Typeset in Times New Roman
by Taylor & Francis Books

Disclaimer
The publisher would like to make readers aware that the chapters in this book are referred to as articles as they had been in the special issue. The publisher accepts responsibility for any inconsistencies that may have arisen in the course of preparing this volume for print.

First issued in paperback 2013

Contents

SPORT IN THE GLOBAL SOCIETY – CONTEMPORARY PERSPECTIVES

Series Editor: Boria Majumdar

GOVERNANCE, CITIZENSHIP AND THE NEW EUROPEAN FOOTBALL CHAMPIONSHIPS

The European Spectacle

Sport in the Global Society – Contemporary Perspectives
Series Editor: Boria Majumdar

The social, cultural (including media) and political study of sport is an expanding area of scholarship and related research. While this area has been well served by the *Sport in the Global Society Series*, the surge in quality scholarship over the last few years has necessitated the creation of *Sport in the Global Society: Contemporary Perspectives.* The series will publish the work of leading scholars in fields as diverse as sociology, cultural studies, media studies, gender studies, cultural geography and history, political science and political economy. If the social and cultural study of sport is to receive the scholarly attention and readership it warrants, a cross-disciplinary series dedicated to taking sport beyond the narrow confines of physical education and sport science academic domains is necessary. *Sport in the Global Society: Contemporary Perspectives* will answer this need.

Titles in the Series

Australian Sport
Antipodean Waves of Change
Edited by Kristine Toohey and Tracy Taylor

Australia's Asian Sporting Context
1920s and 1930s
Edited by Sean Brawley and Nick Guoth

'Critical Support' for Sport
Bruce Kidd

Disability in the Global Sport Arena
A Sporting Chance
Edited by Jill M. Clair

Diversity and Division – Race, Ethnicity and Sport in Australia
Christopher J. Hallinan

Documenting the Beijing Olympics
Edited by D. P. Martinez

Football in Brazil
Edited by Martin Curi

Football's Relationship with Art: The Beautiful Game?
John E. Hughson

Forty Years of Sport and Social Change, 1968-2008
"To Remember is to Resist"
Edited by Russell Field and Bruce Kidd

Global Perspectives on Football in Africa
Visualising the Game
Edited by Susann Baller, Giorgio Miescher and Raffaele Poli

Global Sport Business
Community Impacts of Commercial Sport
Edited by Hans Westerbeek

Governance, Citizenship and the New European Football Championships
The European Spectacle
Edited by Wolfram Manzenreiter and Georg Spitaler

Indigenous People, Race Relations and Australian Sport
Edited by Christopher J. Hallinan and Barry Judd

Reviewing UK Football Cultures
Continuing with Gender Analyses
Edited by Jayne Caudwell

Soccer in the Middle East
Edited by Issam Khalidi and Alon Raab

South Africa and the Global Game
Football, Apartheid and Beyond
Edited by Peter Alegi and Chris Bolsmann

Sport – Race, Ethnicity and Identity
Building Global Understanding
Edited by Daryl Adair

Sport and the Community
Edited by Allan Edwards and David Hassan

Sport, Culture and Identity in the State of Israel
Edited by Yair Galily and Amir Ben-Porat

Sport in Australian National Identity
Kicking Goals
Tony Ward

Sport in the City
Cultural Connections
Edited by Michael P. Sam and John E. Hughson

The Changing Face of Cricket
From Imperial to Global Game
Edited by Dominic Malcolm, Jon Gemmell and Nalin Mehta

The Containment of Soccer in Australia
Fencing Off the World Game
Edited by Christopher J. Hallinan and John E. Hughson

The Flame Relay and the Olympic Movement
John J. MacAloon

The Making of Sporting Cultures
John E. Hughson

The Politics of Sport
Community, Mobility, Identity
Edited by Paul Gilchrist and Russell Holden

The Politics of Sport in South Asia
Edited by Subhas Ranjan Chakraborty, Shantanu Chakrabarti and Kingshuk Chatterjee

The Social Impact of Sport
Edited by Ramón Spaaij

Who Owns Football?
The Governance and Management of the Club Game Worldwide
Edited by David Hassan and Sean Hamil

Why Minorities Play or Don't Play Soccer
A Global Exploration
Edited by Kausik Bandyopadhyay

INTRODUCTION

Governance, citizenship and the new European Football Championships: the European spectacle

Wolfram Manzenreiter[a] and Georg Spitaler[b]

[a]*Department of East Asian Studies, University of Vienna, Austria;* [b]*Department of Political Science, University of Vienna, Austria*

Introduction

For any well-informed observer of European affairs, the cultural significance of football in Europe is evident to such a degree that football must be appraised as the one ubiquitous exception to the 'largely un-European mental universe of most Europeans'. Notwithstanding the pluralities of nations and political systems or the competition between regions and economies, '… what really united Europe was football', said the late New York-based scholar of European history Tony Judt.[1] The centrality of football in European cultures and societies has been established over time by its unique position as the national sport in almost any European country. In terms of popularity, participation rates, spectator turn-out, media presence, market size and marketing appeal, European football has not stopped growing in significance, even though tremendous changes have been set into motion over the past one or two decades. Processes of Europeanization in the fields of economy and politics provided the larger background for transformations of the production and consumption of football on a transnational scale, impacting upon its international framework as well as national institutions and local traditions. In particular, the growing dominance of the free market, which has been championed by the European Union ever since the Maastricht Treaty was launched in 1992, left its mark on club squads, national league rankings and the comparative significance of national and international tournaments. During the course of these new arrangements, Europe's inter-regional football tournaments like the UEFA Championship (hereafter the EURO) or the European Champions League transmogrified into mega-events and media spectacles of the first order, attracting ever-growing audiences within football stadia, host cities, European member nations and beyond.

Writing about football in 'The New Europe', Anthony King argued that a Durkheimian approach to the 'European ritual' of club football unearths the larger transformations of social relations and institutions within the political economy of a consolidating Europe.[2] His observation of the decentring of national or nationalist dimensions and the emergence of an embryonic 'European consciousness' among football fans is partly echoed by Levermore and Millward, even though they are aware of the fact that football can be simultaneously used as a vehicle to resist the formation of any such pan-European identification and to protest against the forces behind the processes of transnationalization in Europe.[3] Our very own contribution to the ongoing debate on football in the European mind is based on a multidisciplinary reading of the EURO 2008 and some of its ramifications, past and present. We agree with many commentators on the general observation that the European football mega-events, including the championship of national teams and club teams, have gained in significance in economic and cultural terms. We also consent to the claim that these and other transformations have been primarily triggered by a changing political environment and economic interests seeking to maximize profit-making under renewed legal conditions. We would not take issue with the general assertion that the realignment of fan solidarities across regions has a potential impact on the definition of new transnational collective identities, even though we do not foresee the complementary development, and ultimately acceptance, of Europe as a 'Nation XL'.[4] However, there is something more we have come to notice, and this is of great concern for the future of citizenship and governance within a European context.

Forestalling our conclusions, we dissociate ourselves from a reading of football as European ritual in which 'the social relations and social groups which are central to European society emerge with a clarity and force which is often absent elsewhere'.[5] Instead, we consciously employ the notion of 'European spectacle' when referring to the EURO in order to highlight the opalescence and opaqueness of a progress in which football has transgressed its traditional boundaries and expanded into new realms of public space and public sphere. The notion of spectacle is particularly well suited to emphasize a number of basic presuppositions we have on the nature and provisional outcomes of this transformation. First, the spectacular of the football tournament is very useful in practical terms to cover all the paradoxes, fissures and dissonances associated with the European multitude. As a matter of fact, Europe means different things to different people, and the intellectual labour of deconstruction which challenges and debates European identity is part of its cultural heritage.[6]

The following section of our introduction to *Governance, Citizenship and the New European Football Championships: The European Spectacle* will demonstrate the plurality and variability of the sometimes fragile, but in any instance fabricated, concepts of Europe in the particular contexts of political integration, the European framework of football bureaucracy and territorial spread. Second, and more to the point of the political consequences, the spectacle form conceals the transformation of organizational forms of power which are largely occurring without open public debate. The football spectacle is part of a wider process of the spectacularization of society in the sense that the definition of the public is increasingly subjugated to the needs of those forces that are emerging as the new political and economic elite within the context of Europe. These changes of governance, which impact on the definition of the public as much as on the notion of citizenship, may have started in the fields of sports and football but they do not end there. Hence their impact extends to any European citizen and the conceptualization of subject and state under the new forms of governance, as we discuss in the third section. We deal with the issue of spectacle and its political functions in greater detail in the fourth part of our introduction. In the final section, we summarize the debate on the 'New European Football Championships' asking what has changed, what is likely to be changed in the future and what are the conditions for its economic, cultural, as well as democratic sustainability?

What do they know of Europe, who only of Europe know?

Kipling's well-known lamentation on the ignorance of his English fellowmen who failed to recognize how much their social and economic way of life was owed to the oppressive conditions of colonial rule has been rephrased in various situations of relevance to the relationship between sport and the politics of representation. Most famously, C.L.R. James asked 'What do they know of cricket, who only of cricket know' to point at the working of colonialism and empire in the British game, which he criticized as an instrument of power and agent of political ideology.[7] In *The European Ritual*, Anthony King asked 'what do they know of Europe, who nothing of football know' to emphasize the significance of football for the symbolic display of social relations and passions within Europe and its potential impact on forging new identities in contemporary Europe. With regard to the EURO, we agree that a comprehensive knowledge about the production, management and governance of the football tournament will generate new insights into the meaning of Europe, or actually the making of meanings of Europe in progress. As stated above, we are more than just sceptical about the role of the EURO as a ritual in the sense that it symbolically displays the fabrics and principles of social reality; rather we believe that the European spectacle simulates an image of Europe that downplays the very concrete interests at stake in arbitrating the diversity of 'Europes' in terms of inclusion and exclusion, integration and boundary making.

Processes of Europeanization in football inevitably are bound to questions of territory and cultural identity. Yet to the geographer, Europe is something different than to the historian or the politician as the continental reference can relate to a physiographic distinction as well as to a cultural or a political one. Not only in the east and south-east with its seamless transition into Asian territory, boundaries often vary according to the positioning of the cartographer, historical conditions and particular objectives of parties involved in drawing the boundaries. In football, Europeanness is first of all defined and made visible by the right of a region to participate at European championships. For this purpose, a nation or a state must have its national association in charge of football be admitted by the governing body of European football, UEFA. The continental federation has recently seen its membership rapidly increasing after the downfall of the Iron Curtain and the dissolution of the former Soviet Union and its satellite states, and the Yugoslavian Republic, in the 1990s. Armenia, Georgia and Kazakhstan are some of UEFA's recent new-entrants from a region going beyond Europe's eastern geographical boundaries of the Ural Mountains or the Black Sea. In the south, Malta has long been considered part of Africa, like Cyprus, whereas Iceland in the north is geographically closer to Greenland than to the European continental shelf. Like Turkey and Israel, these 'fringe nations' have all been awarded formal European membership status as they are among the 53 UEFA member nations.

The expansion from the inaugural 25 members to its current size has impacted on the scope, duration and procedure of UEFA-owned and managed tournaments, their reach and relevance, market value and marketability. It has also affected the way the federation itself is organized and regarded as a political force and negotiation partner within different European frameworks. Internally, the diversity of members as well as the plurality of standards of membership have made any attempt of forging European unity and identity in football increasingly difficult. Fringe nations are not only located at the periphery of Europe, as Marschik reminds us in this issue; others are more centrally placed but have no entitlement to qualify for the European championships. Among them there are nations with a distinct language, tradition and collective consciousness of a cultural or ethnic community like the Basques or Catalans that even have a football association, but no state sovereignty. Others like Kosovo or Vatican City are sovereign but also not UEFA members. Then there are the irritating cases of

England, Northern Ireland, Scotland and Wales which have no state sovereignty but are recognized by UEFA as separate football associations for historical reasons and therefore expand the group of European Union-based football federations to a quantity exceeding the proper number of EU member states.

The European Union with its hybrid character of being a political project, a legal framework and a common market exerts strong and diverting influences on the conceptualization of Europe in the context of football. Particularly in political science, there is a tendency to limit the scope of Europe to the realm of the European Union. In this strict sense, Europeanization stands for 'the impact European integration is having on the individual nation states' as well as 'the strategies the individual Member States have adopted to respond to the challenges posed by European integration'.[8] For the level of European sports, this means that 'more and more legal instruments that are being adopted at European level also effect competences for sport. (…) At the same time, more and more decisions have been taken in the field of sport regarding the requirements the European Union is expected to meet.'[9] As a consequence, the conditions under which football now operates as an industry in each of the European nations are increasingly Europeanized. Switzerland, co-host of EURO 2008 together with Austria, is deliberately a member of UEFA but non-member of the European Union. Hence questions of the country's placement within Europe through football and the impact of the European Championships on Swiss national identity have evolved quite naturally, as Koller points out in this issue.

One of the key aspects of the European Union's policy in regard to sport has been the protection of the single-market principles. The Bosman ruling in 1995 implemented the liberalization of the European labour market for professional football and had considerable consequences on transfer regulations and nationality restrictions of national associations. Even those countries which are not bound to EU legislation have felt the impact of the European Court of Justice's ruling and the symbiotic relationship between football and media organizations as their citizens became equally targeted as players by the hiring policy of Europe's better- and best-paying clubs. UEFA contributed to the 'EUization' of European football by intentionally producing rules that are compatible with EU law, like the 'UEFA homegrown player rule' and the 'UEFA club licensing policy'. These rules are virtually defining a cross-European space in which the football industry operates. The centralized monitoring of club finances is promoted to secure 'financial fair play' and planned to be obligatory for any club performing in European competitions. As a best practice, licensing as a new standard of governance is hoped to filter down gradually into the regulatory inventory of national associations, which would be another significant step in the Europeanization of football. UEFA, which has started to offer 'European solutions to Europeanized problems' of competitive imbalance, has assumed a privileged position to mitigate between the EU and national members throughout the larger Europe.[10]

It must be noted that the dynamics inherent in this particular version of Europeanization are largely top-down. Brand and Niemann point to the fact that bottom-up and transnational processes and attempts to analyse their interplay have entered the debate only recently. Using the example of football, they argue for an understanding of Europeanization as a two-way process which is shaped by the interdependence of European and domestic levels. Moreover, they emphasize the fact that 'Europeanisation does not equate "EUisation"': 'Rather the EU is only part (albeit an important one) of the wider fabric of cross-border regimes in Europe in which other (transnational) institutions and frameworks also play a role'.[11] This can be exemplified by the type of agency generating or resisting change, either by creating transnational spaces that impact on the governance of football or by reacting towards attempts of EU regulation. This view is further elaborated in Brand, Niemann and Spitaler's examination of the Austrian example and the case of broadcasting rights, the Bosman ruling and the impact of the UEFA Champions League and UEFA Cup (now Europa League) on Austrian football in this issue.

Armstrong and Mitchell, using Borneman and Fowler's conception of Europeanization,[12] point to bottom-up practices of Europeanization that are not confined to elite actors and institutions but include 'everyday forms of social exchange which see "Europeans" increasingly interact with each other and thus practicing – if not "imagining" – a European community'. Sport, and especially the new European football, might be seen as a key site of such processes.[13] It could be argued, however, that football has played this role for a long time in the twentieth century (see Mittag and Legrand on historical phases in the evolution of the UEFA European Championships in this issue). Several authors have pointed to the role of the new European club football system – especially the UEFA Champions League – as a source of Europeanization,[14] and the televised European football market has been termed as a 'European public space'.[15] This has been observed in particular on the level of fan practices. It has been argued that the diversity of club teams players' line-ups in the post-Bosman era and the fact that many of the fans' favourite players at their local clubs are now non-nationals could change the fans' notions of representation and their 'existing identity patters' and create 'more "European" allegiances'.[16] The border-crossing popularity of some clubs from the big four European leagues (England, Germany, Italy, Spain) throughout Europe among many fans and *flaneurs* points to emerging transnational, post-traditional and de-territorialized fan cultures[17] and to a 'Euro-cosmopolitanisation' of football cultures.[18] Anthony King, emphasizing the importance of 'new localistic' ties and forms of solidarity that are increasingly differentiated from national identifications or at least have led to 'overlapping and even contradictory groupings and affiliations between clubs and the national team', has pointed to a developing European consciousness among football fans that is evolving out of a higher number of away games in European cup competitions, knowledge of transport systems and cities, as well as contacts with other European fans.[19] But it must be noted that this consciousness is not based on a common European identity or history, but rather on the desire of most fans of bigger clubs to see their team recognized on a European level.[20]

In his analysis of the UEFA Under-17 Championship 2009 in Germany, Tagsold (in this issue) highlights that questions of 'Europeanness' are also negotiated at smaller European tournaments among organizers, participants and local audiences.

In marked contrast to cosmopolitan optimism, Markovits and Rensmann, in their comparison with the US–American sport space, emphasize the prevalence of 'collective particularism' in European football that manifests itself in a high interest in national teams and national sport stars, whose sporting careers are followed by their fans also when playing for other European clubs.[21] This particularism has also been observed by Sanna Inthorn in her analysis of British and German media coverage of EURO 2008 (in this issue) and in several recent studies on media sport discourse and the production of national stereotypes through coverage of national teams.[22] Still, Markovits and Rensmann argue that national sports cultures, characterized by national, regional and local collective identities, have been altered by the effects of post-industrial globalization and have, for instance, led to more inclusive, post-religious and post-ethnic constructions of identity. Like Levermore and Millward, they see football both as an agent of Europeanization, but also as a space for contesting and resisting these changes.[23] Such a complex approach is capable of coming to terms with the politico-cultural schizophrenia in tolerating the apparent contradictions involved in anti-Europeanism on a societal level of everyday life as against the passionate pro-Europeanism of club supporters.

Hence it must be stated that monolithic concepts of identity are too static and simplistic to grasp the overlapping and multidimensional aspects of identifications in today's Europe. In this respect, it might be useful to differentiate between European identity and European identification, following Levermore and Millward's distinction between 'territorialized' concepts of collective identity and a more fluid 'sense of belonging'. They argue that the latter can be increasingly observed in the field of sport where consumer identities are generating 'more cosmopolitan forms of belonging' and 'the notion of a territorialized collective identity is (…) challenged by "transversal" interactions, resulting in a "sense of belonging" that can be shared by peoples across regions, thus transgressing local, national and continental boundaries'.[24] Pan-European identification is therefore less distinguishable and more transversal than national identity, encompassing a broader dimension that espouses a tolerance for diversity; a consciousness that complements, rather than replaces, national and regional identities and one that is 'de-spatialized and multi nodal', based on 'networks and flows' rather than the concept of territoriality.[25] Using Appadurai's theory of globalization, Martin emphasized the role of transnational *mediascapes* for creating 'new forms of social identity' and speculated to what degree this could lead to a *community of affect* (Dick Hebdige) 'based on Europe'.[26] However, the question remains whether such an 'emotional community' is in fact based on Europe, and not on football.

Football, governance and citizenship

Public responses to the process of Europeanization are to some degree characterized by assumptions that are often not made explicit, as has been the case within debates on globalization during the past two decades. In both instances, critical voices are abundant of the lurking suspicion that processes of integration and harmonization are in fact standing in the service of the neoliberal project. Governments giving up parts of their autonomy and regulatory power are said to be increasingly forced to adapt to forces beyond their control. As a consequence, the homogenizing impact of a common market and transnational fields of consumption threaten to undermine local traditions and cultural diversity. In marked contrast to such a taking of globalization, however, there are certain institutions that definitely are responsible for those transformations in Europe, at least within the limited realm of the European Union. Local and national actors are put under practical constraints by transnational laws and regulations that have been devised by elected politicians and the European Union bureaucracy. As we have argued, their impact can also spread beyond the political project. Hence, what we can observe is the emergence of new forms of *governance* within Europe, involving the cooperation of national governments, transnational agencies and non-governmental organizations.

Within political science, the concept of governance has become a useful tool to analyse the interplay of the classic political institutions of the nation state with new emerging international or supranational institutions and private or corporate actors. The 'governing' of citizens and the formulation of policies are no longer confined to the nation state. Sport, with its institutional history and ideology of 'subsidiarity',[27] its traditional embeddedness in the 'third sector'[28] and its national and international governing bodies, which have been partly transformed into global corporate organizations, has been identified as a field of governance par excellence.[29] This view can further be supported with a look on Foucault's original use of the term 'governmentality' ('gouvernementalité') as the 'managing of bodies', linked to 'the transformation of sovereignty from legitimacy to technique'.[30] European sport policy can thus be understood as a 'regime' with different governmental and non-governmental actors who engage in the regulation or 'governmentality' of sport.[31] However, we want to argue that the social, cultural and political impacts of today's sport mega-events, among them the European Championships, have transgressed the realm of sport governance. In fact, the political significance of these spectacles lies in their consequences for the overall governance of citizens, first of all in the host countries and host cities, but also beyond those demarcated places. The EURO affects the lives of millions of Europeans, not only football fans.

Moreover, both football's mega-events and the high-profile European club events also affect issues of *citizenship*.

First, the transformation of football in the last decades has produced conflicts that revolve around the question who 'owns' football. Male supporter cultures have resisted the restriction of their self controlled areas on the terraces through the introduction of new surveillance technologies, the designing of new all-seater stadiums and legal measures against football violence that were introduced throughout European football in the aftermath of the stadium disasters of the 1980s.[32] Some organized football fans have also opposed a number of the consequences of football's incorporation into a global 'media–sport complex'[33] that led to new forms of corporate club ownership or the adaptation of kick-off times to the dictate of television broadcast companies. Thus, the relationship between fans, clubs and sports governing bodies has been *politicized* since the 1990s throughout Europe.[34]

These struggles can be partly understood as conflicts around questions of community and representation.[35] Some fans came to the conclusion that they could not longer support 'their' clubs and founded new (amateur) clubs that – for them – epitomized all the values and traditions that their old clubs had lost. These new *fan-owned football clubs* – that often bear the names of the fan's former teams – have been founded in several European countries in recent years, following the English examples of AFC Wimbledon and FC United of Manchester. On a theoretic level, this can be understood as active participation in civil society and part of *cultural citizenship*, a concept that has been introduced to understand engagements in popular culture and acts of fandom as potentially political and democratic practice.[36]

Conflicts between football fans and (sports) governing bodies could also be observed in the run-up to EURO 2008 when organized Ultrá fan groups in Austria and Switzerland boycotted the European Championship as a symbol of the 'modern football' that they reject.

Second, crowd control in and around football stadiums since the 1980s throughout Europe has evoked discussions about the gradual suspension of *civil rights* in the context of football events. Security measures, such as CCTV, were introduced in football surroundings and later employed in other public areas. With the new urbanization of football's mega-events, the spatial logics of the stadium have been extended to the cities. This involves the partial privatization of public space through the advent of fan zones and new forms of crowd management within cities (see the contributions of

Hageman on 'Host Cities in a State of Emergency' and Lauss and Szigetvari on 'The Appealing Power of Fan Zones' in this issue).

Third, a major democratic issue involves the question about who governs, decides about, and profits from football mega-events. This issue can both be raised on the level of football governance, where a 'democratic deficit' regarding spectators as citizens has been observed,[37] but also with regard to institutionalized politics in the nation state and on a regional level. In the case of EURO 2008, and especially in Austria, the federal government, provinces and local host cities co-financed the football event, providing football arenas, related infrastructure and supporting programmes. Such processes leading towards the spending of public funds trigger questions of the EURO's economic, cultural and democratic sustainability (see Hachleitner and Manzenreiter and Horne in this issue).

Politics by other means: the European spectacle

Issues of governance and citizenship are inextricably linked with the form of the spectacle. Appealing and pleasing as the extraordinary event is, it is a useful device concealing the less-pleasant consequences of the introduction of new forms of governance, and even in the cases where these consequences are apparent, the spectacle helps reduce resistance against the transformations. As a unique performative genre, the spectacle draws on two different cultural traditions deeply rooted in European history. On the one hand, it features core elements from the ritual and festival of folklore culture. As Bakhtin's theory of the carnival explained, ritualized masquerades enabled all members of a social community to experience the inversion of everyday hierarchies, the transgression of social boundaries and the subversion of established orientation guides for a predetermined time–space.[38] Like the carnival, football historically emerged as a festival of status inversion, serving the double purposes of strengthening communal bonds and re-legitimizing power relations. For a certain time, when a state of exceptional circumstances framed the local community, everyday power relations were suspended and the austerity of the normal course of life was replaced by the excess and immoderateness of the festival. In a similar fashion, the modern sports spectacle offers itself as a time–space of merry-making, masquerade and deferral from the constraints of everyday life. Sports jerseys in the colour of the nation team, funny costumes playing on national stereotypes, beer-drinking in public before noon, hilarious acting in front of strangers, and spontaneous forms of fraternization with complete unknowns are some of the carnevalesque side effects that are acceptable within the context of the spectacle, but hardly beyond.

On the other hand, spectacles are informed by influences from baroque theatre and the market fair. The theatre of the spectacle was the dominant propaganda art of the counter-reformation, which attempted to replace medieval chaos by mannered and passive spectator crowds attending public ceremonies within zoned spaces and under police surveillance. Forging collective identity by means of spectacle did not work on the premise of conviction, but of overpowering, and since such demonstrations of state power were extremely expensive, the making of spectacles required the close collaboration of organizers and authorities. Market fairs enacted a different mode of social contract based on a particular conditionality of belief – the double spectacle of commodities and amusement, of merchandise and magic tricks, invited spectators not only to suspend, but also to sharpen their disbelief – and the secular social bond of exchange and commerce.[39] This implies, first, that spectacles have been associated with commercial purposes from early times and second, that this relation was commonly accepted as long as merchants/artists and consumers/visitors were equally aware of the double nature of the spectacle. As the aura of the 'spectacle as-if' is sustained by an economy of knowledge that enables all sides to behave as if the pretensions of the spectacle can be taken at face value, organizers of spectacles utilize a sophisticated machinery of information and disinformation in order to hold up the illusion of the spectacular event by promoting an official image of the spectacle for public consumption. Hence the spectator at the EURO usually believes they see a game, a play of two teams trying to excel at ball skills and technique, team play and fighting stamina. Yet s/he can equally well watch a number of well-paid specialists at work, the replay of national rivalries or the proxy competition for market leadership between rivalling sportswear brands.

In contemporary media-saturated times, spectacles are increasingly drawing on the stage techniques and narrative technologies provided by television and other modern media. As a media spectacle, the football contest is at the same time centred on a particular idea of a place and de-centred because it takes place in millions of places, in homes, sport bars and public viewing areas simultaneously. In doing so, it crafts the symbolic centre which is the represented place of the event. This should not be mistaken for the physical, geographical locality of the action. The symbolic place is constructed for and by the audience, and its meanings are mediated through its perception by the audience. Such a process of co-production is indicative of a shift from place-bound techno-industrial production of material objects to the multi-placed character of late modern production of symbolic goods, commodities and spaces.[40] Echoing the meta-social critique of Guy Debord's *La société du spectacle*, Kellner declared the 'sports entertainment colossus' to be responsible for the transformation of sports into a forum that sells the values, celebrities and institutions of the media and consumer society.[41] For Debord, who used the notion of the spectacle as a metaphorical key towards understanding the consumer society, the spectacle exceeds the cultural form of the mediated event by a long way. Although the mass media provide its most glaring superficial manifestations, the spectacle is not just a mere visual deception produced by mass-media technologies: it is a view of a world that has become objective, a social relation, mediated by images, and thus the ultimate commodity. In marked contrast to orthodox Marxism, power relations in the society of the spectacle are not reproduced in the world of labour, but in the cultural sphere of consumption. Yet the fetishism of the commodity prevents the subject from satisfying her/his actual human needs; it destroys any collective form of society by individualizing the subjects who are nonetheless forced into uniformities of action and thought for the purpose of stabilizing the structures of domination.[42]

Debord's cultural critique has been criticized as sociologically incomplete 'because it conflates the spectacle into the central dynamic of capitalist social relations, eliding it with the commodity form'.[43] But he certainly deserves acclamation for placing a kind of cultural analysis at the centre of political economy, a programme that has been further elaborated by microsociological and cultural studies approaches towards popular culture. Similarly to the French situationist, Abercrombie and Longhurst claimed that the world is constituted as an event, because everyday life has been deeply saturated by the media. But their notion of the event is based on its constitutional performative quality: 'the objects, events and people which constitute the world are made to perform for those watching or gazing'.[44] Seen as a performative genre, spectacles premise agency by dissolving the strict separation of actors/

performers from audiences/spectators. They do not discriminate between natives and strangers, and encourage active participation and even shares. Under the gaze of the watchful surroundings, spectators themselves turn into performers of their own script which is organized in relation to the core action of the protagonists but does not necessarily comply with it. Again it is the mediated character of the spectacle and the chance of instant stardom that amplifies the urge for rewards through performativity. Camera crews scrutinize the seating rows and insert particular eye-catching shots into the main action on the large stadium screen or the broadcasting feed.

Whereas traditional community unanimously agreed on the meaning of public rituals and communal festivals, late-modern society hardly can. As complex social formations replaced traditional communities, functional differentiation distinguished participants from spectators, actors from audiences and regular attendants from casual by-passers, whose insights, involvement and interests largely differ. Modern spectacles therefore are multi-vocal, and they have to be so because otherwise they would fail in communicating to multiple audiences, bridging the gap between frontstage and backstage, and in demarcating a time–space for performances of the self. In closing this discussion, we suggest grasping the EURO as a spectacle in the sense of the overpowering function of make-believe which mediates between frontstage and backstage programmes. Like any other spectacle, the EURO aspires after grandeur and acknowledgement for being unique, exclusive and extraordinary. Ritual symbolism, various staging techniques and the distributional channels of national and international media networks are used to achieve these goals. As the whole spectacle adapts itself around its own sensual, audiovisual potentials, it is the sensually stimulating, dynamic and exciting form that attracts mass participation and gives the spectacle its distinctive visual appearance. Success or failure is measured according to the extent to which mass participation and public acclamation for being a great event can be obtained.

Conclusion: what is new about the European Football Championships?

We hope to demonstrate with this issue that what separates the new European Football Championships from earlier stages of European football is exactly the new centrality of European sport mega-events for questions of governance, citizenship and Europeanization. The EURO spectacle transgresses the field of sport, and its cultural, economic and political impacts are reshaping the public space, as exemplified by the 'urbanization' of football. More and more, the governing of football seems to offer a showcase for new forms of governance and the reconfiguration of citizenship and civil rights in Europe. The 'footballization' of public spheres is evident in the amount of media coverage on football's mega-events or the need for political actors to link with the events and images of sport. Political rhetoric highlights the impact of the European Championships on national economies in the hosting countries (see Hachleitner and Manzenreiter in this issue).

With regard to processes of Europeanization and on an everyday level, high-profile European club competitions such as the UEFA Champions League and the recently introduced Europa League seem to have a stronger impact on European consciousness and new European senses of belonging among fans. Here, in the words of Tomlinson and Sudgen, 'people congregate around football (...) to make strong public declarations of who they are, what groups they identify with, what they stand for, and who and what they stand against'.[45] European Championships, by contrast, attract audiences far beyond the football community.

In both cases, football as a major social and cultural phenomenon plays a dual role in the formation of European citizenship as a site for social cohesion and integration as well as a site of social and cultural division and exclusion.[46] It has the power to generate audiences and to create affective and passionate identifications among consumers and fans. This gives sport a strong position to deliver social policy messages and to offer inclusive potentials. However, exclusionary practices in football can sometimes serve as the best examples for the very social problems that football is attributed to 'solve'. Social inclusions and exclusions on lines of faith, nationality, gender and disability are commonly discussed, albeit not always comfortably, whereas anti-homophobia policies have appeared in less than a handful of federations to date.[47] It might be argued that the modern 'particularistic' face of football is still more present in the (football-) nation-based European Championships than in late-modern European cup competitions.

This ambivalent dualism was also present in debates and social campaigns that were linked to EURO 2008 and several case studies in this issue highlight this fact: With the example of the EUROSCHOOLS learning project, Horvath and Rosenberg point to the pitfalls of anti-racist campaigning that tries to build on images of a 'Europe of nations', and Kimm and Sauer analyse the example of feminist anti-trafficking campaigns during the World Cup 2006 and EURO 2008. Selmer and Sülzle describe Austrian and German discourse on women and gender around EURO 2008 where women, in contrast to domestic club football, were portrayed as constitutive for a peaceful European 'football family'.

It remains an open question how the new European football will develop in the future and what the conditions for its economic, cultural and democratic sustainability will be. The financial crisis that has rocked the global economies since 2007 also had impacts on the neo-liberal, transnational European football project. A return to the old Fordist Keynesian regulatory regime seems unlikely, but King (in this issue) sees the emergence of a 'regulated transnationalism' in which 'the major clubs and their transnational interconnections will remain central features of the new era but their activities will be monitored and controlled by an regulatory complex consisting of national and international federations, European institutions, national governments and the clubs themselves'.

For us, two future scenarios of a UEFAesque Europe could be drawn: Europe may be in the process of becoming a 'new Empire' uncertain of the frontiers of its own discourses. This Empire could be the market and a set of arrangements assuring the surrender of state sovereignty to the movement of economic forces which exercise the ultimate authority in human affairs.[48] In this sense, we can expect the aggravation of concerns with the growing integration of sport and media, in particular television broadcast; the commercialization of sport enhancing the inequality in wealth which is endangering the sport's traditional role of solidarity; and the perceived threat to the 'European model' of sport, based on civil society actors.

Or, new partnerships between the state, sport associations and citizens are becoming engaged in the governance of football as well as other fields of public service, based on an emergent European 'public space'. Debates on financial fair play have already expanded into the public domain and mobilized in a transnational manner many of football's stakeholders, as well as national governments and European institutions; and football supporters constitute an opinionated, vocal community, where everyone has his view, including about the future of the sport and how it should be governed.[49]

In this collection on *Governance, Citizenship and the New European Football Championships: The European Spectacle* the reader will find evidence for both scenarios. However, most contributions point to the struggle over articulating marginalized voices and interests within existing hegemonies and power structures of the new European football.

In deciding on the title for this issue, we had to reflect on these conflicts over definitions; our initial idea was to use the title 'Football and the Production of EURO™pe', thus highlighting the way European (football) realities are shaped by discourse and power.

After consulting the journal editors, we opted for the current title. A decisive factor was legal concerns about the use of a trademarked term but also the editors' remark that the branded term EURO, let alone 'EUROpe', would not be self-explanatory, at least in English-speaking countries where UEFA's European tournament of national football teams is mostly still called the *European Championship*. The latter aspect might be seen as encouraging from a critical point of view and evidence for the open future of European football and the European project as a whole.

Notes

1. Judt, *Postwar*, 782.
2. King, *The European Ritual*.
3. Levermore and Millward, 'Official Policies and Informal Transversal Networks', 158–9.
4. Bernard-Henri Lévy, quoted by Frans Timmermans in a speech on the occasion of the opening of the academic year, Maastricht University, September 6, 2004.
5. King, *The European Ritual*, 16.
6. Pocock, 'Deconstructing Europe', 302.
7. James, *Beyond a Boundary*.
8. Groll *et al.*, 'Political Aspects of Sport in the European Union', 15.
9. Ibid.
10. Hill, *UEFA and the European Union*; Parrish and Miettinen, *The Sporting Exception in European Union Law*; García, 'UEFA and the European Union'.
11. Brand and Niemann, 'Europeanisation in the Societal/Trans-National Realm', 184–5.
12. Borneman and Fowler, 'Europeanization'.
13. Armstrong and Mitchell, *Global and Local Football*, 5.
14. Brand and Niemann, 'Europeanisation in the Societal/Trans-National Realm', 193–4.
15. Brown, 'European Football and the European Union', 142.
16. Brand and Niemann, 'Europeanisation in the Societal/Trans-National Realm', 194.
17. Mikos, 'Imaginierte Gemeinschaft', 102.
18. Roche, 'Europe, "the Cosmopolitan Condition"', 2.
19. King, *The European Ritual*, 11, 28, 202–3, 247.
20. Ibid., 203–5.
21. Markovits and Rensmann, *Querpass*, 22–5.
22. Crolley and Hand, *Football, Europe and the Press*; *Football and European Identity*.
23. Markovits and Rensmann, *Querpass*, 25, 42–4; Levermore and Millward, 'Official Policies and Informal Transversal Networks', 158–9.
24. Levermore and Millward, 'Official Policies and Informal Transversal Networks', 145.
25. Roche, 'Europe, the "Cosmopolitan Condition"'.
26. Martin, 'The "Europeanization" of Elite Football', 360–2.
27. The principle of subsidiarity (competences should remain at the smallest or lowest level) has been maintained by sport's governing bodies to claim organizational independence and autonomy from (national) governments.
28. Non-profit and non-governmental organizations, partly based on voluntary work.
29. Groll *et al.*, 'Political Aspects of Sport in the European Union', 13.
30. Miller *et al.*, *Globalization and Sport*, 97–109
31. Groll *et al.*, 'Political Aspects of Sport in the European Union', 11.
32. King, *The End of the Terraces*.

33. Maguire, *Global Sport*, 144.
34. King, *The European Ritual*, 170.
35. Brown, '"Not for sale?"'
36. Hermes, *Re-reading Popular Culture*, 21–40; Van Zoonen, *Entertaining the Citizen*, 63; Miller, *Cultural Citizenship*.
37. Brown, 'European Football and the European Union', 142.
38. Bakhtin, *Rabelais and His World*.
39. Roberts, 'Typology and Genealogy of the Spectacle', 65.
40. Bolin, 'Visions of Europe', 202–3.
41. Kellner, 'The Sports Spectacle', 40.
42. Debord, *Gesellschaft des Spektakels*.
43. Tomlinson, 'Theorising Spectacle', 57.
44. Abercrombie and Longhurst, *Audiences*, 78.
45. Sugden and Tomlinson, *FIFA and the Contest for World Football,* 4.
46. Brown, 'European Football and the European Union', 131.
47. Groeneveld, 'European Sport Governance, Citizens and the State', 429.
48. Pocock, 'Deconstructing Europe', 305–9.
49. Hill, 'UEFA and the European Union', 11.

References

Abercrombie, N., and B. Longhurst. *Audiences. A Sociological Theory of Performance and Imagination.* London: Sage, 1998.

Armstrong, G., and J. P. Mitchell. *Global and Local Football. Politics and Europeanisation on the Fringes of the EU.* London: Routledge, 2008.

Bakhtin, M. *Rabelais and his World.* Cambridge, MA: MIT Press, 1968.

Bolin, G. 'Visions of Europe. Cultural Technologies of Nation-States'. *International Journal of Cultural Studies* 9, 2 (2006): 189–206.

Borneman, J., and N. Fowler. 'Europeanization'. *Annual Review of Anthropology* 26 (2007): 487–514.

Brand, A., and A. Niemann. 'Europeanisation in the Societal/Trans-national Realm: What European Integration Studies can Get out of Analysing Football'. *Journal of Contemporary European Research* 3, 3 (2007): 182–201.

Brown, A. 'European Football and the European Union: Governance, Participation and Social Cohesion – Towards a Policy Research Agenda'. *Soccer & Society* 1 (2000): 129–50.

Brown, A. '"Not for Sale"? The Destruction and Reformation of Football Communities in the Glazer Takeover of Manchester United'. *Soccer & Society* 8, 4 (2007): 614–35

Crolley, L., and D. Hand. *Football, Europe and the Press.* London: Cass, 2002.

Crolley, L., and D. Hand. *Football and European Identity. Historical Narratives Through the Press.* London: Routledge, 2006.

Debord, G. *Die Gesellschaft des Spektakels* [The society of the spectacle]. Hamburg: Ed. Nautilus, 1978.

Garcá, B. 'UEFA and the European Union: From Confrontation to Co-Operation?' *Journal of Contemporary European Research* 3, 3 (2007): 202–23.

Groeneveld, M. 'European Sport Governance, Citizens, and the State. Finding a (Co-)Productive Balance for the Twenty-First Century', *Public Management Review* 11, 4 (2009): 421–40

Groll, M., M. Gütt, and J. Mittag. 'Political Aspects of Sport in the European Union. Status Report within the Framework of the Project "Sport in Europe – Social, Political, Organisational, Legal Transparency in Europe"'. German Sport University Cologne, Institute of European Sport Development and Leisure Studies. http://www.sport-in-europe.eu/images/stories/PDFFiles/politische%20aspekte_final_end_1201.pdf

Hermes, J. *Re-Reading Popular Culture,* Malden, MA: Blackwell, 2005.

Hill, J. *UEFA and the European Union: The Green Shoots of a New European Public Space?* Unpublished paper, 2007.

James, C.L.R. *Beyond a Boundary.* London: Stanley Paul, 1963.

Judt, T. *Postwar: A History of Europe since 1945.* London: Heinemann, 2005.

Kellner, D. 'The Sports Spectacle, Michael Jordan and Nike: Unholy Alliance?'. In *Michael Jordan, Inc. Corporate Sport, Media Culture, and Late Modern America,* ed. D. Andrews, 37–64. Albany, NY: SUNY Press, 2001.

King, A. *The End of the Terraces. The Transformation of English Football in the 1990s.* London: Leicester University Press, 1998.

King, A. *The European Ritual: Football in the New Europe.* Aldershot: Ashgate, 2003.

Levermore, R., and P. Millward. 'Official Policies and Informal Transversal Networks: Creating "Pan-European Identifications" through Sport?'. *The Sociological Review* 55, 1 (2007): 144–64.

Maguire, J. *Global Sport. Identities, Societies, Civilizations.* Cambridge: Polity Press, 1999.

Markovits, A.S., and L. Rensmann. *Querpass. Sport und Politik in Europa und den USA.* Göttingen: Verlag die Werkstatt, 2007.

Martin, P. 'The "Europeanization" of Elite Football. Scope, Meanings and Significance.' *European Societies* 7, 2 (2005): 349–68.

Mikos, L. 'Imaginierte Gemeinschaft. Fans und internationaler Fußball in der reflexiven Moderne'. In *Medienfußball im europäischen Vergleich,* ed. E. Müller, and J. Schwier, 92–119. Cologne: Herbert von Halem, 2006.

Miller, T. *Cultural Citizenship. Cosmopolitanism, Consumerism, and Television in a Neoliberal Age.* Philadelphia: Temple University Press, 2007.

Miller, T., G.A. Lawrence, J. McKay, and D. Rowe. *Globalization and Sport. Playing the World.* London: SAGE, 2001.

Parrish, R., and S. Miettinen. *The Sporting Exception in European Union Law.* The Hague: TMC Asser Press, 2008.

Pocock, J.G.A. 'Deconstructing Europe'. In *The Question of Europe,* ed. P. Gowan, and P. Anderson, 297–317. London: Verso, 1998.

Roberts, D. 'Towards a Genealogy and Typology of Spectacle. Some Comments on Debord'. *Thesis Eleven* 75 (2003): 54–68.

Roche, M. 'Europe, "the Cosmopolitan Condition" and International Sport: "Cultural Europeanisation" and EU Regulation in the Case of European Football'. Working paper presented at 'Europe and Cosmopolitanism' conference, Royal Holloway College, London University, 2004.

Sugden, J., and A. Tomlinson. *FIFA and the Contest for World Football.* London: Polity, 1998.

Tomlinson, A. 'Theorising Spectacle: Beyond Debord'. In *Power Games. A Critical Sociology of Sport,* ed. J. Sugden and A. Tomlinson, 44–60. London: Routledge, 2002.

Van Zoonen, L. *Entertaining the Citizen. When Politics and Popular Culture Converge.* Lanham, MD: Rowman & Littlefield, 2005.

Towards a Europeanization of football? Historical phases in the evolution of the UEFA European Football Championship

Jürgen Mittag and Benjamin Legrand

The Institute for Social Movements, Ruhr-University Bochum, Germany

In the last three decades, the importance of European football has grown considerably, both for national teams and for clubs. Today, European Championships and team competitions such as the UEFA Champions League attract nearly as much attention as the World Cup – even beyond the European continent. This historical overview shows the divergent and heavily disputed origins of Europe-wide national football competitions and traces the phases of the European tournaments. Particular attention is given to the driving forces and ideas that have influenced this trend. As a key issue, this overview explores how far this trend has led to the 'Europeanization' of football.

Introduction

At the beginning of the twenty-first century, the UEFA European Football Championship is considered to be not only a resounding success story, but also one of the world's most important sporting events – even beyond the borders of Europe. The recognition the tournament currently experiences has been present only since the 1980s, however, when the finals first began to be played in a format similar to the World Cup. In stark contrast, the first qualifiers in the late 1950s achieved considerably less impact and took place under comparatively tricky circumstances. But how is it possible to explain this discrepancy and also the relatively late adoption of a pan-European national tournament, while Latin America already had the *Campeonato Sudamericano* by 1916 and the continent-wide national team tournament of *Copa América* by 1975?[1]

Just how difficult and drawn-out the establishment of a European Football Championship was can be seen by looking at its forerunners of the 1920s. The first European national team tournaments in the late 1920s received only limited attention, because only a very geographically narrow range of countries decided to hold a football tournament of nations. The revival of these tournaments in the 1940s and 1950s remained, at least initially, just as limited to specific parts of the continent. But at what point and for what reasons did football achieve its Europe-wide dimension? This question is at the heart of this article, which presents an overview of the central strands of development and periods in the history of the European Football Championship. Particular attention is given to the development of UEFA, whose founding in 1954 was connected above all with the aim of adopting a pan-European Championship of national teams, although that was not established until 1958–60. The ultimately successful – but by no means straightforward – course that the European Championship took to the present will thereafter be considered as a 'tour d'horizon'.

With a view to the topic of 'Europeanization', which since the middle of the 1990s has received increasing attention from the academic community, this article investigates the still under-researched question of the extent to which the Europeanization of football can be identified. Europeanization, in terms of political science, is understood principally as the effects of European or European Community/European Union (EC/EU)-level politics on the member states of the EU. Europeanization in this sense is defined as a process 'by which domestic policy areas become increasingly subject to European policy-making'.[2] This view has been criticized, however, because not only the effects of European integration on member states or on individual actors and arenas, but also their repercussions on the European level have to be taken into consideration.[3] Consequently, the changing logical processes of national political bargaining are subsumed beneath Europeanization when they are directed towards the European level.

In the past few years, historical works on the concept of Europeanization have begun to expand beyond their narrow political scopes: notable key features are generally given processes and structures as well as the preconceived ideas and perceptions of internal European links that initiate transnational acts of exchange, interdependence or convergence. The reference point for Europeanization is determined not only by the political territory of the EU, but frequently also by the geographical construct of Europe. Given this broad definition, political science and historical approaches can be focused on the central question: what is being Europeanized, and to what degree? In order to produce results relevant to the issue of the European Football Championships, an expanded notion of Europeanization will, in this article, be taken as a basis. It will also include European awareness, as the following analysis relies primarily on media coverage.[4]

From an academic perspective, it should be noted that the history of the European Football Championship – and that of UEFA – has thus far received comparatively little attention. Although FIFA and the World Cup have been researched in detail,[5] the only available studies on the European dimension of football, aside from the usual event-orientated photo books, remain restricted to just a few analytical papers[6] and statistical overviews[7] on the history of the European Football Championship[8] and also on the genesis of club-level competitions.[9] In addition, there have recently been some political science[10] and legal studies[11] on the topic of the Europeanization of football. The early history of the European Championships and the European national team tournaments of the 1920s has barely been researched at all, nor have the organizational structures and the system of national federations. UEFA itself has been discussed principally in two publications on the occasions of the 25th and 50th anniversary of its founding, although only the second publication includes contributions from professional academics.[12] In light of the current state of research, the need for more in-depth studies on European-orientated football is apparent.

Predecessors and early tournaments

With the exception of the British Championship (the Home International Championship), which in 1883 had staged the world's first national team championship with the associations of England, Scotland, Wales and Ireland, the earliest transnational championships began with the football tournaments that have been played in the Olympic games since 1908.[13] Before World War I, the idea of Europe did not receive much attention, but by the 1920s – accompanied by a stronger public European consciousness[14] – a Europe-orientated perspective had become widely accepted.

The practice of regional championships in Europe, like those in Great Britain, also gained adherents in Scandinavia, where from 1924 to 1977 a Swedish-dominated Scandinavian Championship (the Nordic Championship) was played. A further step towards the establishment of a stronger pan-European football framework began with the Mitropa Cup, the first European club tournament. It received considerable attention, at least in those countries that took part.[15] The establishment of the Mitropa Cup in the 1920s is closely tied to the popularization and professionalization of football after World War I. By the 1920s, football had developed conclusively into a socially transcendent mass phenomenon in most European nations.[16] Fundamental impulses towards professionalization came in this context from the Austrian functionary Hugo Meisl, whose primary motive for establishing a European cup tournament was the drive for new sources of revenue. The implementation of the Mitropa Cup was ratified in July 1927 by representatives from Austria, Hungary, Italy and Czechoslovakia at a meeting in Venice.

Because it was impossible to obtain a majority in favour of the project of a European Championship of national teams at the December 1926 FIFA Congress in Paris, Hugo Meisl concentrated his plans on those countries in which professional football already dominated. At the same 1927 meeting in Venice where the Mitropa Cup was ratified, it was also agreed to establish a European tournament of national teams. Both tournaments were designed from the beginning to achieve a financial surplus for the participating clubs and federations.[17] Just two months later, on 18 September 1927, the first match of the so-called 'Švehla Cup' tournament was held in Prague between Czechoslovakia and Austria.[18] The tournament was formed as a series of two legs on a home-and-away basis which stretched over a long period, so that the first tournament lasted from 1927 to 1930. Included among the participating nations were those who also took part in the Mitropa Cup, that is the four founding countries from the Venice meeting: Austria, Italy, Czechoslovakia and Hungary, and also joining later Switzerland and Yugoslavia.

According to contemporary press reports, the new tournament was well-received by fans, and the relatively high number of spectators all but guaranteed its financial success. Although the leading European football nations played in Švehla Cup, the other nations of Europe expressed only a limited interest in the tournament and almost totally neglected any media coverage.[19] Nonetheless, the tournament had imitators, and soon several similar region-specific tournaments were established, including the 'Baltic Cup', which was first lifted in 1928, and the 'Balkan Cup' in 1929. These tournaments resulted in little more than regional interest and response, however.

During the period before the end of World War II, the concept of a European Football Championship was already present, if only in the thoughts and discussions of those involved, most notably in the ambitions of Hugo Meisl and general secretary of the French football association Henri Delaunay. But the time was not yet ripe for a European-wide championship. This was due to some prevailing attitudes that were diametrically opposed to professional football, but also to technical restrictions (consider the travel times) and the resistance of FIFA, which was devoting itself entirely to the preparations required for the World Cup, whose success was at this time by no means certain.

The idea of a European cup for national teams was quickly seized upon by the member countries of the Mitropa Cup, again after World War II. By 1948, a new tournament had begun under rules and a timeframe similar to the Švehla Cup. The first post-war winner was Hungary over Czechoslovakia in 1953. A second round of the newly renamed 'Dr Josef Gerö Cup' was played from 1954 to 1960, but by then, it was already overshadowed by the establishment of UEFA.

The founding of UEFA

Although South America had already founded a continental association (CONMEBOL) in 1916, there were no such moves to do likewise in Europe for a long time. In general, this was due to the fact that Europe was dominant within FIFA: its headquarters were first in Paris then, from 1923, in Zurich, and the head of FIFA was always from a European country. Even as late as 1954, four of five FIFA vice presidents came from Europe. Just as in other areas of European society, the end of World War II caused sweeping changes in the structures of football. At this time, many new states joined FIFA as a result of de-colonization, resulting in the European associations being left behind even in terms of pure numbers. Therefore, at the 1950 FIFA congress in Rio de Janeiro, there was a marked increase in support for the idea of establishing a continental association within Europe, along with a European championship and a European league tournament.

The first overtures towards the founding of an umbrella federation came from the trio of Ottorino Barassi (president of the Italian football federation), José Crahay (general secretary of the Royal Belgian Football Union) and Henri Delaunay (general secretary of the French Football Federation).[20] On 27 May 1952, the three pioneering federations were joined by 13 others at a meeting in Zurich to develop the first outline for a European football union.[21] That initiative failed, but at an extraordinary convention in Paris in November 1953, FIFA amended its statutes and permitted the setting up of continental federations. After several additional informal meetings, on the eve of the 1954 World Cup, the decisive step was taken to establish UEFA. On 15 June 1954 – during the World Cup finals in Switzerland – a joint umbrella organization of European football federations 'in an as yet undecided form' was concluded in Basel.[22] The invitation included 25 of the 31 European federations, but ultimately 29 were listed as founding members because certain delegations joined during the course of the World Cup and others delegated their mandate. The 'Group of European Federations' as it was then known, voted the Dane Ebbe Schwartz as president on 22 June 1954.

From the end of October 1954, the 'Union of European Football Associations' was established as a (con-)federation. The individual member federations maintained their sovereignty and, with the exception of voting procedures, decisions had 'the character of recommendations'.[23] Only after the rule changes in 1961 would UEFA's resolutions become binding for all member federations. The difficulty of finding common positions in the initial phase was demonstrated at the first UEFA convention, which took place between 2 and 3 March 1955 in Vienna. The newly founded UEFA did not immediately succeed in organizing a European Championship, something that was presented not only in the press but also in a statement by UEFA president Schwartz as the central motivation behind its founding. Only 10 (other sources speak of 18) from a total of 30 of the federations in attendance supported holding a European Championship, with a clear majority of the supporters coming from Eastern Europe. In this context, the appointment of a commission to check and finalize the plans was at first the lowest common denominator that could be agreed upon.

Humble beginnings: the first phase (1955–1968)

After Delaunay's death in 1955, his son Pierre followed in his father's footsteps and pursued the idea of a European Nations' Cup. The proposal presented at the second UEFA congress in July 1956 in Lisbon again received no majority, with many nations expressing reservations. It was argued that the international match calendar would be too full, the recently healed war wounds would be re-opened, and the dangers of commercialization would arise. Against this backdrop of criticism, Pierre Delaunay developed a new system for a single tournament played over two years with a short final stage, which he duly presented at a meeting of the UEFA executive committee in Cologne and then at the third UEFA congress in Copenhagen on 28 and 29 June 1957. Delaunay once more met with renewed and hefty criticisms. Critics of the idea argued that this new tournament would disrupt the preparations for the World Cup and hinder the formation of new teams during the period between World Cups.[24] In addition, they did not want to give up on friendly matches, because this was a lucrative source of income for the federations.

The closeness of the final decision for a European Championship is not only reflected in the results of the vote - fourteen ayes and seven nays with five abstentions – at the UEFA congress in Copenhagen in June 1957. In order to achieve the 16 scheduled teams, the registration deadline had to be extended by another four months. Only by the UEFA congress of 1958 in Stockholm had 17 of the 33 European federations finally joined the European Nations' Cup. The heavyweights of the football world – such as Italy, England and Germany, as well as Belgium, the Netherlands and Switzerland – ultimately passed on the chance to take part. With only 15 votes to 13, the realization of the first Nations' Cup came to pass, and in honour of its intellectual father it was proposed to be named the 'Henri Delaunay Cup'.[25]

The Švehla Cup and the other European nation tournaments of the interwar period acted as role models, as documented by the fact that the tournaments initially used the format of a lengthy series of heats that stretched out for almost two years, as opposed to the large final round as in the World Cup. In contrast to its predecessors, these tournaments were based on a knockout system of home and away matches. On 27 September 1958, the first match took place in Moscow, with a lively crowd: over 100,000 spectators packed into the Lenin Stadium for the premiere.[26] After a total of 22 months and a four-day final round in France (6–10 July 1960) with only four teams, the Soviet Union was declared the first 'European Champion'. Only 18,000 spectators attended the final between the USSR and Yugoslavia. The first quarter final between France and Austria had, in the December before, attracted 45,000 spectators in the Parisian Stade Olympique Yves-du-Manoir in Colombes.[27] This was almost as many as an average World Cup qualifying match at the time.[28]

The second 'European Championship', which began with qualifying matches from 1962 to 1963 and culminated in the finals in 1964, received much more attention. In total, 29 UEFA member federations registered for the tournament. With the notable exception of Germany, it included all major European football nations. The final in the Bernabéu Stadium, where the Spanish defeated the Soviet Union 2-1, was seen by considerably more than the official 79,115 spectators (estimates go as high as 125,000). As more and more teams began to take part in the tournament, the media naturally started to pay more attention; for example, the final was shown on German television for the first time.[29] Even though the tournament's attendance rose, its corresponding impact was anything but robust, however; this can be seen in the result pages of the daily newspapers. Even in April 1968, the European Football Championship results were printed in fourth place in Germany. Evidently it was more important – from a German perspective – to show the results of the Bundesliga, the European Champion Clubs Cup and Germany's western regional league.[30]

Growing attraction and consolidation: the second phase (1968–1980)

By the third tournament in 1968, the informally used moniker 'European Football Championship' was officially adopted, although the name took a little while longer to establish itself fully, as for a long time, it was referred to as the 'European Nations' Cup' in reports.[31] Because 31 of the 33 federations had registered – the exceptions were Iceland and Malta – the format of the European Championship qualifiers was changed from knockout rounds to a system of groups. Nevertheless the finals remained with four participating teams.[32]

Looking at the media coverage, it is clear that there was a noticeable increase in attention given to their own side's matches. German journalists were even beginning to travel to European Championship away matches. Reporting extended beyond the game to encompass the host countries themselves. In addition to the change in the amount and context of coverage in the print media, coverage on radio and television also changed; the 1968 European Championship saw the new medium of television explore its possibilities and limits. Although the match between Albania and Germany could only be broadcasted on German TV late in the evening on the following day,[33] the German home match against Yugoslavia was a first in Europe: it was – at least for the first half in which there was sufficient daylight – the first 'outdoor original broadcast in colour'.[34] The growing media presence at the tournament corresponded with the increase in both the importance of sport and the enthusiasm of the football supporters. All three factors re-enforced each other markedly and allowed the European Championship to consolidate during the decade after the final in Italy (1968).

As the significance of the tournament grew for the federations, so did its importance for the players. Before the 1968 tournament, German team captain Willi Schulz remarked in an interview when asked if players would hold back during international games in favour of league matches: 'Although I also like to earn a lot of money, it is always a huge honour for me to be able to wear the national strip, especially as the player's value is increased'.[35] The European Championship was lucrative in its own right, however. Whereas a German national team player in 1967 received 'at best' the equivalent of €125 per European Championship match regardless of the result, Yugoslavian footballers earned €250 from a win.[36] Nine years later it was even more rewarding to take part. Every Dutch player in 1976 received around €7500 if the team reached the finals, while the German players had to be content with €5000 for winning second place. Even though the number of spectators for the 1976 European Championship remained low until the final in Belgrade (a total of 106,087 spectators for four games), the European Championship had managed to establish itself firmly with the fans, players and the media.

UEFA responded to the period of consolidation by enlarging the European Championship tournament itself. By 1980, with eight finalists now in Italy, the format became increasingly similar to the World Cup. In conjunction with this expansion, there was also the hope that, after the financial losses of the 1972 and 1976 European Championships, a profit could be turned. UEFA president Artemio Franchi assured 'sparkling revenues' at the title matches, which were being plugged as a 'mini World

Cup', and predicted average visitor numbers of around 50,000 per game. The German Football Association (DFB) 'cautiously' projected proceeds of an equivalent of €250,000.[37] They were wrong. As indicated in Table 1 the average number of spectators at the European Championship in Italy was only around 25,044. Barely any enthusiasm from the fans and disappointing games of the lowest calibre – that was the judgement of contemporaries after the finals. Even the opening match between Czechoslovakia and West Germany only managed an official audience of 10,500 at the Olympic Stadium in Rome. For the final between Belgium and Germany, 47,860 tickets were sold for the Olympia Stadium, but 80,000 spectators could have got their hands on a ticket. Only for the host Italy did 148,304 people travel to its three group matches, but even these matches were not sold out.

The officially sanctioned research into the causes of this limited success drew out several different factors: the aftermath of the bribery scandal in the Italian league, the excessive temperatures and the times of the matches clashing with the Giro d'Italia cycling tournament were just some of the many put forward.[38] UEFA president Franchi spoke of a 'series of errors', but stressed two factors in particular: first, the kick-off times were so close to each other that the spectators could not return home to watch television quickly enough, or vice versa. Second the entrance fee, at an average of €16, was too high.[39]

The matches also managed to bore both the crowds in the stadiums and those in front of their televisions. The reaction to the format change established in 1980 was evaluated critically. The British *Daily Mail* spoke of 'football melancholy', the French *L'Equipe* pointed out only the final's 'European format' and Dutch newspapers were of the opinion that European football had brought shame upon itself with this tournament. The reason for the harsh pronouncements regarding the quality of play and the bad atmosphere in the stadiums can be laid at the feet of the defensive way teams were matched. This tactical strategy appeared to be the result of the format of the tournament itself: the team qualified for the final after only three first-round matches, but because only the leader of the group reached the final, a defeat caused elimination. Even before the final match, a possible solution was discussed at the UEFA congress. Franchi argued for a European Championship in the form of play-offs, but with a knockout system 'so that boring 0-0 matches are no more'. FIFA vice president and DFB boss Hermann Neuberger put forward two alternatives: one was to adopt semi-final matches to 'mitigate the groups'; the other was to play home and away matches as in the UEFA Cup.

New approaches and further expansion: the third phase (1984–1996)

Instead of further shrinking the sessions, UEFA expanded them even further in 1984, when Neuberger's first proposal was implemented and semi-final matches were introduced. This led the teams to place much greater emphasis on offensive play. The number of draws was reduced to three and the average goals scored increased from 1.93 during Euro 1980 to 2.73 in the 15 matches of Euro 1984.[40]

But the TV rights and ticket prices were not touched by UEFA after the Italian debacle. High ticket prices were once again considered as the main reason why the stands remained empty in 1992 in Sweden and in 1996 in England. Television coverage was nevertheless increased instead of reduced, as had been discussed after 1980. Whereas German TV only broadcasted one game per match day live in 1980, by 1984 nearly every match was shown. By this point, TV forged ahead as a medium regardless of the doubts and misgivings of football functionaries.[41] Increasing attention was also being paid by the print media, however, not just to the matches being played by their own team, but also to the preparations and matches of other countries. But it was not only the media coverage that marked a new era for the European Championship in 1984; the fan culture had also changed. For the first time, the fans themselves began to travel en masse. This development was not entirely consistent, dependant as it was on the activities and success of the individual teams, but it was novel and noticeable. While the German team still struggled to fill the stadium in the border town of Lens,[42] the Danes came in droves to France. Unexpectedly, when the Danish team made it to the semi-finals, they became the 'everyman favourites'[43] not only because of the full stadiums, but also because of the buoyant party spirit that resulted from tens of thousands of fans travelling to the host cities. The successful French team also helped ensure a jubilant party atmosphere at their home European Championship.

This travel mania continued to the 1988 European Championship in Germany, despite the problem of hooliganism. This time it was the Dutch, who even before the first kick-off came to blows over tickets. Tens of thousands of 'Oranje' fans travelled to each Dutch match of the tournament. In total, more than a quarter of the tickets for the 1988 European Championship were sold abroad. With 838,677 official spectators and an average of 55,911 tickets sold per game, EURO 1988 achieved a spectator record that still stands to this day as revealed in Table 1.[44] Even before the start of the tournament, 90% of the tickets were sold, and only four matches were not sold-out in the end. By this point, it had become clear that the format of the tournament was a success.

The spectator figures could not be repeated in the peripheral European country of Sweden in 1992, where the costs and ticket prices were noticeably higher. Whereas in 1988, the most expensive seat cost €50, the price in Sweden had risen to €85.[45] At first glance, the spectator numbers sank again after the climax in Germany 1988, but overall, a gradual increase in the average number of spectators can be observed from the beginning of the European Championship up to 2008. That is particularly valid for all the matches in which the host country did not participate. The number of spectators in the stadiums rose precipitously and stayed at over 80% of capacity up to 2008. The rate of spectators in matches without host participation has risen on average from 22% in 1980 to 67% in 1984 and 81% in 1988. This trend might show improved planning but it also indicates clearly a continuously rising interest in the matches of foreign teams.

Despite all this, EURO 1992 still marked a further expansion in the importance of the European Championship. In accordance with the organizers' motto 'small is beautiful', even with a relatively small audience increased revenues were achieved.[46] Of the organizers' €29m revenue, only €7m came from the sale of tickets. 'I am convinced that the idea of small stadiums was the right one. The big money is made nowadays from the sale of TV broadcasting rights', the president of the Swedish football federation, Lars-Ake Lagrell opined. As host, the Swedish federation received earnings of €1.5m, with each participating federation pocketing a guaranteed €2.3m.

The three finals in France, Germany and Sweden show that a period of expansion had begun. Spectator numbers and revenues reached new heights as the organization and marketing was professionalized. Along with increasing sporting prowess came growing media attention. The finals became increasingly attractive travel destinations for entire legions of fans. By this time, the European Championship has become a pan-European media phenomenon and also a meeting point for fans from a number of nations. The 1980 European Championship may have been a failed experiment, but from it, UEFA learnt and enacted a revised format.

Table 1. Attendance rates: European Championships 1960–2008.

					Matches without participation of host			Matches with participation of host		
European Championship	Host	Average capacity (all stadiums)	Average attendance	Average attendance (%)	Average capacity	Average attendance	Average attendance (%)	Average capacity	Average attendance	Average attendance (%)
1960	France	40,000	19,739	49	40,000	21,575	54	40,000	17,904	45
1964	Spain	107,000	39,063	37	90,000	21,212	24	124,000	56,914	45
1968	Italy	72,500	48,029	66	40,000	21,834	55	83,333	56,761	68
1972	Belgium	51,000	26,737	52	50,500	22,548	45	51,500	30,926	60
1976	Yugoslavia	79,500	26,521	33	79,500	24,334	31	79,500	28,709	36
1980	Italy	79,385	25,044	31	79,58[illegible]	17,767	22	78,900	43,239	54
1984	France	52,074	40,093	77	52,38[illegible]	35,188	67	51,446	49,904	97
1988	Germany	66,605	55,911	84	65,599	53,396	81	69,374	62,829	91
1992	Sweden	32,806	28,632	87	33,645	28,343	84	30,500	29,426	96
1996	England	50,604	41,168	81	44,951	34,411	76	80,000	76,306	95
2000	Belgium-The Netherlands	38,246	35,537	93	34,771	31,236	89	48,237	47,900	99
2004	Portugal	41,879	37,151	89	38,253	32,966	86	56,966	54,588	96
2008	Austria-Switzerland	37,214	36,870	99	35,165	34,780	99	45,754	45,579	100

Source: Authors' calculations based on Grüne 2008.

Challenging the World Cup: the fourth phase since 1996

UEFA drew on this experience and as the EURO 1996 began in England with 16 teams the innovation of quarter-final matches was born. The main reason for this expansion was the series of political developments in Europe since 1989. The developments and factors that had bolstered the European Championship in preceding periods – audience enthusiasm and commercial success – had by 1996 led to an imbalance. The stadiums were often poorly attended, although the host said early on that 90% of all tickets had been sold.[47]

It could hardly be a lack of interest from the fans; EURO 1996 celebrated a total of cumulated 6.9 billion TV viewers in 150 countries delivered via 180 channels, a new record.[48] In Germany alone, the final was seen live by 27.85 million people.[49] That the spectator figures were no longer the sole measure of economic success for the host is underscored by a few other figures: 1996 the UEFA earned 44% (€65m) of the total revenue with ticketing, just 36% (€53m) came from TV contracts. Eight years later ticketing has become just the third most important way of revenue with only 9% (80m) of income. The revenue from TV rights had increased to €560m (66%) in 2004.[50]

Ninety per cent of this income in 1996 was passed on to the participating federations: the European Championship title alone was glided with an extra €6.75m. In its 1992 title win, Denmark had to be content with a mere €4m.

It was not just because of growing spectator numbers that the European Championship was increasingly being compared with the World Cup, however. Egidius Braun credited the number of registered federations: 'Everyone has the aim of joining in such a tournament, particularly one that has almost achieved the level of a World Cup. As, with the exceptions of Argentina and Brazil, the footballing elite are all together in England'. And before the 23rd regular UEFA congress, UEFA president Lennart Johansson praised the level of sporting prowess as well as the significance of UEFA: 'the tournament is of the highest level. The European Championship in 1996 is better than the 1994 World Cup'.[51] All the same, Johansson was not pleased by all of the new innovations. Like his predecessor in office Franchi, who after the introduction of the tournament structure of eight participants in 1980 also planned to return to the status quo ante, the Swede wanted to take a step backwards after the expansion to 16 teams in 1996: 'I have doubts that we can keep this format. We must consider if other formats might not be fairer, perhaps even retuning to the old [format]'.

At the same time, Johansson let it be known that the 16-team format, premiered in England, could not be expanded further. Since then, however, UEFA has decided that the number of teams participating in the 2016 European Championship will be raised to 24.[52] With this, an even stronger rivalry between the World Cup and the European Championship will be apparent. That the European Championship has stood in the shadow of the World Cup can be traced to some extent to the fact that between 1950 and 1975, five of the eight World Cup tournaments were held in Europe, and the European Championship with its shorter finals resulted in only a limited potential for competition. With the expansion of the final rounds in 1980, the professionalization since 1984, the end of the cold war in 1989 – and the numerous newly created states in Eastern Europe – the growing number of participants and the improved performance, the European Championship has become an ever stronger competitor to the World Cup. This is even more apparent as the intervals between World Cup tournaments played in Europe become ever greater.

Conclusions: between Europeanization and 'eventization'

Through the roughly sketched developments of the European Football Championship, several clearly separable periods can be seen. Despite numerous cross-border contacts, football in the first half of the twentieth century was predominantly nationally organized. The second half of the twentieth century looked very different; by the middle of the 1950s, a dense network of border-transcending competitions and common structures within professional football had been formed. In this regard, early attempts at a European Championship were long assigned a subordinate role. By the 1980s, the European Championships could compete on the same level as club tournaments.

Those who seek explanations for the development of the European dimension of football from the mid-1950s are led unavoidably to the contemporaneous process of European integration. With the Council of Europe on one side and the treaties on the European Coal and Steel Community, the European Economic Community and the European Atomic Energy Community on the other, Europe established in the 1950s a variable, but nevertheless increasingly integrated, framework of institutional and rule-based interactions. These steps were flanked by further bi- or multilateral forms of cooperation, such as the formation of the (West-) European Broadcasting Union (1950) or the Eurovision network (1954). With these strands of development, the initial foundation was laid for the unification of the (western) European continent that has served as the basis for the state of integration today. Yet despite the temporal coincidence between the political and football dimensions of Europe, these interactions must not be overemphasized. The founding of UEFA in 1954 was primarily the result of sport-related factors and had little impact on the overall political and economic integration of the continent. The founding of a European football umbrella organization was, in particular, the result of the desire to form a more efficient interest group on the international stage and in regard to FIFA as well. That a tournament of national teams arose as a result of UEFA's founding was not a politically led process; rather it was due much more to the dogged engagement of a few individual actors.

The reasons behind football becoming a more and more important frame of reference for Europe are closely tied to socially, culturally and technically induced processes. During the period after World War II, countless transnational interactions were formed, including technical and economic discoveries, growing migration and increased transnational mobility, as well as cultural transfers and changing methods of communication. The framework of increasingly multifaceted processes of interdependence – consisting of structural connections above and below the level of the nation-state – is mirrored in football. Here, the media in particular acted as a decisive catalyst in football's new European dimension. This increased significance can be seen in the extent to which the media reported on the European Championship. In this regard, it would appear that acts of Europeanization and eventization have mutually strengthened one another. Only after a format was found for the European Championship that could make it attractive both to the television audience of the entire continent and to the spectators in the stadiums, and only after an overarching framework was established – and the atmosphere for fans and partying needs were given greater attention – would the media increasingly take notice. This served to further boost the tournaments' attractiveness and popularity.[53]

It must not be overlooked that the scope of both the European Single Market (Bosman Case) and the formation of the UEFA Champion's League did not necessarily result from Europeanization as a top-down processes and a corresponding convergence, but seen in light of the European Championship, they seem to have come about via other processes of Europeanization. Irrespective of the growing importance of UEFA as perhaps the most important regulatory actor in the European football regime,[54] the Europeanization of the European Championship is to be understood on more socio-economic terms with successive transnational interdependencies, rather than in terms of the reactive processes of convergence in response to challenges on the European level.

Regarding football, it seems that the European dimension has less to do with the narrow EC/EU-level conception of Europeanization grounded in political science, than with the broader and more process-orientated Europeanization approach in the discipline of history. The extent to which it is possible to state further convergence processes in light of this reasoning remains to be seen. Nevertheless, Europe continues to lack media structures that would allow communication to a Europe-wide public, in a common language spoken by all Europeans, and the intermediary actors that would serve as transmission lines between national states and social bonds. Football cannot replace these elements, but through its 'pull' and its potential for mobilization with the media it has the potential to create, at least in part, a European consciousness.

Notes

1. Today there is also a Central American/Caribbean CCCF Championship (founded in 1941), an Asian Championship (1956) and the Africa Cup (1957).
2. Börzel, 'Institutional Adaptation to Europeanization in Germany and Spain', 574.
3. Eising, 'Europäisierung und Integration', 387–416; Radaelli, 'The Europeanization of Public Policy', 27–56.
4. Particular attention will be devoted to the *Westdeutsche Allgemeine Zeitung* (WAZ), which continues to have the highest circulation in the Ruhr, the region that has the strongest football tradition in Gemany, as well as a keen interest in all matters European due to the dominance of the coal and steel industries. Additional sources include the nationwide press of Germany and several other states in Western Europe.
5. Eisenberg *et al.*, *Fifa 1904–2004.*
6. Connelly, *Spirit High and Passion Pure.*
7. Robinson, *Soccer*; Grüne, *Fußball EM Enzyklopädie 1960–2012*; Ionescu, *The Complete Results and Line-ups of the European Football Championships 1958–2008.*
8. Schulze-Marmeling and Dahlkamp, *Die Geschichte der Fußball-Europameisterschaft.*
9. Mittag, 'Europa und der Fußball', 155–76.
10. Brandt and Niemann, 'The Europeanization of German Football'; Mittag, 'Die Europäische Union und der Fußball', 203–18; Brand and Niemann, 'Europeanisation in the Societal/Trans-National Realm', 181–201.
11. Caiger and Gardiner, *Professional Sport in the EU*; Parrish, *Sports Law and Policy in the European Union*; Lehmkuhl, 'Der lange Schatten staatlichen Rechts'.
12. Europäische Fußball-Union 1979; UEFA 2004.
13. The first Olympic football tournament was held in 1900 as a demonstration.
14. Heater, *The Identity of European Unity*; Delanty, *Inventing Europe. Idea, Identity, Reality.*
15. Mittag, 'Europa und der Fußball', 155–76.
16. Eggers, *Fußball in der Weimarer Republik.*
17. Huber, *Die Geschichte des Wiener Fußballs 1923–1998.*
18. Skocek and Weisgram, who in the run-up to Euro 2008 produced one of the few works to date on the early history of the European Championship, have established that this tournament was known in German-speaking areas as the 'Europapokal' or 'Europameisterschaft', and sometimes even 'Internationaler Cup', while it existed under the name of 'Europá Kupa' in Hungary, in Italian as 'Coppa Internazionale', in France as 'Coupe Internationale Européenne' and in Czechoslovakia as 'Mezinárodní Póhar'. Because the then leading Czech politician and Minister Antonín Švehla had donated the victor's trophy it became

known for a time at least as the 'Švehla Cup'. See Skocek and Weisgram, *Die Europameister – Eine Heimkehr*.
19. Still, in the 1934 World Cup between Italy and Czechoslovakia and in the 1938 World Cup between Italy and Hungary, on both occasions the two finalists were member countries of the Švehla Cup.
20. Europäische Fußball-Union, *25 Jahre UEFA*; UEFA 2004, *50 Jahre UEFA.*
21. UEFA 2004/I: *50 Jahre UEFA*, 45.
22. Ibid., 46.
23. Ibid.
24. Schulze-Marmeling and Dahlkamp, *Die Geschichte der Fußball-Europameisterschaft*, 30.
25. Bangerter, 'Die UEFA einst und jetzt', 24.
26. *WAZ*, 28 September 1958.
27. *WAZ* December 14, 1959.
28. *WAZ* June 28, 1957. The qualifying matches were seen at the time as good business. In 45 deciding games prior to the 1958 World Cup 2,153,000 spectators were counted, ~ 48,000 per game.
29. *WAZ* June 20, 1964.
30. *WAZ* April 4, 1968.
31. *WAZ* April 6, 1967.
32. Heimann, 'Die Fussball-Europameisterschaft', 166–8.
33. *WAZ* December 15, 1967.
34. *WAZ* October 9, 1967.
35. *WAZ* December 14, 1967.
36. *WAZ* June 7, 1967.
37. *Frankfurter Allgemeine Zeitung* June 11, 1980.
38. Süddeutsche Zeitung June 11, 1980.
39. *Frankfurter Allgemeine Zeitung* June 23, 1980.
40. Schulze-Marmeling and Dahlkamp, *Die Geschichte der Fußball-Europameisterschaft*, 168.
41. These misgivings led to several attempts at limiting television broadcasting, beginning with the 'Vienna accord' of 1955 up to the 'framework of co-operation between football and TV' in 1978.
42. *WAZ* June 18, 1984.
43. *WAZ* June 28, 1984.
44. The term EURO was established at the 1988 European Championship in Germany and has been used regularly since then, actually becoming part of the logo in 1996.
45. *WAZ* June 10, 1992.
46. With a seating capacity of only 37,725, Ullevi stadium in Göteborg was the largest of this tournament. In total, 431,001 spectators saw the 15 matches. Only five matches – three of them involving the Swedes – were sold-out.
47. *WAZ* June 11, 1996.
48. *Frankfurter Allgemeine Zeitung* July 1, 1996.
49. *WAZ* June 29, 1996.
50. UEFA, Finanzbericht 2007/2008, 46.
51. *WAZ*, June 27, 1996.
52. *Kicker* March 4, 2009.
53. Pyta, 'Nicht mehr im Abseits', 65–77.
54. Garcia, 'UEFA and the European Union', 202–23.

References

Bangerter, H. 'Die UEFA einst und jetzt'. In *25 Jahre UEFA,* ed. Europäische Fußball-Union, 11–50. Bern: UEFA, 1979.

Börzel, T.A. 'Institutional Adaptation to Europeanization in Germany and Spain'. *Journal of Common Market Studies* 37, 4 (1999): 573–96.

Brand, A., and A. Niemann. 'The Europeanization of German Football'. In *German Football: History, Culture, Society,* ed. A. Tomlison and C. Young, 127–142. Abingdon: Routledge, 2006.

Brand, A., and A. Niemann. 'Europeanisation in the Societal/Trans-National Realm: What European Integration Studies Can Get Out of Analysing football'. *Journal of Contemporary European Research* 3, 3 (2007): 181–201.

Caiger, A., and S. Gardiner, ed. *Professional Sport in the EU: Regulation and Re-Regulation.* The Hague: TMC Asser Press, 2000.

Connelly, C. *Spirit High and Passion Pure: A Journey Through European Football.* Edinburgh: Mainstream Publishing, 2000.

Delanty, G. *Inventing Europe. Idea, Identity, Reality.* Houndmills: Macmillan Press, 1995.

Eggers, E. *Fußball in der Weimarer Republik.* Kassel. Agon Sportverlag, 2001.

Eisenberg, C., P. Lanfranchi, T. Mason, and A. Wahl. *Fifa 1904–2004. 100 Jahre Weltfußball.* Göttingen: Die Werkstatt, 2004.

Eising, R. 'Europäisierung und Integration. Konzepte in der EU-Forschung'. In *Europäische Integration,* ed. M. Jachtenfuchs and B. Kohler-Koch, 387–416. Opladen: Leske und Budrich, 2003.

Europäische Fußball-Union, ed. *25 Jahre UEFA.* Bern: UEFA, 1979.

Garcia, B. 'UEFA and the European Union: From Confrontation to Co-operation?' *Journal of Contemporary European Research* 3, 3 (2007): 202–23.

Grüne, H. *Fußball EM Enzyklopädie 1960–2012.* Kassel: Agon Sportverlag, 2008.

Heater, D. *The Identity of European Unity.* Leicester: Leicester University Press, 1992.

Heimann, K-H. 'Die Fussball-Europameisterschaft'. In *25 Jahre UEFA,* ed., Europäische Fußball-Union, 163–77. Bern: UEFA 1979.

Huber, J. *Die Geschichte des Wiener Fußballs. 1923–1998. 75 Jahre Wiener Fußball-Verband.* Wien: Wiener Fußball-Verband, 1998.

Ionescu, R. *The Complete Results and Line-ups of the European Football Championships 1958–2008.* Cleethorpes: Soccer Books, 2008.

Lehmkuhl, D. 'Der lange Schatten staatlichen Rechts: Verrechtlichung im transnationalen Sport'. In *Verrechtlichung – Bausteln für global Governance?,* ed. B. Zangl and M. Zürn, 179–97. Bonn: Dietz, 2004.

Mittag, J. 'Europa und der Fußball. Europäische Dimensionen des Vereinsfußballs vom Mitropa-Cup bis zur Champions League'. In *Das Spiel mit dem Fußball. Interessen, Projektionen und Vereinnahmungen,* ed. J. Mittag and J-U. Nieland, 155–76. Essen: Klartext, 2007.

Mittag, J. 'Die Europäische Union und der Fußball. Die Europäisierung des Profifußballs zwischen Bosman- und Simutenkow-Urteil'. In *Das Spiel mit dem Fußball. Interessen, Projektionen und Vereinnahmungen,* ed. J. Mittag and J-U. Nieland, 203–18. Essen: Klartext, 2007.

Parrish, R. *Sports Law and Policy in the European Union.* Manchester: Manchester University Press, 2003.

Pyta, W. 'Nicht mehr im Abseits. Fußball als Gegenstand bundesdeutscher Geschichtswissenschaft'. In *Fußballsport und Wissenschaftsgeschichte. Jahrbuch 2006 der Deutschen Gesellschaft für Geschichte der Sportwissenschaft e.V.,* ed. J. Court, A. Müller, and C. Wacker, 65–77. Berlin: LIT, 2007.

Radaelli, C.M. 'The Europeanization of Public Policy'. In *The Politics of Europeanization,* ed. K. Featherstone and C.M. Radaelli, 27–56. Oxford: Oxford University Press, 2003.

Robinson, J. *Soccer: The European Football Championships 1958–2004.* Cleethorpes: Soccer Books, 2004.

Schulze-Marmeling, D., and H. Dahlkamp. *Die Geschichte der Fußball-Europameisterschaft.* Göttingen: Die Werkstatt, 2008.

Skocek, J., and W. Weisgram. *Die Europameister – Eine Heimkehr.* Wein: Echomedia, 2008.

UEFA, ed. *50 Jahre UEFA,* 2 Vols. Nyon: UEFA, 2004.

From the stadium to the fan zone: host cities in a state of emergency

Anke Hagemann

HafenCity University Hamburg, Germany

This article focuses on the repercussions of EURO 2008 in the city of Zurich and describes the new urban dimension of large-scale football tournaments, using two complementary developments as a guide: first, the urbanization of football events, since they increasingly involve the host cities and their public spaces; and second, the gradual eventization of the host cities, as they increasingly attempt to use these events to further their own interests. The main thesis is that the stadium has become a spatial prototype for the temporary and long-term changes observable in urban spaces, projecting its functional, economic, social and regulatory conditions into public spaces. Finally, the text accentuates the 'state of emergency/state of exception' as a key phrase in the multilayered discourses around the large-scale event and its instrumentalization for a city's political and spatial reconfiguration.

> During the European Football Championship 2008, all of Zurich is in a state of emergency. This event is not limited to the sportive competition, but it also entails many other interests which are not carried out in the stadiums, but in urban space. For three weeks, Zurich has been transformed into a 'FAN CITY' – a place where special rules apply.
>
> (Project Fancity 2008, Zurich)

> In the last few days, the country has been turned into a fairground. The train stations and stadiums are decked out, the public transit systems are prepared, the security deployments planned and tested.
>
> (*Neue Zürcher Zeitung*, June 7–8, 2008)

Introduction

The UEFA European Football Championship, like the FIFA World Cup, is a nationally organized tournament for which host countries are chosen. However, the cities in which these tournaments take place have gained more and more importance in the last few years. Traditionally, the host cities were merely home to the championship stadiums. But developments such as the growing number of spectators and the establishment of live broadcasts of the games in public spaces have recently transformed the role of the host cities, turning them into significant arenas for mega-sports events. During the UEFA European Championship 2008, the host cities even acted as UEFA's contractual partners, positioning themselves as independent stakeholders in the planning of the tournament, and replacing the centralized national organization committee, which played a leading role in the FIFA World Cup 2006 in Germany. The contractual agreements between the cities and UEFA, called 'Host City Charters', stipulated each partner's interests, regulated the implementation of concrete measures, and allocated costs and benefits between UEFA and the public authorities.

This article is, first and foremost, an attempt to describe the new urban dimension of large-scale football tournaments, using two complementary developments as a guide: first, a phenomenon we can call the urbanization of football events, since they increasingly involve the host cities and their public spaces; and second, the gradual eventization of the host cities, as they increasingly attempt to use these events to further their own interests. Afterwards, we attend to the concrete impact football events have on urban spaces, and the patterns and strategies related to them. The main thesis is that the stadium has become a spatial prototype for the temporary and long-term changes observable in urban spaces, projecting its functional, economic, social and regulatory conditions into public spaces. Finally, the article will deal with the 'state of emergency/state of exception' as a key phrase in the multilayered discourses around the large-scale event and its instrumentalization for a city's political and spatial reconfiguration.

This article focuses on the repercussions of EURO 2008 in the city of Zurich. It is based upon research conducted in the course of a public event series at Rote Fabrik Zurich that dealt in a critical way with the urban impacts of the European Football Championship 2008.[1] Essential sources of information include observations and cartographic documentation conducted in the field, reports in the press and qualitative interviews with experts.

The urbanization of the football event

Today, at large-scale football championships, only a fairly small elite is granted access to the games in the stadiums. Both the fans' mobility and the demand for tickets have grown considerably in recent years; simultaneously, the share of tickets available to the general public has been reduced. In order to compensate for the fact that many fans end up without tickets, big-screen live broadcasts of the tournament games are typically provided in urban public spaces. These broadcasts, which go by the fake-English term 'public viewing' in German-speaking countries, and which were first implemented on a large scale during the FIFA World Cup 2002 in Japan and South Korea, were quickly established as the primary stage for each subsequent tournament. During the World Cup 2006 in Germany, public viewing was declared to be an official, integral part of the tournament in each of the 12 host cities, and dubbed 'FIFA Fanfest'. EURO 2008 adopted and refined the concept, renaming it 'fan zone'.

With the advent of public viewing, the tournament obtains – alongside the generic space of the stadium – a specific place in the heart of the city. The focus of the event is displaced from the actual occurrences of the match to the place where the event is represented through media and collectively received. Whereas the stadiums are mostly filled with guests of honor, VIPs, corporate representatives, the press and some lucky ticket winners, the complementary urban areas are increasingly considered to be the proper arenas for all local citizens and football fans – a place for the common people. Thus, when the media want to show local reactions, they tend to report from public viewing areas, capturing a dynamic atmosphere that can hardly be expected to be found in today's stadiums. The built environment of the cities becomes an experiential space, a stage for the spectacle – with wide-reaching consequences: urban spaces are suddenly expected to act as stadium venues, offering the same qualities and meeting the same requirements in the areas of logistics, security and marketing.

At the same time, the cities' local distinctions and landmarks are used as a high-profile, media-friendly backdrop. Accordingly, the four Swiss host cities chose centrally located and prestigious places for official public viewing in their 'fan zones': Zurich picked the downtown Sechseläutenplatz on its lakefront, Basel used the shore of the Rhine, Geneva the downtown Plaine de Plainpalais and Berne the plaza in front of the Federal Palace of Switzerland. The streets chosen as routes for visitors, referred to as 'Fan Miles' or 'Fan Boulevards', carefully stage-managed the walk through each downtown area to the fan zone.

Thus, the event uses the city as a resource: first of all, public viewing allows for an expansion of the tournament venue. Urban areas can often accommodate many more visitors than stadiums. Zurich's Letzigrund Stadium, for example, offered only 30,000 seats for the European Cup, whereas the city's fan zone allowed for up to 45,000 spectators. The entire Zurich Fan Mile played host to ~ 2.7 million people during EURO 2008.[2] Naturally, this meant an incredibly large opportunity for additional marketing in conjunction with the event: fan zones and Fan Miles transformed downtown public spaces into areas of leisure and consumption, displaying a massive density of gastronomy, entertainment, merchandising products and advertising.

Taking its cues from the FIFA World Cup 2006, UEFA demanded exclusive advertising and sales licenses for its sponsors in the public viewing areas of EURO 2008: within the fenced area of the fan zone in Zurich, all visible advertising belonged to the official sponsors. Searches at the entrances were therefore not only intended to prevent risks to safety; at the same time, they were meant to minimize the introduction of advertising from external sources in the form of printed T-shirts, baseball caps or flyers, as well as to keep visitors from bringing along their own food and drinks. Here, only the sponsors' branded products (such as Coca-Cola, Carlsberg or McDonalds) were to be bought, sold and consumed. All other foods for sale were rendered anonymous, reduced to basic descriptions such as 'chocolate bar' or 'ice cream' and advertised only with neutral illustrations. The fact that in the fan zones and along the Fan Miles, only beer from the Carlsberg Group was allowed, led to longstanding conflicts with local bars and restaurants. When established beer gardens along the Rhine in Basel refused to sell only Carlsberg, they were eventually separated from the public viewing area by a fence.

Additionally, the various surfaces of the city are used as a basis for advertising displays more and more often – either by the event organizers and their official sponsors, or by many other companies who indicate their presence at the event using advertisements with a football theme. In Zurich, a city that has typically been conservative about allowing large-scale advertising, the sight of the EURO 2008 tram cars, covered in advertisements for Coca-Cola, Carlsberg, Swiss Air and Credit-Suisse moving through the city from November 2007, was highly unusual.

Along with the extensive use of existing advertising space, many temporary, object-like advertisements could be found in and around the fan zone and Fan Mile. These included the shells and backs of the event architectures, the flags and banners called 'Host City Dressing', the standardized roofs of the booths, printed sunshades and various furniture systems. Additional distinctive features included the large temporary sculptures built especially as vehicles for advertising. In Zurich, for example, visitors arriving at the central train station were greeted by 11 gigantic figures of football players, so large that they reached to the roof of the station concourse – and wearing Adidas shoes almost as large as compact cars. The temporary brand worlds, designed in the corporate style of big companies as product showrooms or theme parks are taking this commercialization of urban space on another level. In Zurich, you could find the Carlsberg Relax Zone, the Swisscom Showroom or the Family Park of the Migros supermarket chain, consisting of a provisional fast food restaurant and a small leisure park for children. Additionally, in the fan zones and stadiums, special zones were designated as 'commercial display' areas for the official sponsors. In the Zurich fan zone for example, a small passage with corporate pavilions was set up, alluring visitors with information, fun and entertainment.

The European Championship and its presenter, UEFA, thus profit from the host cities in many ways: as a significant enlargement of the venue, as an additional commercial platform, as a vehicle for advertising and as a display for the sponsors. Additionally, UEFA can count on each of these augmentations being largely bank-rolled by public funding and public services. The city of Zurich provided a total budget of CHF18 million for EURO 2008, CHF8 million of which were spent on provisions required for event hosting in the areas of organization, security, traffic control and waste disposal.[3] Substantial public services were additionally financed at the federal level, where a total of CHF82.5 million were earmarked for the European Championship. By contrast, UEFA contributed only a marginal amount of money to the costs of the fan zones and of public transportation associated with EURO 2008.[4] 'It's a general catch phrase that profits are privatized, while costs are democratized,' says Daniel Rupf, head project manager of Zurich's public preparations for EURO 2008. 'Because the UEFA and the FIFA have a very clear monopoly on these types of mega-events, and they know how to use it. But the rules of this game were clear to us from the beginning.'[5]

The eventization of the city

The questions as to why cities are still willing to shoulder the high burdens and costs of hosting a large sporting event, why they allow private organizations to dictate the conditions of these events and why cities even feverishly compete for the privilege of hosting them, are hardly ever asked today. The common-sense notion that host cities will profit from events seems obvious, although the evaluations of the most recent World Cups and European Championships.[6] no longer support the argument that large football events have positive short- or medium-term economic effects.[7] Instead, before and after EURO 2008, Switzerland repeatedly pointed to the inestimable positive effects in destination marketing. 'We are convinced that the marketing of the European Championship is a long-term investment,' said Maurus Lauber of Zürich Tourismus in January 2008. 'We are quite conscious of the fact that we will have fewer visitors in June 2008 than in June 2007, since Zurich will have hardly any business or convention tourism during the EURO 2008. However, our goal is the long-term positive positioning of the destination Zurich, and the EURO 2008 is the springboard for that goal.' Beyond these anticipated image benefits, Lauber mentioned several other desirable effects connected to the football event: Zurich is actively taking part in the world's third-largest sporting event. That advances many projects that would otherwise never have been possible. The Letzigrund Stadium would never have been approved by all of the authorities so quickly if it weren't for the European Championship waiting in the wings. Likewise, during such a large project, so many people who haven't ever spoken to one another before end up working together, whether in the area of security, transportation or marketing. It strengthens us for the time after the EURO 2008, too.[8] The high-profile staging of the city in terms of global destination marketing, the creation of new supporting organizational structures, the truncation of decision-making processes, the learning effects in administration, and the total mobilization of all resources were described by the urban sociologists Hartmut Häußermann and Walter Siebel in 1993 as the central motivation for the 'Festivalization of city politics', by which the event is made into an instrument of urban development.[9] Their thesis seems to be more relevant than ever today.

Host city marketing

'Seize the opportunity' was the motto of city marketing: the enormous amount of media attention for the European Championship was meant to be steered toward Switzerland and the host cities in order to provide for a long-term facelift for the Swiss image and for the largest possible 'return on investment'.[10] Both in Austria and in Switzerland, each host city presented its own EURO 2008 logo – within a set of design guidelines. Additionally, each city had its own slogan, such as 'Berne makes miracles', 'Basel, more than 90 minutes', or 'Living Zurich'; Switzerland had its own advertising campaign with the slogan 'Discover the Plus'. Despite intensive cooperation between the cities, each city was essentially devoted to its own success and competed for overnight guests with the others. At the same time, the two host countries were in direct competition: without the use of targeted marketing efforts, many worried that Austria, a country experienced in self-promotion, would end up attracting most of the attention for itself, and that Switzerland would end up with the short straw – the so-called 'Korea effect' observed during the World Cup 2002 in Japan and Korea.[11] For EURO 2008, Zurich's promotional efforts were mostly directed towards the international press. The city attempted to 'dispense with old, clichéd impressions of the city'.[12] and to present itself as a 'dynamic and creative experience and science destination',[13] a favoured destination for tourism, economic development and lifestyle.

Urban spaces play an entirely new role in this type of marketing: when host cities become the 'calling cards' of a nation, fan zones turn into the cities' 'showcases'.[14] The city is increasingly represented not only by the stadium, but also by the public viewing areas: 'The "UEFA fan zone Zurich" was to be the most beautiful fan zone, the heart of the attractions in Zurich.' Therefore, the choice of a location for the fan zone was not only based on issues of capacity and transportation, but also 'ultimately reasons of location marketing supported the decision.'[15] Through the positioning of the fan zone in the skyline of Lake Zurich, the city was presented as a 'lifestyle metropolis on the water' – with a lovely view of the Alps in clear weather. The Fan Mile on the bank of the Limmat River developed connections to other important sightseeing attractions, such as the Grossmünster Cathedral, whose towers were augmented with LED displays as a part of the 'Kirche 08' initiative. As part of the so-called 'Host City Dressing', the most important pedestrian streets in the city were decorated with official EURO 2008 flags or traditional celebratory flags; the facades of the Swiss Federal Institute of Technology and the University of Zurich, which tower over downtown, were decorated with thematically planned light projections. Spotlights were specially installed to provide attractive nighttime lighting for the buildings on the Utoquai lakeside promenade.

Mobilizing the people

Alongside the provisions for international marketing, Zurich also attributed great importance to internally focused marketing, that is, public relations and offerings intended for the city's own population. 'Zurich's residents should feel free to identify themselves with the football festival and, at the same time, to participate actively.'[16] Even the EURO 2008 slogan 'Living Zurich' (German: 'Wir leben Zürich') appealed explicitly to the city's residents. Citizens' identification with their city was meant to be strengthened across all cultural and social divides.[17] Germany's World Cup slogan 'A Time To Make Friends' ('Die Welt zu Gast bei Freunden') as well as the atmosphere of the 2006 tournament were considered exemplary, making an active and enthusiastic populace an important aspect of Zurich's destination marketing during EURO 2008. At the same time, these types of initiatives are meant to increase residents' acceptance of the event and its various related arrangements and irritating side effects. In this context, Häußermann and Siebel refer to the 'staging of "public spirit"' as well as the concept of 'elating the masses and generating a willingness to follow'.[18]

Pacemaker for urban development

The potential for public mobilization inherent in a major event was, in Zurich, first used to press ahead with the building of the stadium: as it became clear that ongoing legal battles could prevent the timely construction of the stadium planned on the area of the old Hardturm Stadium, authorities saw the accelerated construction of the new Letzigrund Stadium as the only possibility to take part in the European Championship. The Zurich voters' broad approval of the public expenditure for the stadium in June 2005 was interpreted as an official affirmation of the residents' desire to take part in EURO 2008. The construction of the new Letzigrund Stadium could only be finished on time because of the precondition that there would be no objections to the plans and that all parties concerned would cooperate smoothly. Häußermann and Siebel describe such phenomena this way: 'Large events function as "time machines" … which bring about an extreme truncation of normal planning time spans and also allow for frustrating and time-consuming conflicts with a fragmented opposition to be cut off'.[19]

From stadium to fan zone

As a result of the growing mutual and intertwined interests of the event in the city and of the city in the event, urban spaces are, to an increasing degree, temporarily transformed in their physical and functional structure. Within these concrete transformations, patterns and strategies can be identified that reveal the spatial logic of the urbanized event or the eventized city, respectively. The essential thesis is as suggestive as it is plausible: the stadium functions as a prototype for the transformation of urban spaces. Public viewing turns the city into a provisional stadium and the urban spaces are forced to function as event venues: they must accommodate tens of thousands of visitors and offer the same density and atmospheric qualities as a stadium; they must enable frictionless accessibility and make emergency routes available; and they must simultaneously fulfil the same commercial demands and security requirements as a stadium. These conditions give rise to two different spatial strategies: the installation of temporary stadiums in the city, or the conversion of urban spaces into temporary stadiums. The first strategy, which fabricates spaces enclosed by makeshift constructions and separates them from the urban context, could be observed at the 'Adidas World of Football' in Berlin 2006 which was in fact a miniature replica of Berlin's Olympic Stadium, placed in front of the Reichstag. Similarly, the 'UBS Arenas' – public viewing facilities awarded to 16 small Swiss cities by the UBS bank – and the so-called 'ninth stadium' near Basel were all based on a closed, stadium-like model. The four Swiss host cities, however, planned to profit from the high number of expected visitors and international media attention. Their strategy called for their downtowns to be used as a picturesque setting for public viewing. Accordingly, the pretty facades of the buildings facing the Federal Plaza in Berne or those surrounding Basel's market square served as enclosures for an atmospheric urban football arena.

In order to meet the various demands on these spaces, a great deal of effort was invested in physical changes and technical interventions: in order to provide comfort for spectators, not only standing-room areas, but also seating, stands and canopies were provided. Analogous to today's trends in stadiums, public viewing areas were fitted with differentiated hospitality and VIP zones; additionally, television cameras and members of the media required their own places. Last but not least, since the World Cup 2006, it has become obvious that the security implications of massive public viewing events are essentially the same as those which present challenges in football stadiums. With the FIFA Fanfests in 2006, the practice of fencing in public viewing areas and performing security checks on visitors, as well as video surveillance of the entire area and the stewarding and policing by private security firms, became standard. Outside of opening hours or in case of overcrowding, the area could be closed completely. Most of these security measures were only made possible by the fact that the public viewing areas were temporarily placed under the domestic authority of a private organizer; that is, they were temporarily privatized. At the same time, this legitimated the exclusion of unwanted people or objects from the area on the basis of a set of house rules that read exactly like stadium regulations. The stadium-like security standards of the FIFA Fanfests were adopted in their essential form by the UEFA fan zones in 2008.

Just as in 2006 during the World Cup, Zurich's official public viewing took place at the Sechseläuten Platz, a traditional festival area on the shore of Lake Zurich. On game days, the adjacent street was barricaded and incorporated into the fenced area of the fan zone so that it could accommodate up to 45,000 spectators. The different areas for spectators were divided into large standing-room areas that could be used free of charge, 2600 seats on a set of stands with a canopy, and various exclusive areas for the media and VIPs. The seats on the stands, for which CHF15–20 tickets were already on sale in February 2007, were outfitted with separate entrances and electronic ticket control. At the top of the stands, there was a gallery with seven stadium-like 'VIP Sky Boxes' for guests of honor, sponsors and members of the media. Also, so-called 'Party Boxes', which were meant to be affordable for 'ordinary' residents of Zurich, were installed on the stands. In front of the centrally located 62 m^2 viewing screen, there was a canopied stage. On the lake, a 1600 m^2 floating 'hospitality platform' was installed. VIP guests could reach the hospitality platform – with its own gourmet open-air restaurant, lounge area and a separate floating viewing screen – using a footbridge.[20]

The Zurich fan zone can be defined as a hybrid of the two spatial solutions described above: the L-shaped set of bleachers and the accompanying viewing screen composed an arena closed on three sides, which turned its back to the city and was only open toward the lake. According to the spatial principles of the stadium, therefore, the event subjects urban spaces to its own (event-based) logic, classifying the spectators according to their societal status, buying power or consumer preferences and then directing them to various areas using a highly differentiated accessibility system. The increased demand for exclusivity is met by creating privileged areas which are separate from universally accessible urban spaces. Staying with the image of the stadium, it is possible to compare the Fan Miles which lead to the fan zones, and even the tourist attractions of the city, to the increasing multifunctionality in stadiums themselves, additional entertainment and commercial opportunities intended to increase the length of spectators' visits. Just like the stadium's economic considerations, its hermetic sealing and control techniques are also projected into the city. A piece of public space is temporarily cut out of the urban context, fenced and given over to the control of a private event organizer, who is then allowed to economically exploit it and regulate the ways in which it will be used.

The staging of a state of emergency

During the implementation of EURO 2008, martial terms such as fan invasions, first-aid staging points, airspace surveillance and rescue corridors were present in public discourse. 'At times, it seemed as if the city were preparing for a military battle or at least for a siege,' wrote the *Tages-Anzeiger* on June 19, 2008. The media often adopted the German word 'Ausnahmezustand' (state of emergency/state of exception) in order to describe the circumstances of EURO 2008. The fact that international football tournaments are increasingly conceived of as a type of popular festival, encompassing all aspects of society, is also suggestive of the exceptional circumstances historically associated with festivals: the Brockhaus encyclopedia defines festivals as 'temporally bounded', 'excessive' and 'staged events', which 'suspend everyday rules of conduct' for a certain amount of time. Häußermann and Siebel, too, speak of the state of exception as a 'powerful mobilizer' in the 'festivalization of city politics'.[21]

The political and media discourses surrounding the implementation of EURO 2008 in Zurich reveal the frequent rhetorical use of the term 'Ausnahmezustand' to justify regulatory exceptions, financial expenditure or other special measures which would never have been enforceable under normal circumstances. The state of exception itself is construed not only as positive and desirable, but also as volatile and dangerous. In a positive context, for example, the chance to hold the third-largest sporting event in the world is described over and over as a unique opportunity. The 'tremendous chance to present our city to the world'.[22] was a constant refrain among Zurich's location marketers. Accordingly, the Zurich-based urban event manager Martin Heller interpreted the football tournament as a very welcome challenge, because 'these types of events generate a sort of exceptional situation in which many things which would normally be unthinkable are suddenly possible.... The staging of this type of event is something like the simulation of an emergency which requires the mobilization of all possible resources.'[23]

However, a much more prominent aspect of the rhetoric of a state of emergency was that of the threat scenarios, conjured up by politicians and the media in the run-up to the football event – for example, the invasion of violent hooligans from near and far, the spread of crime associated with the event (such as fraud, pick-pocketing, forced prostitution or organized crime) or the risk of high-profile and disastrous terrorist attacks, but also the enormous number of spectators and the inherent dangers of organizational failures, accidents or mass panic.[24] In order to 'get hold' of the imminent 'state of emergency',.[25] it appeared an equally exceptional array of extraordinary measures and regulatory exemptions were necessary.

Switzerland and Austria had already given UEFA blanket security guarantees in their application for the European Championship in 2002. However, just how this security was to be established was a problem that would have to be solved and politically legitimated after the fact. It soon became clear that Switzerland was about to see a police operation of unprecedented dimensions and that Switzerland's force of ~ 16,000 police officers alone would be inadequate to both satisfy the security requirements of EURO 2008 and provide basic law-enforcement services. Therefore, new institutions had to be established so that the federally organized police force could coordinate its actions across the borders of the cantons. Approximately 1000 police officers were placed at Switzerland's disposal by Germany and France using bilateral agreements, but without any clear basis in constitutional law. Additionally, in March 2007, the Swiss Parliament approved the 'presumably largest deployment' of the Swiss Army 'since World War II': up to 15,000 soldiers and military equipment were to be allocated for the implementation of EURO 2008 in the areas of physical protection, logistics, transportation, emergency management and border control.[26] Military observation drones were to be deployed for the surveillance of crowds' movements within the host cities and stadiums from the air.[27] Lastly, private security services were given the responsibility for a great deal of the policing and stewarding, especially in the stadiums and public viewing areas. All that, as well, occurred without any clear regulatory framework. In order to ensure effective action against presumed hooligans, the Federal Parliament enacted an amendment to the homeland security law,.[28] which was often described as the 'hooligan law' in the media. It included the introduction of a 'hooligan databank' as well as preventative police operations against suspicious individuals. Because the legislative authority in this area actually belongs to the cantons, this in fact unconstitutional law was passed as an exceptional, temporary measure in hopes that the cantons would ratify it retroactively.

In addition, many other extraordinary measures and regulatory exceptions can be mentioned – not all of them only in the name of security. For example, the recruiting of ~ 5000 volunteers who worked without pay in both Austria and Switzerland,.[29] the authorization of longer opening hours for shops during the European Championship, the enhancement of border patrols, the introduction of a special EURO 2008 visa for visitors from non-EU countries or the intermittent curtailing of bans on night flights.

The effects of this well-organized state of emergency naturally made themselves noticeable in urban spaces as well, not only due to the presence of security personnel in various uniforms, the makeshift stationing areas of the riot police, first aid personnel or emergency preparedness crews, or the constantly audible movements of the helicopter patrols, but also because of the multiple partitions, barriers and fences between different areas of the city and within its public spaces. The rhetoric of exceptional circumstances not only legitimates temporary regulatory exceptions; it also leads to the creation of spatially confined zones in which established rules are suspended.

The most striking example is certainly the 'special case of the fan zone',.[30] where the temporary privatization of a confined area lent potency to exceptional regulations dealing with the control of entrances and exits, video surveillance or the exclusivity of certain products, none of which would have normally been possible in a public space. Although the fan zone Zurich was very compact compared to the fan zones in, for example, Vienna or Berlin, it still had sweeping effects on the city. Because important thoroughfares had to be closed during its opening hours, districts south-east of the fan zone were cut-off from downtown in the afternoons and evenings. Many people found themselves forced to make long detours in order to follow their daily routines.

The European Championship stadiums presented a comparable situation: UEFA demanded an extended security perimeter around each stadium. Using extensive fenced enclosures, large portions of the public space were temporarily incorporated into the 'outer security ring' and subjected to the stadiums' house rules. Furthermore, on match days, another wide-ranging ban zone for motor vehicles was set up around the EURO 2008 stadiums. Around Zurich's Letzigrund Stadium, all access roads were blocked with concrete barricades and heavy military vehicles. Residents of the area were forced to apply for special clearance far in advance in order to drive in and out of their neighbourhood on match days. In addition, a no-fly zone for civilian air traffic was declared for a 22-km radius around the stadiums.

Physically imperceptible, but geographically defined and legally operative, zones called *Rayone* were specified by the police in several Swiss cities in the run-up to the European Championship. According to the new 'hooligan law', individuals who had made themselves conspicuous could be banned from the *Rayone* at specified times. These zones – abstract rectangles on the urban plan – covered, for example, wide-ranging areas around Zurich's stadiums, its central train station and its fan zone. By contrast, the makeshift 'special prisons' established in the four Swiss host cities in order to provide efficient mass processing and temporary imprisonment of a large number of arrestees can be considered clearly physically defined zones. In Zurich, the canton police force's barracks yard was transformed into a 'detention street' constructed out of tents and containers.

Moreover, in many parts of the city, urban spaces were dissected into more or less exclusive privately organized public viewing locations, hospitality areas and VIP lounges with restricted access or paid admission. Areas of public parks were fenced off in order to protect them from being used as toilets or campsites. Other places were declared 'football-free zones' in contrast to the ubiquitous EURO 2008-related activities. The all-encompassing presence of the event did, in fact, have the character of an extraordinary situation. In hindsight, this puts the various exceptional measures and zones in a context that makes them appear self-evident.

Likewise, in the discourses surrounding the legitimating of the exceptional regulations described above, the 'state of emergency' was often depicted as less of a self-imposed challenge and long-planned event and more of an unchangeable, catastrophic or quasi-religious phenomenon, which demanded sacrifices and followed its own laws. According to Luzius Theiler, a EURO 2008 critic from Berne, the local decision-makers allegorize the football event as a storm breaking over the city of Berne, 'creating an extra-constitutional state of emergency' and justifying the suspension of valid laws and democratic procedures.[31] 'But we're not in a state of emergency,' argues the constitutional scholar Rainer J. Schweizer in an interview with the *Neue Zürcher Zeitung*. Even in the context of EURO 2008, 'we can proceed in a framework of clear-eyed, orderly legislative processes.' But, 'the media and the citizenry are not asking enough critical questions. Nobody wants to spoil the party.'[32] The 'mobilization of all available resources'.[33] under the constraints of exceptional circumstances excludes controversial discussions or possibilities of opposition. The few critics of EURO 2008 who refused to join in the consensus were quickly stigmatized as spoilsports and narrow-minded defeatists.

Nevertheless, opposition to the implications of the event came from various directions. The rather conservative residents and business owners in the Zurich neighbourhood of Seefeld fiercely resisted plans to block traffic in the area of the fan zone. In Berne and Winterthur, leftist splinter parties mainly criticized the commercial implications of the event and initiated referenda against the cities' EURO 2008 budgets. One referendum successfully prevented the UBS public viewing arena in Winterthur, while in Berne the vote of 48% almost jeopardized the city's hosting of EURO 2008. In addition to dedicated football fans, leftist–alternative cultural institutions and initiatives, and a few critical voices in the mainstream media, the civil rights organization grundrechte.ch offered potent criticism of the measures associated with EURO 2008. The event, says grundrechte.ch, brought with it exorbitant security measures, the gradual militarization of internal affairs and the curtailment of basic civil rights.[34]

However, the extraordinary security measures cannot be understood as a mere reaction to the necessities of the 'exceptional circumstances' of the European Championship. In fact, grundrechte.ch suggests that EURO 2008 provides a 'basis for legitimization and a testing ground, opening the door' for the establishment of more-restrictive security and surveillance methods or a new justification for the military.[35] Many of the 'new laws and the resources and methods established in the context of the EURO 08 will remain in force after the event is over'.[36] However, within these processes, protective niches and very different kinds of exceptional circumstances are still possible. A few days after the end of the European Cup, Zurich's Hardturm Stadium, which was about to be torn down, was squatted by activists and declared a temporary open space for the weekend-long 'Brotäktschen Games'.[37] These 'non-commercial, self-determined' and 'unregulated' games were a subversive answer to EURO 2008: 'Brotäktschen created an open space for itself and showed that major events can take place without sponsoring, absurd special regulations, a police force of thousands, military deployments and drone surveillance.'[38]

Conclusion

First of all, how should the tendency towards collective experiences in public spaces and the increasing significance of urban space in the implementation and marketing of football tournaments be interpreted? Is this the ultimate appropriation and celebration of public space? Or, considering the temporary privatization of public urban areas and the dominance of private corporate interests, is it exactly the opposite? Regina Bittner speaks of the experience-driven society's 'obsession with urban space': 'The city and the event appear to be deeply connected in our postindustrial present. The new interest for the city feeds out of the contemporary hunger for experience, a hunger that is driven by the longing for locality and identity.'[39] For sociologist Christian Schmid, urban mega-events accelerate the commodification of urbanity: the city is being 'sold to the highest bidder'. Thus, 'certain parts of the city are ceded to the event organizers, who in turn sell their sponsors the right to these spaces' as a matter of course.[40] In order to make the rich and diverse experiences promised by the cities into sellable, consumable wares, they are standardized and robbed of any actual quality.[41] In 1967, Guy Debord had already polemically described the scale of this commodification: 'The spectacle is the moment when the commodity has attained the total occupation of social life. Not only is the relation to the commodity visible but it is all one sees: the world one sees is its world.'[42]

The urbanization of the event and the eventization of the city are two intertwined patterns of development which describe the interplay of city and event and the accompanying issues, strategies and effects on various levels. At first glance, it is easy to get the impression of a 'win–win situation' for the event and its organizers on the one side and the city on the other side. Although football tournaments of global significance are highly dominated by the profit expectations, demands and rules of UEFA or FIFA and the scope for individual decision-making on the city's part is quite small, these types of large events can by now be considered part of the toolkit of entrepreneurial urban policy. Countries and cities compete for hosting the tournaments in order to deploy the event strategically – whether for image benefits in the context of location marketing, to create excitement and consensus among residents, as a driving force for urban development or as a test bed for new organizational forms. The asymmetrical power dynamic between the event organizers and the city, the high public costs, the unfortunate side effects and the constraint of democratic decision making processes – all of these manifest themselves in this context – are systematically ignored or depicted as unavoidable constraints of hosting an event.

Simultaneously, the two patterns of development suggest two different concepts of the city itself: eventization turns the city into a virtual construct intended to provide collective identity internally and formulaically project the location's special qualities to the outside world. The urbanization of large football tournaments, by contrast, places a new emphasis on the physical qualities of urban spaces. However, its direct physical presence and experience in the built environment are accompanied by numerous pictorial representations, whether in the form of transmissions in the media, advertising displays or urban backdrops. In this context, strong similarities between the visual and linguistic advertising strategies for commercial products, on the one hand, and for location marketing, on the other hand, can be observed. Through the promises made by the city's and the event's marketing divisions and the experimental set-up of public viewing, the Fan Mile and supporting events, the concrete way in which visitors experience the city is already highly structured. The eventization of the city and the urbanization of the event are two sides of the same coin: the promise and its fulfilment, the advertisement of a product and its consumption, the marketing and the commodification of urbanity.

The transference of the spatial principles of the stadium into the city is a constituent element of these developments. The event appropriates the city as a venue, demanding the spatial preconditions for its frictionless implementation and economic profit. The city seizes this as a chance to stage and market its best qualities. The model of the stadium can be used to describe the concrete consequences of the event's presence in urban space – its differentiation, segmentation, privatization and exclusivity. If these temporary reconfigurations slowly become a new state of normality, however, the stadium also becomes a prototype for long-term urban transformations. Perhaps it can then be considered, along with shopping malls and airports, as another paradigmatic type of place in postmodern urban development. It would be interesting to explore to what extent the stadium can also be conceived of as the materialization of a societal trend: has it become necessary to manufacture collective experiences – with the stipulation of frictionless procedures, maximal comfort, and the exclusion of every possible risk – in order to unite our fragmented society into temporary communities? Is the creation of political consensus today only possible through large, popular events, as Häußermann and Siebel explain?.[43] Is the stadium not the perfect architectural counterpart for the 'instrument of unification' of Guy Debord's spectacle, which admittedly only produces a type of unification that 'is nothing but an official language of generalized separation'?[44]

In the context of the event and the city, the rhetoric of a state of emergency does not only serve as a justification for extraordinary regulations for the implementation and security of the event. In fact, this rhetoric has already become an autonomous force to legitimate, practice and establish all possible extraordinary measures under the 'exceptional circumstances' of the event. This strategy provides a basis for the restructuring both of governance and security apparatuses, and for the spatial reconfiguration of the cities. With the increase in spatially defined exceptional situations, urban spaces are fragmented, differentiated and arranged hierarchically. Numerous smaller and larger enclaves arise, demarcated with barricades, fences, velvet ropes, signs or invisible legally defined borders, determining different conditions of accessibility and use for different individuals. Here, too, the exceptional circumstances threaten to become rules: spatial patterns are reused and refined from event to event, becoming more and more normal with each new event and establishing themselves in daily urban life. The patterns described above are, of course, not entirely new or surprising. The event is, more than anything else, a symptom of and a pacemaker for the dominant trends in urban development under the conditions of neoliberalism, global competition and societal fragmentation. 'For three weeks, the event showed us a concentrated version of things which usually occur in the form of a subtle and hardly noticed process.'[45]

Notes

1. See www.fancity2008.ch.
2. According to the official estimation of the Zurich municipality, ~ 730,000 guests visited the fan zone. Stadt Zürich. 'Schlussbericht', 55.
3. Not including the construction cost of the new stadium. Cf. Stadt Zürich, 'Weisung zum Objektkredit'.
4. UEFA provided CHF1.2 million and two large LED screens for the fan zone; additionally there was small financial support for public services. Author interview with Daniel Rupf, Zurich, January 11, 2008.
5. Radio interview with Daniel Rupf. Maya Brändli. 'EURO 2008 – was bringt sie und was nicht?' April 3, 2008. 9.05–9.35 a.m., DRS 2
6. Brenke and Wagner, *Zum volkswirtschaftlichen Wert der Fußball-Weltmeisterschaft 2006 in Deutschland.*
7. Still, in the case of EURO 2008, the economic potential had been overestimated: some of the fan zones and Fan Miles were clearly oversized. According to various local media reports, retailers, the hotel industry and restaurants hardly profited from the event. However, UEFA brought in record revenues of €1.3 billion and a profit of €250 million.
8. Interview with Maurus Lauber, Zurich, January 28, 2008.
9. Häußermann and Siebel, 'Politik der Festivalisierung'.
10. Stadt Zürich, 'Weisung zum Objektkredit Euro 2008'.
11. Ibid., 44, 45.
12. Stadt Zürich, 'Schlussbericht', 33.
13. Stadt Zürich, 'Weisung zum Objektkredit Euro 2008', 48.
14. Ibid., 45.
15. Stadt Zürich. 'Euro 2008. Schlussbericht', 45.
16. Stadt Zürich, 'Weisung zum Objektkredit Euro 2008', 50–1.
17. Ibid., 50, 51, 59.
18. Häußermann and Siebel, 'Politik der Festivalisierung'.
19. Ibid., 22.
20. Stadt Zürich, 'Schlussbericht', 45.
21. Häußermann and Siebel. 'Politik der Festivalisierung' 22.
22. 'Ein Test für die Marke Schweiz', *Neue Zürcher Zeitung*, June 7–8, 2008.
23. Author interview with Martin Heller, Zurich, January 7, 2008.
24. Teilprojekt Sicherheit Öffentliche Hand UEFA EURO 2008. 'FAQ Sicherheit EURO 2008', October 31, 2007. Schweiz Tourismus. www.switzerland.com/files/?id=7588.

25. *Neue Zürcher Zeitung*, June 21, 2008.
26. Moosmann, 'Die Schweiz rüstet sich für die Euro 08', 64–74.
27. Eventually, 'only' an average of 4600 soldiers were on duty every day, Moosmann, 'Die Armee auf der Sinnsuche im Innern', 8–9.
28. 'Bundesgesetz über Maßnahmen zur Wahrung der inneren Sicherheit' (BWIS).
29. UEFA Euro 2008 SA, 'Die UEFA EURO 2008™ in Zahlen'.
30. *Neue Zürcher Zeitung*, June 26, 2008.
31. Luzius Theiler in a public panel discussion on 'Schauplatz. Stadt, Event und Vermarktung', *Fancity 2008*, Rote Fabrik, Zurich, March 26, 2008.
32. *Neue Zürcher Zeitung*, December 12, 2007.
33. Interview with Martin Heller, Zurich, January 7, 2008.
34. *antidotincl.* Special Issue: 'Euro 08 versus Grundrechte. Testspiel mit Folgen', October 2, 2008.
35. Ibid., 13.
36. Györffy, 'Euro 08 und Grundrechte', 3.
37. 'Brotäktschen' reads like a sloppy pronunciation of either protection or the German-English combination of 'bread action'.
38. www.raumpflege.org
39. Bittner, 'Die Stadt als Event', 16.
40. *Neue Zürcher Zeitung*, May 31, 2008.
41. Christian Schmid at the public panel discussion 'Schauplatz. Stadt, Event und Vermarktung,' *Fancity 2008*, Rote Fabrik, Zurich, March 26, 2008.
42. Debord, *Society of the Spectacle*, Chapter 2, no. 42.
43. Häußermann and Siebel, 'Politik der Festivalisierung,' 22.
44. Debord, *Society of the Spectacle*, Chapter 1, no. 3, paragraph 3.
45. *antidotincl.* Special Issue: 'Euro 08 versus Grundrechte. Testspiel mit Folgen', grundrechte.ch, October 2, 2008, 18.

References

Bittner, R. 'Die Stadt als Event.' In *Die Stadt als Event,* ed. R. Bittner, 14–24. Frankfurt: Campus, 2001.

Brenke, K., and G. Wagner. *Zum volkswirtschaftlichen Wert der Fußball-Weltmeisterschaft 2006 in Deutschland.* Berlin: Deutsches Institut für Wirtschaftsforschung, April 2007. Deutsches Institut für Wirtschaftsforschung. www.diw.de/deutsch/produkte/publikationen/researchnotes/docs/papers/rn19.pdf.

Debord, G. *Society of the Spectacle.* Detroit, MI: Black & Red, 1977. Marxists Internet Archive. www.marxists.org/reference/archive/debord/society.htm.

Györffy, V. 'Die Euro 08 und die Grundrechte. Sicherheitskonzept mit Nachwirkungen'. *antidotincl.,* October 2, 2008 [Special Issue: 'Euro 08 versus Grundrechte. Testspiel mit Folgen'] 3.

Häußermann, H., and W. Siebel. 'Die Politik der Festivalisierung und die Festivalisierung der Politik. Große Ereignisse in der Stadtpolitik'. In *Festivalisierung der Stadtpolitik. Stadtentwicklung durch große Projekte,* ed. H. Häußermann and W. Siebel, 7–31. Opladen: Westdeutscher Verlag, 1993.

Moosmann, R. 'Die Schweiz rüstet sich für die Euro 08'. *Bürgerrechte und Polizei/CILIP* 89, 1 (2008): 64–74.

Moosmann, Reto. 'Die Armee auf der Sinnsuche im Innern', *antidotincl.,* October 2, 2008 [Special Issue: 'Euro 08 versus Grundrechte. Testspiel mit Folgen']: 8–9.

Stadt Zürich. 'Euro 2008. Schlussbericht.' www.stadt-zuerich.ch/euro2008

Stadt Zürich, Präsidialdepartement. 'Weisung zum Objektkredit Euro 2008 an den Stadtrat' (2006). www.zuerich.com/files/get.cfm?id=4680.

Teilprojekt Sicherheit Öffentliche Hand UEFA EURO 2008. 'FAQ Sicherheit EURO 2008' (October 31, 2007). Schweiz Tourismus. www.switzerland.com/files/?id=7588.

UEFA Euro 2008 SA. 'Die UEFA EURO 2008™ in Zahlen' (Medienmitteilung Nr. 74), May 29, 2008. Nyon: UEFA. http://www1.de.uefa.com/MultimediaFiles/Download/MediaRelease/Competitions/MediaServices/70/28/52/702852_DOWNLOAD.pdf

Governing by fun: EURO 2008 and the appealing power of fan zones

Georg Lauss and András Szigetvari

Department of Political Science, University of Vienna, Austria

Fan zones are envisioned as a place where the expectations, pleasures and desires of visitors shall meet. At the same time, they play an important role in the security architecture. Offering fun and entertainment, fan zones promised to attract thousands of people, mainly those who did not have a ticket for one of the games, but still wanted to become part of the event. 'Fun' was not just a congregational element, but also a specific organizing principle by which order was maintained inside the fan zones. To illustrate the double aspect of fun, we show how a range of devices tried to animate visitors to actively interact and participate in the vision of a peaceful European consumer community. Fans were offered different roles so that their emotions could be positively channelled, and non-violent, friendly relationships between strangers could flourish. Ties between fans were established both by the macro-architecture of the zones and the type of entertainment offered. What we would like to emphasize is that the promise made in the official motto of EURO 2008, 'Expect Emotions', should not only be taken as a marketing slogan, but also be understood as a central regulatory element of such a sports mega-event.

The king felt great displeasure that his son abandoned the streets, to ramble aimlessly cross country to build his own judgement about the world. He gave him a horse and cart. 'Now you do not have to walk any more my son', were his words. 'Now you are no longer allowed to', were their meaning. 'Now you cannot any more', their effect.

(Günther Anders, 1956)

We can no longer fight back against this centennial event. The fans from all over Europe will come (...). And these fans will infect us with their good mood. We will not be able to elude them.

(Austrian Football Association President Friedrich Stickler, June 6, 2007[1])

Introduction

In 2008, the finals of UEFA's four-year European Championships, the world's third largest sports event, were staged in Austria and Switzerland. EURO 2008 was a mega-event, not only in sporting and commercial terms. As a mass-mediated spectacle, the football tournament was at the centre of European and even global publicity. In this respect, the event was a symbolic play, in which the political vision of a peaceful, competitive and unified Europe could be manifest. To present this spectacle of a United Europe, an elaborate security policy was orchestrated in which the newly devised 'fan zones' of host cities played a central role.

Fan zones, their composition and roles as part of the logic of the entire event, have increasingly been gaining scholarly attention. This article is based upon a fresh reading of existing studies and may serve to expand the horizon of their perspective. The article argues that the establishment of security and order in the fan zone is not only guaranteed by erecting zones and borders, by setting rules and enforcing them with police or private security companies, or by the surveillance of individuals and groups and the categorizing of areas. Instead, we want to highlight the double-faced application of 'fun' in the context of fan zones: on the one hand, its role as a congregational element, its ability to gather; and, on the other hand, its function as a specific organizing principle. The promise made in the official motto of EURO 2008, 'Expect Emotions', should be taken not only as a marketing slogan, but also as a central regulatory element of this event.

According to Michel Foucault, 'governing by fun' lies at the heart of what has been labelled as the core question to answer for those who govern within a framework of liberal governmentality: 'The problem', for them 'is how they can say yes; it is how they can say yes to [individual] desires'?[2] We want to emphasize that 'fun' as referring to a particular form of pleasurable leisure activity must be differentiated from the concept of 'entertainment'. Whereas entertainment typically refers to the passive expenditure of time, 'fun' demarcates a process in which desires, understood as the pursuit of individual interest, become translated into particular (social) action. Hence 'fun' resembles more closely 'recreation' and therefore emphasizes a more active and participatory mode of activity than entertainment.

Hagemann (in this issue) offers an exciting interpretation of the fan zone. In her opinion, fan zones expand the logics of the football stadium into the urban area. Whatever is allowed to happen in the stadium will follow a similar pattern when exported to the city. This translation concerns not only the sphere of business and marketing, but equally the countless security measures that have been tried and tested in football arenas over the years. Klausner evaluates this phenomena from a 'surveillance studies' perspective and applies the main focus of attention to technologies of security that provide control and order in and around the fan zones.[3] Risk areas are highlighted and rigid controls ensure that unwanted persons cannot infiltrate the event. Within the designated areas, hi-tech CCTV monitoring disciplines the crowd present and differentiates between specific areas. In addition, hundreds of police and private security guards ensure both security and order. Surveillance and admittance remain the responsibility of the private organizer, and the public authorities play only a small role.[4]

This article makes two additions to the previous research. The first is the subject of the analysis. Whereas previous studies have focused on the technology involved in surveillance and security, which seek to ensure peace and control within the fan zone, this article focuses on the fan zone *itself* as a technology of security. The second aspect extends the analysis of security technology by shifting the focus onto fun as an additional element. Any analysis of surveillance and security issues presupposes undisturbed entertainment as a basic condition of the event. The techniques used to manufacture individual conformity establish control through a combination of threat and repressive violent measures, on the one hand, and surveillance and control regimes, on the other hand. This article focuses on the analysis of the specific construction of the 'fan zone choreography', and especially how the configuration of a fun-producing milieu can be understood as a security element in itself. It will be shown how a number of devices animated the visitors to actively interact and participate in the vision of a compacted, peaceful, European, consumer community.

A combination of three different methods of inquiry was employed in order to collect empirical material for this study. First, nine qualitative interviews were conducted with representatives from the Viennese police forces, fan workers, the marketing department of an international sponsor, the Austrian EURO organization committee and UEFA; all interviewees had been active in the planning and proceedings of the fan zone in Vienna. Second, this text is supported by participant observation, which was conducted over a three-day period and at different times of the day in the Viennese fan zone. Third, press material and media reports were collected and an analysis of the contents was carried out.

The core concern of this article is to portray the activating, or better the appealing, part of power. Political technology, the code of which is decrypted here, tends towards the creation of a fun-producing milieu, whereby a sharp categorical differentiation between the football core event, brand and city marketing, and security interests can no longer be sustained in a meaningful way.

Contextualizing the 'fun factor': rearranging the European security environment

It can be argued that only within the political framework of a united Europe do fan zones become an indispensable, political instrument. Since the middle of the 1990s the number of visitors flocking to international football championship matches, and most significantly the number of fans travelling without match tickets, has exploded. Yet the celebration of a temporarily united Europe in the European Football Championship initiated a tightened safeguarding of national territorialism. From June 2 to July 1, 2008, Austria and Switzerland intentionally suspended the Schengen Agreement (providing for the removal of systematic border controls among EU member states) in order to prevent hooligans from attending the event. The enforced border controls actually inversed the selective penetrability of national demarcation because borders became more permeable to police officers from neighbouring EU countries. Active exchange of security concepts and technology was made not just at governmental level.

Unprecedented in Austria was the support from the German federal government, which deployed 850 police officers to assist the Austrian police. German police were granted 'full powers of arrest'[5] equalling the sovereign rights of local forces. Alongside this, exchanges of current security situations were conducted between the two states. In addition, UEFA sent its own security experts from Nyon to advise the Viennese police. On an organizational level, the arrangement of the fan zone was devised in close consultation between the local organizer and UEFA.

International border-crossing interactions also took place among non-governmental organizations participating in the event. In all host cities, Football Supporters International (FSI) and the Football Against Racism in Europe (FARE) network, which operates throughout Europe, established official 'fan embassies' in public areas. Both organizations had 'foreign' employees operating in the vicinity of the venues. Knowledge transfer also took place on a European scale.

A short history of the fan zone

Although 'fan zones' entered the level of broader public awareness only during the World Cup in 2006, first – unsuccessful – attempts to create 'fan miles' date back to the early 1990s. Prior to this, visitors to both the World Cup and European Championships were 'widely left to themselves' which often led to frustration and aggressive behaviour, as a German fan worker reports:

> The hooligan problem became apparent in the 1980s. Hooligans disturbed both local residents and away supporters and were responsible for an increasing amount of criminal damage within urban areas. Official security policy relied upon isolating the hooligan groups and focused on maintaining order in all public areas by identifying potential groups that may instigate disturbances. Over the years, this attitude has changed to a concept of 'hospitality': if people feel well received, the motivation to cause disturbances and trouble is a lot lower.[6]

In fact, a surprising turnaround has taken place within a decade. Earlier fan zones were either erected half-heartedly or completely rejected by officials. In 1992, the Swedish organizers of the first ever fan zone at a European Championships still asked visitors for an entry fee. Unlike in Germany 2006 or Austria/Switzerland 2008, where fan zones were set up at the centre of the host cities, the Swedish fan zones were located on the periphery of the city. Accordingly, fan attendance was low.

Discussions on how to handle fans that travel to the venue without tickets for the games remained confined within fan worker networks until the 1996 European Championships in England. A German fan guidebook quoted the official organizers as saying that 'there will not be any accompanying event programmes for fans during the 96 European Championships'.[7] The official position remained distanced. In the run-up to the World Cup 1998, the English Football Association spent over £1m on a campaign with the motto 'If you don't have a ticket, stay at home.'

A series of violent incidents during the 1998 World Cup in France and EURO 2000 in Belgium and the Netherlands, like the brutal attacking of French policeman Daniel Nivel by German hooligans who did not have tickets for the game in Lens, contributed to a revision of top ranking officials' attitudes towards fan zones. A German fan worker remembers:

> As the German eleven played in Lens, three or four sport halls were designated for public viewing, but they were hard to reach and badly advertised. Apart from that, it was a very hot day, with temperatures of more than 30 degrees. So it came as no surprise that nearly nobody went there, which also favoured the attack on Daniel Nivel because the fans that didn't have tickets couldn't watch the game anywhere.[8]

The pivotal question is not whether there is a direct connection between violence and the degree of entertainment offered to fans. But it is important to note that various actors increasingly started to see this connection as real. The complex issues of security and entertainment began to intertwine. During EURO 2000, fan workers and the media speculated about a connection between the lack of public viewing areas and incidents of violent outbursts by fans. After a clash between England and German fans in the Belgian city of Charleroi, *The Guardian* wrote:

> Uefa in its wisdom made things even worse by putting the England–Germany match (…) in one of the smallest venues available. That bizarre choice created a large cohort of potential 'hooligans' – thousands of fans who wanted to go to the game but couldn't get anywhere near the stadium. (…) And what did Charleroi do to accommodate them? Zero. In Place Charles II, the big central square where the 'riot' occurred, there were no outdoor television screens, no loudspeakers, not even a scoreboard.[9]

And a German fan worker warned of the event in the *Jenaer Allgemeinen Zeitung*:

> There will be hardly any screen in the vicinity of the games, where fans from all over Europe can congregate and watch a game that they don't have tickets for. (...) The result is the fans will be forced into pubs. From a security aspect, that can't be worse than allowing them to gather in large, public areas.[10]

The reconsideration process was quickly set into motion by many countries: recommendations[11] by the Council of Europe on how to avoid violence at large sporting events, especially football, did not mention fan zones or public viewing areas in 2003. But five years later, Alan Ridley, UEFA Head of Sponsorship and Event Promotion, said that 'generally the idea is, that people have a better time, if they have things to do. They are happier, and then they behave probably in a better way'.[12] The same rationale was stated by a Viennese police expert: 'A good atmosphere and good communication are natural methods to prevent violence.'[13] Swiss authorities posed similar arguments: '[P]ublic viewing also has a preventive character: It offers all those persons who have no tickets an opportunity to get close to the action. From this perspective, public viewing reduces the frustration and risk potential.'[14]

Fan zones offering the opportunity of having fun were expected to attract fans without match tickets and to keep them under control. For that reason, the Viennese municipality argued for locating the fan zone in the city centre: 'Fans tend to gather in city centres. Because of this, it makes sense to build a fan zone in the city centre. And of course it is easier to control them [the fans] in that way'.[15] Similarly, a German fan worker summarized his experience from the World Cup 2006: 'Attempts to clear the city centre from fans have failed in the past. Especially international fans prefer to stay in the centres, no matter if public viewing areas are available or not.'[16] In Vienna, a decision was made for a very attractive location. The central ring road around the inner district bypassing famous sights such as the Austrian Parliament, the City Hall and one of Vienna's most famous theatres was chosen to host the fan zone. All traffic was temporarily excluded from a section of the ring road linking two central squares of the city, the 'Heldenplatz' and the 'Rathausplatz', with the fan zone.

From our interview partners we learnt about other relevant aspects of 'fun' for the ability to govern mega-events. Different stakeholders all agreed that nobody should 'miss out on the fun', no matter how the event was to be governed or regulated in detail. Police operations succumbed to the premise that people having fun are more peaceful. Günther Marek, security director of EURO 2008 in the Austrian Interior Ministry, said before the start of the tournament: 'I do not believe that something will happen in the stadiums or in the public viewing areas. Where a positive environment reigns, there is no nutrient for violence'.[17]

The city of Vienna and its tourist board hoped to broadcast positive images showing peaceful, celebrating visitors. Local co-organizers wanted to demonstrate that they could cope with an event of this magnitude and to generate the same positive atmosphere as the sponsors, who rely on placing their brands in a positive environment. Finally, fan networks such as FARE and FSI, which had previously been critical of the UEFA marketing machine, also embraced the core notion of peaceful fans gathering for a good time and tried to dispel local fears about the arrival of violent hooligans in the run-up to the event.[18]

The fun aspect was successful in bridging the divide between the organizing partners, and was also used as an argument to legitimize the disturbance the event would cause to public transport. After erecting the fan zone in the centre of Vienna on the always-busy ring road, one of the main arterial roads in the city was blocked for five weeks. The municipality was able to justify the nuisance as long as it could demonstrate that the fan zones were meeting public demand for the whole day and period of the tournament. Officials therefore developed a programme to encourage schools to visit the fan zones during the day, with 13,000 school children and youths accepting the invitation.[19]

Choreographing security at a sports event held in a city milieu

The first sections of this article have shown how, within just a decade, fan zones have edged into the centre of large sporting events. On the one hand, they combine city tourism and a 'stadium feeling' for fans that had not received tickets for the proper match. On the other hand, fan zones and public viewing areas have become of major interest to security experts. In the following, we demonstrate how the concept and vision of the fan zone materialized within the context of Vienna, during the 2008 European Championships. For this purpose, we will, in a literal sense, present a tour through the Viennese fan zone. We will see modern surveillance technology and practises of selection, classification, distribution, labelling and (re)arrangement – in short, the principles and practises of differentiating between specific spatial areas.[20] Most importantly, we will encounter devices and their arrangement, which are trying to facilitate the production of '[t]he collective interest through the play of desires'.[21]

From a security point of view, the fan zone represented both an answer and a new problem to the organizers of EURO 2008 in Vienna. The fan zone in Vienna was, as highlighted above, an integral part of the security strategy, with its main function being to channel, gather and contain crowds of fans in a host city. However, this strategy gave rise to a new trouble spot, because it was to be expected that through the concentration of the crowds and their heterogeneity, the danger of crowd disturbances within the city centre could increase considerably. Keeping fans and visitors in the fan zone under control became a newly created challenge. The existing city area had to be reconfigured to meet this new challenge and similar security tactics and methods were put in place at both the stadium and the fan zone (see Hagemann in this issue).

In a sense, such problems were not new to city areas. The city is an arrangement which has become used to finding answers to questions that arise from a multiplicity of relationships and exchanges between all sorts of different people, generally unfamiliar with each other. The concept of the fan zone therefore amplified the problem of urban coexistence, which at its core, is to devise a way strangers can socially interact with one another. For sociologist Richard Sennett, this constellation of urban coexistence posed a central question on 'which societal conditions encourage people to display their feelings to others in such a way that some sympathetic response, some arousal, occurs'.[22]

When there is a strong public life, according to Sennett, there should be affinities between the domains of stage and street. 'There can arise in a city rules for making believable appearances before strangers that have a continuity of content with the rules governing response to the stage at the time'.[23] Public life needs choreographies that provide codes for interesting and peaceful performances. To determine – as unambiguously as possible – the best operational tactics for the specific area of operation, every public space must first of all be marked, defined and confined.

At the Vienna fan zone in 2008, the logic of the urban area had to be re-choreographed so that peaceful 'fun' could take place in the fan zone. Around the fan zone, a 3-km-long fence was erected. In addition, the organizers made use of a 1-km-long historical fence, which surrounded public park areas. The perimeter fences were used to prevent unwanted people and items from entering the fan zone and to channel all subjects and objects through security gates where a search for weapons and random checks of personal details routinely took place. But the fence itself also became a security problem. The Vienna Fire Brigade repeatedly pointed out that in the case of an emergency the fence would encumber mass evacuation of the area. The fan zone organizers, the Vienna Marketing and Prater Service Company, which is fully owned by the city of Vienna, first considered a fan zone without barriers, which would have preserved the festive appearance. But this idea was quickly discarded because the city was obliged by contract to safeguard the commercial interests of the UEFA 'official sponsors' inside the zone. The fence was a way of guaranteeing exclusive rights to the official sponsors, and gate controls made enforced restrictions on alcohol and small-sized beverages within the area possible.

Clearly, the fence is a barrier refusing entry to some people while granting access to others. Here we would like to focus our analysis on the function of the admittance procedure, which induces, in combination with the specific configuration of the interior of the fan zone, transformative processes of subject positions. Upon entering the fan zone, subjects are immediately incorporated into this artificial area. The pivotal point is that organizing a fan zone equates with the making of a milieu which is embedded in a particular 'liberal' governmentality and security strategy in a Foucauldian sense.

The fan zone is, to all intents and purposes, a 'social product'[24] that programmes certain types of coexistence. It has been envisioned as a place to serve the entrants' expectations, desires and pleasures. Entrants are performing the visitor role which allows the positive channelling of their emotions and the flourishing of friendly relationships between strangers. The macro-architecture structures the ties between the visitors, as in the case of the large video screens that focus attention and directivity while enabling the crowds to disperse all over the area instead of congregating in one place. As Barry[25] reminds us, active and responsible citizens cannot be presupposed; they must be formed and created. Devices that are built on an interactive model do not just discipline the subject. This sort of technology operates better through guidance than through rules.[26] Many of these devices were spread throughout the Vienna fan zone, offering the subject the chance to perceive, discover and experience oneself as an individual and part of the crowd. In the following section, we present a number of these devices. Moreover, we explain how insecurity is absorbed through the introduction of a specific choreography of space and the codes on offer at this specific public area.

Governing by fun

You are part of it all

Admittance to the Vienna fan zone did not follow the same pattern during the day. Security personnel were fewer in the morning when the rush was small, and the liminal gate control was easy to pass. But in the afternoon, especially before games involving the Austrian team which caused the largest influx of fans, or on the days of the semi-finals and final, the scenery was characterized by dynamics familiar from the stadium. Thousands of people queuing, their noisy babble drowned-out by loudspeakers transmitting the voices of Austrian TV moderators who used the fan zone as the atmospheric background to their live broadcasts.

The inside of the fan zone was conceived as a huge entertainment area. The event sponsors used the opportunity to attract new customers for their brands by handing out samples and give-aways, mostly interactive devices. These devices potentially enabled football fans to become active participants in the choreography of the fan zone. The fan zone offered them a number of roles and models. As a consumer, designer, sportsman and football fan, concert-goer and entertainer, as VIP and city tourist, visitors at the fan zone could become part of a vision of peaceful sport competition in a consumer society.

Consume and design your own product

The first significant and visible attraction near one of the two main entrances was a temporary McDonalds' fast food stall. About 80 more stands, all offering snacks and refreshments, were spread throughout the fan zone. In the central square (Heldenplatz), sports apparel maker Adidas had erected its own complex including the 'Biggest Shoebox in the World'. Inside the cube, consumers could design their own shoes. Outside they were encouraged to prove their talents at various games while sporting the newest Adidas sport shoes. The fusion of interactive entertainment and consumerism was apparently very appealing as the Adidas box was always crowded whenever we conducted our observations there.

Be a (sport) star

Opportunities for participatory behaviour were abundant. For example, there was a special programme for children and youths, mainly concentrated at Heldenplatz. There was also a rodeo for kids on a 'wild' football, a bouncy castle, bungee-running and a 'Moby Dick' inflatable slide. Face painting was offered by staff members of the Austrian Federal Railways (ÖBB) on the ring road. Next to it, Korean car-maker KIA operated a human-sized table football game inviting fans to perform as tabletop football players. The 'ContiFanCenter' (by the tyre-maker Continental) encouraged visitors to compete against each other in online football games. Next to the largest stage in the fan zone, motor oil company Castrol invited fans to play on a street kick pitch. The screen above the pitch was showing the 'Castrol-Performance-Index' which documented individual players' movements and analysed key moments of the games. The same software and technology that was also in use by Austrian TV broadcasters to analyse the 'real' EURO games gave amateur players the opportunity of improving their game.

Be your own entertainer

Part of the entertainment was created by the crowd's reflection of itself. Within the areas in front of the large stages, cameras filmed the football party and live images of the hilarious behaviour were instantly displayed on the giant screens. Watching themselves on the screens has usually been a major incentive for fans maximizing the merry-making performance. During half-time breaks in EURO matches, television companies would usually broadcast live from the fan zone. The programme included fans randomly picked to come up to the stage from where they commented on their team's game and progress, how they felt to be at the event and whom they forecast to win the EURO. Sponsors also offered the opportunity of self-expression: the Austrian tabloid newspaper *Kronenzeitung* presented a front-page of their paper on an LED wall. Every day new pictures of fans from the fan zone were published in the online paper. Self-entertainment was also offered by JVC and the Austrian mobile phone provider A1. JVC recorded fan messages and A1 photographed fans and invited them to pose for placards. Communication and interaction were key technologies to promote the enthusiasm of the fans.

Let me entertain you

Alongside the interactive offerings, there was a broad range of stage shows which gave visitors to the fan zone the possibility of swapping roles and turning into concert-goers. The main stage featured mostly stars from the Austrian music scene. At the official opening of the event, the Vienna Philharmonic Orchestra and the Vienna Boys' Choir performed on behalf of the EURO. The choice for the opening performance impressively demonstrated that the event would not only be about entertainment, but also about advertising Austria as a tourist destination. Cultural events such as concerts should keep the fan zone attractive and appealing to visitors, even on days when no games would take place. Alongside this, sponsors created some additional events, with the likes of Zinédine Zidane and Arsène Wenger attending celebrity football games in the fan zone.

Discover the beauty of Vienna

By locating the fan zone in the city centre, on the Imperial Ring Road, the City of Vienna designed glorious scenery to leave both fan zone visitors and the TV audience with unforgettable impressions of the beauty Vienna has to offer. By including city landmarks in the fan zone, or at least in its close vicinity, the stage was set for the city to market itself. 'Self-assured, the city declared it would turn into the fan zone of Europe.'[27] Whoever wished to follow a game at the Rathausplatz in front of Vienna's scenic town hall could choose between two giant screens. One was immediately in front of the city hall, which was built toward the end of the nineteenth century, the other was next to the Burgtheater, one of the most famous theatres in the German-speaking world, facing the town hall.

The magnetic effect of the fan zone on the international media was shown by the location of the media communication centre between the landmarks of the town hall and the theatre. An average of 25 television broadcasting companies reported daily from the Vienna fan zone into Europe and beyond. In total, more than 500 broadcasters and 4000 media representatives visited the communication centre.[28]

Conclusion

In the planning and execution of EURO 2008, and embedded in a multitude of legal, disciplinary and precautionary measures, 'fun' was a key factor in regulatory security policies. In addition, the often-differing economical and political interests of the stakeholders behind the fan zone could be harmonized by 'fun'.

Fun should unite and bind the crowd. Mediated through entertainment elements, even the most critical fan workers could bond with UEFA's economic goals. Transnational sponsoring brands expected a huge advertising effect and designed interactive concepts for fans that dominated the interior of the fan zone. In much of the fan zone, regulatory power was based less on rules and surveillance technology, and more on the realization of an entertainment milieu. Such milieus were to activate, excite and awaken visitors' interests and involve them in specific choreographies of space. In the fan zone, things should not just be forbidden; on the contrary, everything should flow. This strategy did not always succeed, and maybe that is where the problem lay: it is telling that the fan zone management decided to create another entry to the fan zone during half-time in the event due to the low number of visitors.

The strategies of governmentality on which we have focused worked less with the 'suppression' of subjects, but rather through the allocation of role models and under the aid of interactive devices, to produce certain subject positions that could be articulated with specific governmental objectives. Fun was not only a goal of the Viennese fan zone to be realized with rigid preventive measures, but rather it was a strategy of governmentality by which people and objects could be put into an ordered context. The exceptional thing about this strategy is that the totality of this thought barely allows for resistance: Who would hold something against people amusing themselves? 'Irony of this deployment is', said Foucault, 'in having us believe that our "liberation" is in the balance'.[29]

Notes

1. *News* 23/07, June 6, 2007.
2. Foucault, *Security, Territory, Population*, 73.
3. Klausner, 'Spatial Articulations of Surveillance'.
4. Roost and Schöning, 'Public Screens and Public Screening'.
5. *Die Presse*, December 13, 2007.
6. Interview of Michael Gabriel, 'Koordinationsstelle Fanprojekte bei der Deutschen Sportjugend' (KOS), December 12, 2008.
7. Koordinationsstelle Fan-Projekte, *Das Euro Fanzine*, 4.
8. Interview Michael Gabriel.
9. Reid, *The Guardian*, June 22, 2000.
10. Jenaer Allgemeine Zeitung, June 14, 2006, 5.
11. Council of Europe, 'Recommendation Rec (2003)1 of the Standing Committee'
12. Interview with Alan Ridley, October 28, 2008.
13. Interview with Philipp Koloszar and Herwig Lenz, Federal Criminal Police Office, Department for Crime Prevention & Victim Support, November 5, 2008.
14. UEFA EURO 2008 Public Authorities Security Sector Coordination, 18.
15. Interview with two representatives of Municipal Department 36, September 16, 2008.
16. Koordinationsstelle Fan-Projekte. *Fans willkommen*, 69.
17. *Profil* 19/2008, May 5, 2008, 103.
18. Interview with Heidi Thaler, Fair Play. Different Colours. One Game, October 15, 2008.
19. Koordination UEFA Euro 2008 im Bundeskanzleramt, 35.
20. Klauser, 'Spatial Articulations of Surveillance at the FIFA World Cup 2006™ in Germany'.
21. Foucault, *Security, Territory, Population*, 73
22. Sennett, *The Fall of Public Man*, 28.
23. Ibid., 38.
24. Löw, *Raumsoziologie*, 129.
25. Barry, *Political Machines*, 127.
26. Ibid., 129.
27. Die UEFA Euro 2008. Der offizielle Turnierführer, UEFA, 99.
28. Koordination UEFA Euro 2008 im Bundeskanzleramt, 35.
29. Foucault, *The History of Sexuality*, Vol. 1, 159.

References

Barry, A. *Political Machines: Governing a Technological Society*. London: Athlone, 2001.
Council of Europe. 'Recommendation Rec (2003) 1 of the Standing Committee on the role of social and educational measures in the prevention of violence in sport and handbook on the prevention of violence in sport'. Council of Europe. http://www.coe.int/t/dg4/sport/Resources/texts/sprec03.1_en.asp

Die UEFA Euro 2008. Der offizielle Turnierführer, UEFA. Gütersloh: Chronik Verlag, 2008.
Foucault, M. *The History of Sexuality, Vol. 1: An Introduction.* New York: Vintage Books, 1980.
Foucault, M. *Security, Territory, Population: Lectures at the College de France 1977–1978.* New York: Palgrave MacMillan, 2007.
Klauser, F.R. 'Spatial Articulations of Surveillance at the FIFA World Cup 2006™ in Germany'. In *Technologies of InSecurity. The Surveillance of Everyday Life,* ed. K.F. Aas, H. Oppen Gundhus, and H. Mork Lomell, 61–80. London: Routledge, 2008.
Koordinationsstelle Fan-Projekte. *Das Euro-Fanzine.* Frankfurt: KOS, 1996.
Koordinationsstelle Fan-Projekte. *Fans willkommen – Das Fan- und Besucherbetreuungsprogramm bei der WM 2006.* Frankfurt: KOS, 2006.
Koordination UEFA Euro 2008 im Bundeskanzleramt. Fussball Verbindet: Endbericht Koordination Bund zur UEFA Euro 2008™ in Österreich. Vienna, 2008.
Löw, M. *Raumsoziologie.* Frankfurt: Suhrkamp, 2001.
Reid, T.R. 'Hooligans? I didn't see any'. *The Guardian,* June 22, 2000.
Roost, F., and B. Schöning. 'Public Screens and Public Screening'. In *Heimspiel 2006 – Standort, Sport, Spektakel,* ed. Neue Gesellschaft für Bildende Kunst, 36–39. Berlin: NGBK, 2006.
Sennett, R. *The Fall of Public Man.* New York: W.W. Norton, 1992.
UEFA EURO 2008 Public Authorities Security Sector Coordination with the participation of the Confederation, the cantons and the host cities. FAQ Security EURO 2008. Questions and answers on safety and security at the EURO 2008. Solothurn, May 20, 2008.

Interviews

Michael Gabriel, 'Koordinationsstelle Fan-Projekte bei der Deutschen Sportjugend' (KOS) (via e-mail), December 12, 2008.
Philipp Koloszar and Herwig Lenz, Federal Criminal Police Office, Department for Crime Prevention & Victim Support, November 5, 2008.
Alan Ridley, UEFA Head of Sponsorship and Event Promotion, October 28, 2008.
Heidi Thaler, Fair Play. Different Colours. One Game (fan work coordinator), October 15, 2008.
Two representatives of Municipal Department 36 (Authorisation of events), City of Vienna, September 16, 2008.

Football negotiating the placement of Switzerland within Europe

Christian Koller

School of History, Welsh History and Archaeology, Bangor University, Wales

Although hosting the 'Union Européenne de Football Association' (UEFA) and having co-organized the 2008 European Championship, Switzerland is deliberately still a non-member of the European Union. This evokes the question about football's role in the negotiation of Switzerland's placement within Europe. Football and 'Swissness' have been linked at several times in modern Swiss history, even though the record of the Swiss national football team is rather poor, unlike Switzerland's political stability, economic prosperity and democratic traditions. This article will first give a concise overview of modern Switzerland's placement within Europe in general. The second section explores the relationship between football, national consciousness and Switzerland's place in Europe from the late nineteenth to the early twenty-first centuries. In the third section, the link of this triangle to the relationship of Switzerland's linguistic communities is analysed, and the last section discusses the impact of the 2008 European Championship on Switzerland's placement within Europe.

Introduction

Switzerland is by no means a successful nation in the football world. Unlike her political stability, economic prosperity and democratic traditions, the record of her national football team is rather poor, the greatest success still being a silver medal in the 1924 Olympic tournament. Nevertheless, football has been regarded as a national sport in Switzerland since the inter-war era and football and 'Swissness' have been linked at several times in modern Swiss history. Thinking of Switzerland as a 'Sonderfall' (special case) committed to neutrality and political independence shaped external football relations at several moments and in different ways. Although hosting UEFA and having co-organized the 2008 European Championship, Switzerland is deliberately still a non-member of the European Union. This evokes the question about football's role in the negotiation of Switzerland's placement within Europe. This article will first give a concise overview of modern Switzerland's placement within Europe in general. The second section explores the relationship between football, national consciousness and Switzerland's place in Europe from the late nineteenth to the early twenty-first centuries. In the third section, the link of this triangle to the relationship of Switzerland's linguistic communities is analysed, and the last section discusses the impact of the 2008 European championship on Switzerland's placement within Europe.

Switzerland and Europe

Switzerland's placement in Europe has been and still is to a certain degree determined by a myth of 'Sonderfall'. Although Switzerland has been highly transnationalized in her economic relations, as well as regarding cultural exchange, since at least the nineteenth century, the dominating discourse was about independence of a small, allegedly peasant nation. From 1848 to 1914, Switzerland as a democratic republic was a special case in Europe indeed as far as her political constitution was concerned. Yet, adherents of the myth of 'Sonderfall' would hardly argue with the 1848 constitution, which resulted out of a short civil war between liberals and conservatives, but is used to stress the mythical foundation of the allegedly already democratic and 'free' confederation in 1291, which in reality was a local peace alliance among peasant elites like many others at that time.

Swiss neutrality became another central pillar of the myth of 'Sonderfall'. In fact, neutrality had been forced upon Switzerland by the 1814/5 Vienna Congress, especially as Russia did not want the country to become a sphere of influence for one of her neighbouring powers. Whilst neutrality was dealt with quite flexibly throughout the nineteenth century,[1] it became a crucial element of Swiss national consciousness in the 'fin de siècle' and even more important during World War I, when partisanship for one of the belligerent coalitions threatened to split the country. After World War I, Switzerland joined the League of Nations, however not before having her neutrality granted within the newly established system of collective security. In the 'spiritual national defence' of the 1930s, neutrality was even more hypostasized. In May 1938, Switzerland abandoned the principle of 'differential neutrality', which allowed participation in economic, but not in military, sanctions concluded by the League of Nations, and returned to so-called 'integral neutrality'.[2]

Neutrality, together with low taxes, made Switzerland an attractive host for international organizations, not only for the League of Nations, which settled in Geneva in 1920, but also for sport federations. After Pierre de Coubertin moved the headquarters of the International Olympic Committee to Lausanne in 1915 in an attempt to preserve the Committee's global character, the Socialist Workers Sport International was founded in Lucerne in 1920 and when FIFA eventually established an administrative headquarters in 1932, Zurich was chosen as its host city. Following World War II, UEFA, founded in 1954, moved to Berne in 1959 (and from there to Nyon in 1995).

Despite spatial proximity to crucial international organizations, attempts to initiate a process of European integration did not meet much enthusiasm in inter-war Switzerland. The Swiss government greeted French foreign minister Aristide Briand's famous 1929/30 initiative regarding its part on the liberalization of trade, although obviously not appreciating the plan's political implications. The pan-European movement, initiated by Count Richard Coudenhove-Kalergi in 1923, nevertheless managed to establish two Swiss branches, which merged into the 'Europa-Union' in 1934. After World War II, this movement organized a conference of European federalists, which took place in September 1946 in Berne and Hertenstein, and resulted in the foundation of the 'Union Européenne des Fédéralistes' (UEF). At the same time, on 19 September 1946, Winston Churchill delivered his famous speech 'The Tragedy of Europe' at the University of Zurich, in which he claimed the formation of 'a certain kind of United States of Europe' and ended with the pathetic call 'let Europe arise!'[3]

The influence of organizations in favour of European integration, however, was very limited in post-war Switzerland. After the country had been spared by World War II, the myth of 'Sonderfall' seemingly gained new evidence. The fact that her fascist neighbours had not attempted to invade Switzerland was not attributed to her wide-ranging integration into the Axis powers' economic system, but to her alleged military strength as well as her 'eternal' neutrality. The country, although according to its economic and political structure an integral part of the anti-Communist world in the Cold War era, would stay apart from military alliances and from any processes of integration threatening to go beyond mere free-trade aims. The 'spiritual national defence' adapted relatively smoothly to the changed geopolitical constellation.[4] This spirit even resulted in plans for nuclear armament of the Swiss army in the 1950s and 1960s.[5]

Switzerland also stayed apart from the United Nations Organization and was very sceptical when it came to initiatives for the establishment of supranational structures in Europe.[6] In 1948, Switzerland was a founding member of the Organization for European Economic Co-operation (OEEC), however, it claimed a special clause of abstention. As for the European Council, founded in 1949, at first Switzerland did not join because of the organization's political impetus, which allegedly threatened the country's neutrality and its plebiscitarian political system. Switzerland restrained her involvement to technical co-operation and only became a full member in 1963.

In 1951, Swiss political elites overwhelmingly rejected the Schuman Plan for the establishment of the European Coal and Steel Community. Also, the 1957 Treaties of Rome, founding the European Economic Community and the Atomic Energy Community, did not meet with much enthusiasm. As a reaction, in 1960, Switzerland became a founding member of the European Free Trade Association (EFTA), which was designed as a purely economic alternative to these communities.[7] In 1972, 72.5% of the Swiss electorate approved of a free-trade agreement with the European Community. However, there were heavy debates during the electoral campaign, when some right-wing opponents even went as far as to compare the European Community with the Third Reich.

After the collapse of the Eastern bloc, Switzerland's placement within Europe had to be renegotiated. In May 1992, the Swiss government submitted an application for membership to the European Community. This application was frozen soon afterwards, after the Swiss electorate rejected the treaty on the European Economic Area (EEA) in December 1992. Only 49.7% approved of the treaty. A clear majority of the cantons had rejecting majorities with, however, the French-speaking part of the country overwhelmingly approving the treaty. However, membership of the European Community would officially remain a strategic goal of the Swiss government. In the run-up to the referendum on the EEA treaty, heavy debates on Switzerland's placement in Europe had taken place. Although the government, three of the four governing parties, employers organizations and trade unions were in favour of the treaty, opponents formed an unholy alliance between national conservatives, led by far-right populist Christoph Blocher, and green forces. Nationalist opponents went as far as to denouncing the EEA as a colonial treaty.

After the lost referendum, the Swiss government pursued a policy of bilateralism, leading to the conclusion of a first bundle of treaties with the EU in 1999. These included regulations on the free movement of people, air and road traffic, agriculture, technical trade barriers, public procurement and science. In 2001, new negotiations began, which resulted in a second bundle of treaties (so-called Bilaterals II) in 2004 on issues such as security and asylum (including Schengen membership) and cooperation in fraud pursuits. Although in the electoral campaign against the EEA treaty, far-right opponents had praised bilateralism as the proper Swiss way to negotiate the country's placement within Europe, they now partially took an even more isolationist stance, opposing also the bilateral treaties. The Swiss electorate, however, supported the policy of bilateralism in several referenda. With the ratification of the second round of bilateral treaties, the Swiss government downgraded their characterization of full EU membership from a 'strategic goal' to an 'option' in 2006.

Football, national consciousness, and Switzerland's place in Europe

Football has played a remarkable role in negotiating Switzerland's placement within Europe at several key moments. Sometimes, it stressed Switzerland's position as a modern and cosmopolitan country interested in transnational relations on a cultural and economic level and wishing to contribute to peace and stability in Europe. On other occasions, football helped to demonstrate Switzerland's willingness to remain an independent and partially isolated 'Sonderfall' and to strengthen the Swiss people's national consciousness. Thus, it somehow reflected Swiss perceptions of the 'outside' world and desirable relations to it.

In its pioneer phase, football clearly reflected Switzerland's quality as a quickly modernizing country that disposed of many transnational links and networks all over the continent. From the late 1860s on, Switzerland became a bridgehead in the game's cultural transfer from the British Isles to the continent. Many British students attended elite schools at Lakes Geneva and Constance and made their fellow pupils familiar with the kicking game. Thus, it was from Switzerland that the spread of the game over large parts of Central, South and Eastern Europe started.[8] Many football pioneers first kicked the ball while studying in Switzerland. Furthermore, many Swiss merchants, academics and teachers would promote football in other European countries. Hans 'Juan' Gamper founded FC Barcelona in 1899, Gustav Kuhn, together with French, Swiss, Spanish, German and Italian friends, founded FC Bari in 1908, Enrico Hintermann founded Internazionale Milano in the same year, and Louis Rauch founded FC Bologna in 1909.

After World War I, football contributed to Swiss attempts to re-establish her neighbour Germany as a respectable member of the international community. Although the losers of World War I had been banned by FIFA and were thus theoretically excluded from all international games, Swiss clubs started to play friendly matches against German teams soon after the end of the war. In Easter 1919, FC Nordstern Basle played some games against clubs from southern Germany. In November 1919, the football associations of the neutral states of Denmark, Finland, the Netherlands, Norway, Sweden, Spain and Switzerland held a conference at which they passed a resolution against the exclusion of any member from FIFA for other than sportive reasons.

In April 1920, the football associations of Switzerland and Germany concluded a friendly international. This game was sponsored by the German government, who had become aware of the importance of sports in overcoming Germany's isolation.[9] After the conclusion of the game had become known, protests were launched against Switzerland, especially by the football associations of France, Belgium and England. Switzerland's French-speaking community also protested and would not let their players participate in the game. The latter took place all the same on 27 June 1920 in Zurich and ended with a Swiss 4–1 victory. The return match in Frankfurt in March 1922 was a mass event, when 40,000 German fans welcomed the Swiss team and German officials' speeches stressed the political impact of the 1920 game and neutral Switzerland's mission as an agent of peace and humanity.

Towards the end of the 1930s, football became a catalyst for Swiss national consciousness and thus contributed to the placement of Switzerland in a Europe that was dominated more and more by fascism. The seminal event in this respect was the 1938 victory against 'Greater Germany' in the preliminary round of the World Cup in France.[10] After a 1–1 draw in the first game, Germany led 2–0 in the replay after just 20 minutes, but in the end, Switzerland won 4–2. This victory triggered an outburst of patriotic enthusiasm. Immediately after the radio had heralded the end of the game, spontaneous celebrations took place in many Swiss cities and villages. The press glorified the game as a proof that even a small nation was able to survive in an environment dominated by great powers. Minister of Defence Rudolf Minger congratulated the victorious team 'with confederate salute'[11] and many Swiss citizens would send patriotic telegrams to Paris. A week after the Paris game, an article in the newspaper *Sport* claimed that football should become a compulsory subject in Swiss schools, for, as the victory against 'Greater Germany' had shown, it promoted patriotism and could thus become an agent of 'spiritual national defence'.[12]

The cultural policy of 'spiritual national defence', officially formulated by the Swiss government in their 1938 'message on the preservation and propaganda of Swiss culture',[13] defined Switzerland's placement within Europe as that of an independent, democratic, federative and pluricultural nation, and was directed against both communism and fascism.[14] However, the 'spiritual national defence' would sometimes include nationalistic elements hardly different from those of the neighbouring fascist powers' propaganda and has thus even been characterized by some scholars as a form of 'helvetic totalitarianism'.[15]

The spiritual national defence's ambivalent character was also inherent in the football games between Switzerland and several fascist powers during World War II. From September 1939 on, Switzerland played 11 official internationals against the Axis powers and their allies (Germany, Italy, Hungary and Vichy-France) as well as two games against the fascist neutrals Spain and Portugal and three nonofficial internationals against the Ustashe state of Croatia. In particular, the games against Germany had an ambivalent character, stressing good neighbourhood, but at the same time Switzerland's claim to remain an independent and democratic country.[16] Thus, these games quite accurately reflected Switzerland's policy of wide-ranging economic cooperation with the Axis powers without political or ideological integration into their European system of power. The two friendly internationals against Sweden in 1942 and 1943, by contrast, were widely interpreted as a 'peaceful demonstration of the neutral stance'.[17]

The post-World War II internationals reflected the country's placement within a newly structured Europe.[18] In April 1945, even before the fighting in Europe had ended, Switzerland played a friendly game against liberated France, which the Swiss press explicitly linked to football's alleged commitment to international understanding.[19] From 1945 to 1948, four internationals between Switzerland and England took place. This was quite remarkable as England played all their other 'victory internationals' exclusively against World War II allies. Although Switzerland's economic cooperation with the Axis powers was hardly appreciated by the U.S. government, the British preferred to sympathize with Switzerland's quality as one of the few European democracies in the early 1940s.[20] The encounter in July 1945 was attended by General Henri Guisan, commander-in-chief of the Swiss army, Federal Councillor Kobelt as well as British ambassador Norton. The newspaper *Sport* interpreted this game as a 'demonstration of the spiritual solidarity of two democratic countries'.[21]

For a short time immediately after the war, there were also Swiss attempts to establish good relations with the Soviet Union. Although the Swiss government had pursued an extremely anti-Bolshevik policy from 1918 to 1943, this stance would change shortly after the Battle of Stalingrad. Thus, having prohibited the Swiss Communist Party in 1940, the government allowed the formation of a new Communist Party organization in the last months of the war. Football became involved into this short-lived change as well. In 1934, the government had refused entry visas to the Soviet national team, which had been invited by the Swiss Association of Communist Red Sports Footballers.[22] After the Soviet victory in World War II, the Swiss envoy to Moscow arranged a friendly international in Switzerland, which was scheduled for spring 1947. However, the game had to be cancelled due to an overburdening of the Soviet team with internationals. Thereafter, the emerging Cold War made an encounter with the Eastern superpower no longer desirable. Only in April 1966, would the first game between the national teams of Switzerland and the Soviet Union take place.

Yet it was not just the negotiation of Switzerland's relations with the victorious countries that football was involved in after World War II. In November 1946, the Swiss team played a friendly game against Austria in Berne, and the Swiss reserves travelled to Innsbruck for an encounter with a Tyrolean selection. In this context, Swiss football officials expressed their hopes that there should be a free and independent Austria soon, and the Swiss players gave their Austrian counterparts food packets as presents.[23] Last but not least, as after World War I, Swiss footballers would also break the boycott against Germany. In April 1947, the newspaper *Sport* stated that the democratic structure of Swiss sports should be an example for Germany.[24] In 1946 and 1947, several Swiss teams travelled to southern Germany to play friendly games there. In September 1948, FC Wiesloch was the first German team to travel abroad, playing a game against FC Schlieren, which was considered by officials of both teams as a contribution to international understanding.[25] Three weeks later, city selections of Zurich, St. Gall and Basle played friendly games in Stuttgart, Munich and Karlsruhe. Although they were heavily criticized by the countries that had been occupied by Nazi Germany, the Swiss Football Association would only penalize the organizers with a symbolic sum.

In the same year, the Swiss Football Association tried to obtain Germany's reentry to FIFA, however, it would fail at first. At least, FIFA permitted international games against German club teams in May 1949, whereupon 1st FC Nuremberg were the first German elite class team to travel abroad, playing against Young Fellows Zurich. In 1950, after intensive lobbying by the Swiss Football Association, the FIFA congress decided to lift their ban against Germany.[26] The first international of the newly established Federal Republic of Germany took place on 22 November 1950 in Stuttgart against Switzerland and was attended by 115,000 spectators. Whereas the Swiss newspaper *Sport* commented that the game was a 'symbol of peace' and stressed neutral Switzerland's duty to create 'bridges over ditches of hatred and pain',[27] the German *Sportbericht* stated that Switzerland was 'a great power of goodwill, to whom we have to be eternally grateful'.[28]

In the Cold War era, football would hardly play a role in negotiating Switzerland's role within Europe, which stood firm as a neutral country even outside the United Nations Organization, but ideologically, and regarding its political and economic systems, clearly belonging to the 'West'. The 1954 World Cup hosted by Switzerland had an impact on Western Germany's self-consciousness[29] and the preparations for the event triggered some debates about the relationship between Swissness and cultural modernity,[30] Switzerland's placement within Europe, however, was not really at stake.

Only in the 1990s, with the end of global bipolarity and the post-modern shattering of all certainties, would football again play a role in Switzerland's placement within Europe and the world. It was, however, no longer primarily the choice and boycott of partners for friendly internationals that was crucial in this context, but the very composition of the Swiss national team. From the late 1980s on, the latter had become a more and more multicultural event.[31] As the Swiss football pioneers before World War I had been emblematical of Switzerland's quality as a transnationalized emigrant country, the multicultural national team around the turn of the millennium became the symbol of an immigrant society. The news magazine *Facts* stressed this in 2004 by titling 'Hopp Schwiic', thus linking the traditional slogan 'Hopp Schwiiz' to the typical suffix of Serbo-Croatian names.[32]

However, Swiss national players with foreign roots are not a new phenomenon of the post-Cold War era. Already from the 1920s to the 1950s, the most successful period in Swiss football history, some of the most important players such as Severino Minelli, Sirio Vernati and Hans-Peter Friedländer were sons of immigrants from neighbouring countries. Génia Walaschek, a striker with Czech, German, Swiss, Russian and Hungarian roots, even played some time for Switzerland as a stateless person. From the late 1980s, the number of national players with a migrant background, often referred to as 'secondos', increased dramatically. Kickers with roots in the neighbouring countries of Italy, Germany, France and Austria would still dominate, but players from Turkey, Spain as well as the former Yugoslavia, and even Congo, the Ivory Coast, Colombia and Argentina also became members of the Swiss national team.

Although national coach Köbi Kuhn praised in 2005 the plurality of mentalities in the Swiss team and the boulevard weekly *Sonntags-Blick* stated that the national football team was a good example of how Swiss and foreigners could learn from each other,[33] far-right voices would criticize the 'overforeignization' of Switzerland in general and of the national football team in particular.[34] Isolationism regarding Switzerland's participation in the process of European integration, xenophobia and opposition against the deployment of 'secondos' in the national football team emanated from the same political circles. On an electoral level, the achievements of 'secondo' players for the Swiss national team had hardly any impact. In October 2004, two proposals for a quicker naturalization of second- and third-generation foreigners were rejected by 56.8 and 51.6% of the electorate, despite the national team being an issue in supportive propaganda and Spanish-born national player Ricardo Cabanas actively participating in the electoral campaign.

The two qualification games against Turkey for the 2006 World Cup were another episode of placing post-Cold War Switzerland in Europe.[35] Although the adversary was a country with an active application for full EU membership, the Swiss media, especially the boulevard newspaper *Blick*, would nevertheless portray Turkey in a quite traditional manner as an uncivilized nation. The riots in the Sükrü Saraçoglu Stadyumu in Istanbul after the second game in November 2005 activated perceptions of the Turks that can be traced back to early modern fears of the Ottoman Empire[36] and experienced a renaissance in the discussions on Turkey's attempts to join the EU. In particular, German politicians and scholars opposed to Turkey's membership of the EU would rather argue with prejudices drawn from Samuel Huntington's 'Clash of Civilisations'[37] than with Turkey's ongoing official denial of the 1915/6 Armenian genocide that had been a result of the Young Turks' embrace of European nationalism. On balance, discourses around the two Swiss games against Turkey in 2005 would fit quite well into euro-centrist perceptions of the 'Orient'[38] and thus implicitly take Switzerland's position as an integral part of Europe for granted, without, however, reflecting on her relationship to the EU.

Swiss football and the 'Röstigraben'

Football's remarkable role in negotiating Switzerland's placement within Europe has sometimes been closely linked to internal issues, especially to the relationship between her two largest linguistic communities, German-speakers and French-speakers. Conflicts between these two communities are usually referred to as the 'Röstigraben' (literally 'Rösti ditch'), from the name of the national Swiss–German potato dish Rösti.[39] At several moments in modern Swiss history, the 'Röstigraben' was closely linked to conflicting notions of Switzerland's placement within Europe. In the late nineteenth and early twentieth centuries, and especially during World War I, German-speakers were under strong cultural and political influence from Germany, whereas French-speakers were in favour of closer connections with France. In the late twentieth century, the French-speaking parts of Switzerland supported the country's membership in the EEA and even had strong sympathies for full EU membership, whereas isolationism was much stronger in the German (as well as in the Italian and Romansh)-speaking parts of the country.

These debates would affect football as well. Already in 1899, the clubs of the French-speaking part of Switzerland had left the national football association and founded the 'Ligue Romande'.[40] However, this split did not result from political animosities, but from the question of Sunday games. The leading figures of the 'Ligue Romande' were not French-speaking Swiss, but Germans and British. In 1920, however, another split threatened, which was clearly motivated by politics. After the aforementioned friendly international between Switzerland and banned Germany, and after the Swiss Football Association had recalled their participation in the 1920 Olympic football tournament, partly for financial reasons, but partly in order to protest against the exclusion of Germany, Austria and Hungary, long debates between the delegates from the two linguistic communities followed at the association's general assembly in August 1920. The French-speaking delegates even threatened to found an autonomous 'Union suisse romande de football et d'athlétisme'. These debates resulted in the adoption of a new mode of conduct for the association's 'foreign policy', which from now on was to be pursued by two international delegates, one originating from the German-speaking part of the country and one from the French-speaking part.[41]

In the 1990s, the link between the 'Röstigraben' and Switzerland's placement within Europe spilt over to the sphere of football once again; however, it would not reach an intensity comparable with the time after World War I.[42] After the French-speaking part of Switzerland had been overruled in the 1992 EEA referendum, a series of three referenda on the weekend before the start of the 1994 World Cup showed an analogous outcome. On 12 June 1994, majorities of 51 and 52.8% of the countrywide electorate approved of a constitutional article for the promotion of culture and the acceleration of the process of naturalization for young foreigners. However, both proposals, which had gained considerable support in the French-speaking part of Switzerland, failed, because a majority of the cantons, especially the small conservative ones in German-speaking central and eastern Switzerland, had rejected them. On the same day, 57.2% of the electorate rejected Swiss participation in future UN peacekeeping operations. Here again, German-speakers had overruled French-speakers.

Commentators interpreted the outcome of these three referenda as another defeat for the cosmopolitan and Europhile French-speaking part of the country against the isolationist and conservative German-speaking part. Many journalists recommended football as a means to reconcile the two linguistic groups. Furthermore, the Swiss national team was seen as ambassadors of a more progressive Switzerland, who should overcome the country's image abroad as a nation of isolationist and conservative rejecters, ready to defend their fatherland with their rifles and hostile against every foreigner.[43] After the Swiss team had won their second World Cup game against Romania 4–1, cultural anthropologist Arnold Niederer commented in the weekly *SonntagsZeitung* that football was much simpler than politics, everybody would understand the game. That is why football was able to create national enthusiasm and build bridges over political and confessional ditches.[44]

The 2008 European Championship and Switzerland's place in Europe

How did the 2008 European Championship (EURO 2008), hosted jointly by Switzerland and Austria, affect Switzerland's place in Europe? To anticipate the result of this section, it has to be said that the EURO 2008 hardly played a political role in the way outlined above. The deployment of many 'secondo' players in this event did not change notions of Swiss citizenship, nor was the overall criticism of the EU's governance model affected. The fact that approval for the Swiss government's European policy was slightly higher in a referendum in February 2009 than in previous referenda in 2005 and 2006 can hardly be traced back to the experience of EURO 2008, but rather to the imminent economic crisis and to the internal problems of far-right opponents.

Switzerland's joint application for the EURO 2008 together with Austria was hardly a political statement, but resulted from several failed attempts by Austria to organize the championship as the 'Danube games' together with Hungary, the Czech Republic or Croatia. The Austrian Football Federation was obviously planning an event, in which it could dominate its partner financially and which should be linked to the concept of 'Mitteleuropa' (Central Europe).[45] Only after these attempts had failed in 1999, was Switzerland considered as viable partner for a joint application on an equal footing, which was successful in 2002. For the Swiss side, it was clear from the beginning that an application for this event was only possible with a partner, and Austria was the only neighbouring country of comparable size that might be interested in such a partnership.

Enthusiasm about the event was not unanimous with local populations. A project for a new football arena in Zurich, which would host some of the EURO 2008 games, was rejected by nearly 40% of the city's electorate in a referendum in September 2003 with a rejecting majority even in the concerned quarter of the city, the multicultural 'Industriequartier', mainly inhabited by students, immigrant workers, artists and leftist alternatives.[46] In the following months and years, construction of the stadium was prevented by several appeals.[47] According to opinion polls conducted by DemoSCOPE, 51% of the Swiss population were looking forward to the event in January 2007, with 3% being angry and 44% not interested. A year later, 54% were looking forward, 6% were angry, 38% not interested and 2% had no opinion. However, in January 2008, a relative majority of 49% (compared with 43% the year before) thought that EURO 2008 would cause unnecessary costs for Swiss taxpayers and 43% (compared with 31% the year before) feared an increased risk of terror attacks in

Switzerland due to the event. However, 80% agreed that EURO 2008 would improve Switzerland's image in the world and also boost the Swiss economy.[48]

Although the joint application for the championship was not meant to promote Switzerland's integration into the EU area, it nevertheless had some impact technically leading in this direction. For the duration of the championship, a joint EURO 2008 visa for both the Schengen area and Switzerland was created. After Russia had reached the quarter-finals, Swiss border police even allowed Russian supporters who could produce only a Schengen visa to travel to Basle, thus anticipating Switzerland's entry to the Schengen area half a year before its completion. Furthermore, the policing of the tournament also deepened existing cooperations between Switzerland and Germany.

Altogether, however, EURO 2008 did not much affect Switzerland's cooperation with the EU and her members. Because the performance of the Swiss team in the tournament was rather poor, the latter had hardly any emotional impact that would have affected the country's mental placement within Europe either.

Notes

1. Mittler, *Der Weg zum Ersten Weltkrieg*.
2. Bonjour, *Geschichte der schweizerischen Neutralität*, 275–6.
3. Koller, 'Kriegsende und Friedensprojekt', 41–4.
4. Tanner, 'Zwischen "American Way of Life" und "Geistiger Landesverteidigung"', 351–63.
5. Metzler, *Option einer Nuklearbewaffnung für die Schweizer Armee 1945–1969*.
6. Jost, *Europa und die Schweiz 1945–1950*.
7. Maurhofer, *Die schweizerische Europapolitik vom Marshallplan zur EFTA*.
8. Coviello, *Die Macht der Disziplin*; Lanfranchi, 'Football et modernité', 76–88; Koller, '"Little England"', 11–22; Ghanbarian-Baleva, '"Ein englischer Sport" aus der Schweiz', 155–82; Emeliantseva, 'Sport und urbane Lebenswelten', 31–76.
9. Koller, 'Das Boykottspiel', 27–37; Eggers, *Fussball in der Weimarer Republik*, 104–5.
10. Koller and Brändle, '"Man fühlte, dass die Eidgenossen eine Grosstat vollbracht hatten"', 177–214.
11. Cited in *Neue Zürcher Zeitung*, June 10, 1938.
12. *Sport*, June 17, 1938.
13. 'Botschaft des Bundesrates an die Bundesversammlung über die Organisation und die Aufgaben der schweizerischen Kulturwahrung und Kulturwerbung vom 9.12.1938', *Bundesblatt*, 90 2 (1938): 985–1033.
14. Mooser, 'Die "Geistige Landesverteidigung" in den 1930er Jahren', 685–708.
15. Jost, 'Bedrohung und Enge', 131, 175–6.
16. Koller, 'Fussballerische Landesverteidigung an Führers Geburtstag', 63–75.
17. *Neue Zürcher Zeitung*, November 16, 1942.
18. Brändle, 'Von der Politik der guten Dienste bis zur WM im eigenen Land', 95–118.
19. *Tages-Anzeiger*, April 7, 1945.
20. Wylie, *Britain, Switzerland, and the Second World War*.
21. *Sport*, July 13, 1945.
22. Koller, 'Proletarische Verbrüderung auf exterritorialem Gebiet', 51–61.
23. *Sport*, November 13, 1946.
24. *Sport*, April 30, 1947.
25. Hochstrasser and Stahel, *Jubiläumsschrift*, 34–39.
26. Wahlig, *Ein Tor zur Welt?*, 102–111.
27. *Sport*, November 22, 1950.
28. Cited by Brändle, *Von der Politik der guten Dienste*, 104.
29. For example, Gehrmann, 'Le sport comme moyen de réhabilitation nationale', 231–3. Brüggemeier, *Zurück auf dem Platz*, has recently challenged the traditional notion of the 1954 World Cup as seminal event for West Germany's national consciousness.
30. Brändle, *Von der Politik der guten Dienste*; Koller, 'Das dramatische Duell', 77–88.
31. Koller, 'Wer ist ein echter Schweizer?', 51–62.

32. *Facts*, July 15, 2004.
33. *Sonntags*-Blick, November 21, 2005.
34. For example, Weltwoche, June 17, 2004; Schweizer Demokrat, September 2004.
35. Hellmüller, *Fussball zwischen Himmel und Hölle*; Lischer and Zibung, *Mediale Berichterstattung über Türkinnen und Türken*; Knellwolf, '"Mit dem Einzug in den Fussballhimmel geantwortet"', 143–52.
36. Kissling, 'Türkenfurcht und Türkenhoffnung im 15./16. Jahrhundert', 1–18; Höfert, *Den Feind beschreiben*. For the early nineteenth century: Grimm, 'Das "Türkenbild" der philhellenischen Freischärler', 87–99.
37. Huntington, *The clash of Civilizations*.
38. Said, *Orientalism*.
39. Büchi, *Röstigraben*.
40. Koller, 'Jamais le dimanche', 60; Ligue Romande de Football: 100 ans de joli jeu.
41. Ruoff, *Das Goldene Buch des Schweizer Fussballs*, 46; Koller, 'Das Boykottspiel'.
42. Beer, '"Jetzt müssen die Welschen endlich Tore schiessen"', 131–41.
43. For example, *Journal de Genève et Gazette de Lausanne*, June 27, 1994; *Der Bund*, June 11, 1994; *SonntagsZeitung*, June 19, 1994.
44. *SonntagsZeitung*, June 26, 1994.
45. See on the concept 'Mitteleuropa' in general Emeliantseva, Malz, and Ursprung, *Einführung in die Osteuropäische Geschichte*, 14. On its application to sports: Marschik, 'Mitteleuropa: Politische Konzepte – sportliche Praxis', 88–108; Marschik and Sottopietra, *Erbfeinde und Hasslieben*.
46. *Tages-Anzeiger*, September 8, 2003; *Neue Zürcher Zeitung*, September 8, 2003.
47. *Tages-Anzeiger*, June 11, 2005; June 15, 2005; *Neue Zürcher Zeitung*, June 15 and 22, 2005; *Tagblatt der Stadt Zürich*, June 13 and 15, 2005.
48. 'Die Schweiz freut sich auf die Fussball-EM', DemoSCOPE, Medienmitteilung vom 29.1.2008.

References

Beer, E. '"Jetzt müssen die Welschen endlich Tore schiessen" – Annäherung an die Weltspitze: Schweiz–Rumänien 4:1 (22.6.1994). In *Sternstunden des Schweizer Fussballs,* ed. C. Koller, 131–41. Münster: Lit Verlag, 2008.

Bonjour, E. *Geschichte der schweizerischen Neutralität.* Vol. 3. Basel: Helbing + Lichtenhahn, 1980.

Brändle, F. 'Von der Politik der guten Dienste bis zur WM im eigenen Land'. In *Die Nati: Die Geschichte der Schweizer Fussball-Nationalmannschaft,* ed. B. Jung, 95–118. Göttingen: Werkstatt, 2006.

Brüggemeier, F-J. *Zurück auf dem Platz: Deutschland und die Fussball-Weltmeisterschaft 1954.* Munich: dva, 2004.

Büchi, C. *Röstigraben.* Zürich: Buchverlag NZZ, 2001.

Coviello, M. *Die Macht der Disziplin: Ursprünge des modernen Fussballs in Grossbritannien und der Schweiz.* Zürich: unpublished MA thesis, University of Zürich, 2007.

Eggers, E. *Fussball in der Weimarer Republik.* Kassel: Agon Sportverlag, 2001.

Emeliantseva, E. 'Sport und urbane Lebenswelten im spätzarischen St. Petersburg (1860–1914)'. In *Sport als städtisches Ereignis,* ed. C. Koller, 31–76. Ostfildern: Thorbecke, 2008.

Emeliantseva, E., A. Malz, and D. Ursprung. *Einführung in die Osteuropäische Geschichte.* Zürich: Orell Füssli, 2008.

Gehrmann, S. 'Le sport comme moyen de réhabilitation nationale au début de la République Fédérale d'Allemagne: Les Jeux Olympiques de 1952 et la Coupe du Monde de Football de 1954'. In *Sports et relations internationales,* ed. A. Wahl, 231–43. Metz: Centre de Recherche Histoire et Civilisation de l'Université de Metz, 1994.

Ghanbarian-Baleva, G. 'Ein "englischer Sport" aus der Schweiz: Der bulgarische Fussball von seiner Entstehung bis zum Beginn der 1970er Jahre'. In *Überall ist der Ball rund: Zur Geschichte und Gegenwart des Fussballs in Ost- und Südosteuropa,* ed. D. Dahlmann, A. Hilbrennner, and B. Lenz, 155–82. Essen: Klartext, 2006.

Grimm, G. 'Das "Türkenbild" der philhellenischen Freischärler'. In *Südosteuropa unter dem Halbmond: Untersuchungen über Geschichte und Kultur der südosteuropäischen Völker während der Türkenzeit,* ed. P. Bartl and H. Glassl, 87–99. München: Trofenik, 1975.

Hellmüller, L. *Fussball zwischen Himmel und Hölle: Schweizer Engel – türkische Teufel? Eine empirische Untersuchung der Berichterstattung von Blick, Tages-Anzeiger und NZZ zu den Barrage-Spielen Schweiz–Türkei.* Fribourg: unpublished MA thesis, University of Fribourg, 2006.

Hochstrasser, E., and H. Stahel. *Jubiläumsschrift 75 Jahre FC Schlieren.* Schlieren: FC Schlieren, 1996.

Höfert, A. *Den Feind beschreiben: "Türkengefahr" und europäisches Wissen über das Osmanische Reich 1450–1600.* Frankfurt: Campus, 2003.

Huntington, S.P. *The Clash of Civilizations and the Remaking of World Order.* New York: Simon and Schuster, 1996.

Jost, H.U. 'Bedrohung und Enge (1914–1945)'. In *Geschichte der Schweiz – und der Schweizer.* Vol. 3. ed. B. Mesmer, J.-C. Favez, and R. Broggini, 101–89. Basel: Helbing & Lichtenhahn, 1983.

Jost, H.U. *Europa und die Schweiz 1945–1950: Europarat, Supranationalität und schweizerische Unabhängigkeit.* Lausanne: Chronos, 1999.

Kissling, H. J. 'Türkenfurcht und Türkenhoffnung im 15./16. Jahrhundert: Zur Geschichte eines "Komplexes"'. *Südost-Forschungen* 23 (1964): 1–18.

Knellwolf, T. '"Mit dem Einzug in den Fussballhimmel geantwortet": Türkei – Schweiz 4:2 (16.11.2005)'. In *Sternstunden des Schweizer Fussballs,* ed. C. Koller, 143–52. Münster: Lit Verlag, 2008.

Koller, C. 'Kriegsende und Friedensprojekt – die Anfänge des europäischen Einigungsprozesses nach dem Zweiten Weltkrieg'. *Rote Revue* 83, 3 (2005): 41–4.

Koller, C. '"Little England": Die avantgardistische Rolle der Schweiz in der Pionierphase des Fussballs'. In *Die Nati: Die Geschichte der Schweizer Fussball-Nationalmannschaft,* ed. B. Jung, 11–22. Göttingen: Werkstatt, 2006.

Koller, C. 'Wer ist ein echter Schweizer? Doppelbürger, "Secondos", Ein- und Auswanderer in der Nati'. In *Die Nati: Die Geschichte der Schweizer Fussball-Nationalmannschaft,* ed. B. Jung, 51–62. Göttingen: Werkstatt, 2006.

Koller, C. 'Jamais le dimanche'. *Zwölf – Fussball-Geschichten aus der Schweiz* 4 (2007): 60.

Koller, C. 'Fussballerische Landesverteidigung an Führers Geburtstag: Schweiz – Deutschland 2:1 (20.4.1942)'. In *Sternstunden des Schweizer Fussballs,* ed. C. Koller, 63–75. Münster: Lit Verlag, 2008.

Koller, C. 'Das Boykottspiel: Schweiz – Deutschland 4:1 (27.6.1920)'. In *Sternstunden des Schweizer Fussballs,* ed. C. Koller, 27–37. Münster: Lit Verlag, 2008.

Koller, C. 'Proletarische Verbrüderung auf exterritorialem Gebiet: Schweiz – Sowjetunion 2:5 (22.8.1934)'. In *Sternstunden des Schweizer Fussballs,* ed. C. Koller, 51–61. Münster: Lit Verlag, 2008.

Koller, C. 'Das dramatische Duell der ungleichen Alpenrepubliken: Schweiz – Österreich 5:7 (26.6.1954)'. In *Sternstunden des Schweizer Fussballs,* ed. C. Koller, 77–88. Münster: Lit Verlag, 2008.

Koller, C., and F. Brändle. '"Man fühlte, dass die Eidgenossen eine Grosstat vollbracht hatten": Fussball und geistige Landesverteidigung in der Schweiz'. *Stadion* 25 (1999): 177–214.

Lanfranchi, P. 'Football et modernité: La Suisse et la pénétration du football sur le continent'. *Traverse* 5 (1998): 76–88.

Ligue Romande de Football: 100 ans de joli jeu. Lausanne, 2000.

Lischer, S., and M.R. Zibung. *Mediale Berichterstattung über Türkinnen und Türken anlässlich der WM-Qualifikationsspiele Schweiz–Türkei.* Unpublished paper, University of Fribourg, 2006.

Marschik, M. 'Mitteleuropa: Politische Konzepte – sportliche Praxis'. *Historical Social Research* 41, 1 (2006): 88–108.

Marschik, M., and D. Sottopietra. *Erbfeinde und Hasslieben: Konzept und Realität Mitteleuropas im Sport.* Münster: Lit Verlag, 2000.

Maurhofer, R. *Die schweizerische Europapolitik vom Marshallplan zur EFTA 1947–1960: Zwischen Integration und Kooperation.* Bamberg: Difo-Druck, 2001.

Metzler, D.B. 'Die Option einer Nuklearbewaffnung für die Schweizer Armee 1945–1969.' *Zeitschrift des Schweizerischen Bundesarchivs: Studien und Quellen. Rüstung und Kriegswirtschaft* (1997): 121–65.

Mittler, M. *Der Weg zum Ersten Weltkrieg: Wie neutral war die Schweiz? Kleinstaat und europäischer Imperialismus.* Zürich: NZZ libro, 2003.

Mooser, J. 'Die "Geistige Landesverteidigung" in den 1930er Jahren: Profile und Kontexte eines vielschichtigen Phänomens der schweizerischen politischen Kultur in der Zwischenkriegszeit'. *Schweizerische Zeitschrift für Geschichte,* 47 (1997): 685–708.

Ruoff, P. *Das goldene Buch des Schweizer Fussballs.* Zürich: Domprobstei, 1953.

Said, E.W. *Orientalism.* New York: Pantheon, 1978.

Tanner, J. 'Zwischen "American Way of Life" und "Geistiger Landesverteidigung": Gesellschaftliche Widersprüche in der Schweiz der fünfziger Jahre'. *Unsere Kunstdenkmäler* 43 (1992): 351–63.

Wahlig, H. *Ein Tor zur Welt? Der deutsche Fussball und die FIFA 1945–1950.* Göttingen: Werkstatt, 2008.

Wylie, N. *Britain, Switzerland, and the Second World War.* Oxford: Oxford University Press, 2003.

The Europeanization of Austrian football: history, adaptation and transnational dynamics

Alexander Brand[a], Arne Niemann[b] and Georg Spitaler[c]

[a]*Department of Political Science, Technische Universität Dresden, Germany;* [b]*Department of Political Science, University of Amsterdam, the Netherlands;* [c]*Department of Political Science, University of Vienna, Austria*

In this article we seek to analyse the Europeanization of Austrian football as a consequence of both (1) pressures stemming from the European integration process and (2) changes in domestic football involving other transnational (non-EU) European bodies and phenomena. As for the former, we look at the impact of the 1995 Bosman ruling of the European Court of Justice (both in terms of the nationality regime and the transfer regime) and the European Commission's activities to induce decentralized marketing of broadcasting rights in the EU. In terms of the second aspect, we investigate the impact of the UEFA Champions League and UEFA Cup (now Europa League) on Austrian football and to a lesser extent the role of transnational groupings/club forums and non-governmental organization (NGO) networks. In addition, we analyse the relevance of a 'historically determined' Europeanization process in Austrian football. The hypothesis here is that Austria – as a former dual monarchy and multinational state – has been more internationally oriented right from the beginnings of the game.

Introduction

In the past, studies on Europeanization have often focused on top-down processes of domestic change that were caused by European integration and induced by the institutions of the European Union (EU). Here, we highlight the interdependent two-way character of Europeanization. For us, this term also encapsulates bottom-up or transnational and societal processes that, in turn, impact on European governance, as exemplified by the case of football.[1] Therefore, this article seeks to analyse the Europeanization of Austrian football as a consequence of *both* pressures stemming from the European integration process and changes in domestic football involving other transnational (non-EU) European bodies and phenomena. In terms of the former, we look at the impact of the 1995 Bosman ruling of the European Court of Justice (both in terms of the nationality regime and the transfer regime) and the European Commission's activities to induce decentralized marketing of broadcasting rights in the EU. In terms of the second dimension, we investigate the impact of the UEFA Champions League and UEFA Cup (now Europa League) on Austrian football and look at Europeanizing mechanisms that emanate from transnational groupings/club forums as well as from anti-racism and fan networks. In addition, we analyse the relevance of a 'historically determined' Europeanization process in Austrian football. Our hypothesis in this regard is that Austria – due to its heritage as a fairly multinational state (Austro-Hungarian dual monarchy) – has been more internationally oriented from the beginnings of the game. Thus, it was Europeanized to some degree (as regards the multiethnic make-up of the teams and the almost 'natural' Central European frame of reference for team competition, etc.) long before European integration kicked in. However, some of the more recent Europeanizing dynamics observed in other European leagues, not least in its largest neighbour Germany, are substantially weaker in Austrian football.

Germany serves as a case of comparison throughout the text, not least because of the special and precarious German–Austrian football relationship as neighbours sharing a language and to some degree a historical–cultural heritage,[2] the large versus small country difference, and the allegedly different styles of play frequently invoked, especially by Austrian commentators. However, in some instances, Austrian football has, despite all gestures of dissociation, taken German policies as a point of reference.[3]

This article is structured as follows: the first section discusses Europeanization/internationalization processes before the Bosman era. The second section looks at the nationality issue of the Bosman ruling. The third section deals with the transfer regime aspect of the Bosman ruling and the issue of broadcasting rights. Thereafter, we consider more transnational Europeanization processes by discussing the influence of the Champions League and UEFA Cup, and take up the issue of transnational club forums and anti-racist NGO networks, before drawing some conclusions from our analysis.

Austrian football before Bosman

There is a quite well-researched cultural studies-oriented account of the historical trajectories of football in Austria.[4] Two interesting strands of argument with regard to our concerns in this article are found: on the one hand, the 'Austrification' thesis (Horak), which basically highlights that from its beginnings until the second half of the twentieth century, for the most part, Austrian football meant football in the capital Vienna. On the other hand, the pivotal role of Austrian/Viennese clubs and figures in the creation of a distinctive Central European format and space of the game has received attention (Marschik's treatment of Central European football).

First, Austrification – the idea that a real *Austrian* football has come into play only in the latter half of the twentieth century through a combination of modern economic management strategies, i.e. professionalization and commercialization, and an explicit anti-metropolitan attitude[5] – at first glance seems to contradict the hypothesis of an internationally oriented football. However, a closer look at the contours of Viennese football reveals our idea. Although the equation Austria = Vienna (expressed in the fact that up until the late 1940s the Viennese champion was considered to be the Austrian champion) seems to indicate that the most dynamic development of Austrian football was restricted to a specific space; this very space – Vienna as both the former capital, and the central city of the ancient multinational dual monarchy – and its characteristics as a melting pot of cultures, ethnics, refugees, migrants and inhabitants come into play.

The idea that Austrian/Viennese football was fairly internationalized, especially with regard to Europe, even before World War II is further confirmed by the fact that the most important frame of orientation for Viennese clubs has been the so-called 'Central European triangle', i.e. the tripartite competition between Vienna, Prague and Budapest. As Marschik and Sottopietra have elaborated in depth,[6] the very idea of a

Central European football space – one might say for our purposes, as a transboundary space of action – and a distinctive style of football that developed out of frequent contacts, matches and peer-group orientation can be attributed to a large degree to Viennese clubs and charismatic figures at the national level (most importantly, Hugo Meisl, the General Secretary of the Austrian Football Association, ÖFB, in the inter-war period[7]). This dense network also led to the establishment of the so-called Mitropa[8] Cup (a club competition involving the Central European triangle mentioned above, with Italy and Yugoslavia also incorporated) and the International Cup (national team competition).[9] Both tournaments were forerunners of now well-established competitions at the European level (see Mittag and Legrand in this volume). In this regard, it is important to bear in mind that the 'unofficial' Central European Championships were initially established only on the basis of private arrangements worked out between the participating associations, which underscores the density and depth of the cross-border network. The reasons for establishing these international (albeit regionally bounded) contacts on a regular basis seem to be many-fold: sport may have served as a means by which the respective young states that had belonged to the former empire normalized their relations; this common heritage may, in turn, also explain why contact among these actors evolved in the first place. In any case, business interests and the will to generate extra revenue by establishing an attractive tournament for the masses were a primary incentive.[10] With the occupation of Austria by Nazi Germany in 1938, the Central European dimension of Austrian football to a large extent ceased to exist and did not recover, even after 1945, although there were attempts at revival in the years following World War II.[11]

Thus, it is not too far-fetched to state that the Europeanization of Austrian football has an important pre-Bosman dimension. Whereas in other cases, such as German football, European impulses and orientations can be attributed in large part to the workings of European institutions since the 1990s, Austrian football already had an impressive historical–cultural record with a deep Central European orientation, when Austria became an EU member in 1995.

The Bosman ruling I: the nationality issue

Prior to the Bosman ruling, the migration of (professional) football players towards Austrian clubs had been significantly influenced by rules enacted by the Austrian Football Association (ÖFB), and the professional league (partly induced by Austrian politics), as well as by UEFA and FIFA.[12] The few foreign players that came to Austria in the first years after World War II were mainly refugees. At the end of 1945, there were an estimated one million displaced persons in Austria: (former) forced laborers and prisoners of war, survivors of concentration camps and ethnic Germans fleeing from Eastern Europe. FIFA rules that were implemented in Austria hampered their participation in Austrian football: sportsmen who were members of foreign football associations required the clearance/approval of their home association. Foreign and stateless persons also required the permission of the ÖFB to participate in official games. At the same time, foreign players were regarded with suspicion by some Austrian football officials and in 1949 the newly formed pan-Austrian Football League (Staatsliga) adopted a rule limiting the number of foreign players used in a match to three. This rule survived until the mid-1960s.[13]

The league reform of 1964 led, after heated discussions in the media over 'foreign legionaries' in Austrian football, to a reduction in the number of foreign players per team to two. This was changed back to three in the 1970/1 season. Although the proportion of foreign players decreased in the mid- and late 1960s, it increased to 15% in 1973. The oil crisis of the same year and the subsequent recession led to a general halt in the recruitment of foreign workers (through the social partners) in Austria, a step that was paralleled by the ÖFB, which ruled that clubs in the two professional leagues could not contract any additional foreign players. In 1977, the Austrian Football Association again liberalized the rules governing the use of foreign players to two. At the same time, players who had already played for a club in the 1976/7 season were not counted towards the respective foreigners contingent. This was largely in line with the rule enacted by UEFA in 1978, after negotiations with the European Commission, in which it recommended allowing at least two foreign players, although excluding 'assimilated' players (that had been in residence in the respective country for at least five years) from this restriction. As a result, the proportion of foreign players in Austria's first league increased again, from 6.7% in 1976/7 to 11.8% in 1978/9.[14]

The fall of the Iron Curtain in the late 1980s increasingly turned Austria into a country of transit and immigration. The political changes also affected the football migration regime, especially in Central and Eastern Europe. Transfer rule restrictions were gradually abolished and players increasingly made use of their freedom to travel. This led to an increase in the numbers of, especially of Hungarian and Czechoslovakian, players in Austrian football,[15] however, this mostly affected the lower leagues, amateur teams and 'commuters' (*Pendler*), who continued to live in their home countries, but played/worked for a certain time in Austria. Within professional football, this surge was not felt that much, not least because Austria lost more and more of its special appeal as a destination for Central and East European players. Before 1989, the geo-political position of Austria as a neutral state in Central Europe gave Austrian clubs a privileged position in their negotiations with communist sport authorities in Eastern and Central Europe to receive approval for contracting players or managers from these countries (mostly from Czechoslovakia or Hungary; even the first Soviet player in the West signed a contract in Austria with Rapid Vienna). After 1989, it increasingly became a transit country in this regard.

With Austria's accession to the EU in 1995, the Bosman ruling of the same year also became effective. Players with an EU/EEA nationality were on a par with Austrians from 1996/7, as a result of which any restrictions limiting their numbers were now illegal. But Austria went further. In 1996, the competent federal ministry ruled that up to five third-country nationals were allowed per club.[16] In 1998, the ministry liberalized the rules further by putting third-country nationals that had been in residence for longer (and those with a trainee player qualification) on a par with Austrian players. In 2001, the ministry extended the maximum number of third-country players to seven.

There seem to be several explanations for this liberalization beyond that strictly required by the Bosman ruling. First, Austrian professional clubs obviously expected to gain a certain advantage through this extensive liberalization. The two professional leagues principally attracted (and still attract) players from Central and Eastern Europe, including the former Yugoslavia. Clubs sought to continue to make use of these players, given that they were and still are relatively moderately priced and thus affordable for Austrian clubs. Second, it could be argued that the Europeanization pressures were accompanied and paralleled by more general trends towards globalization, liberalization and deregulation.[17] In this regard, professional football increasingly came to be seen as a distinct field of business, although nevertheless part of a neo-liberally restructured economic sphere.[18]

As a result of such liberalization, the proportion of foreign players increased sharply in the post-Bosman era. Whereas in 1995, 19% of top league football players in Austria were foreign, this percentage had doubled by 2000. This increase constituted the biggest change in terms of the composition of club teams in the last 40 years. In terms of regional tendencies, there has also been a shift since 1995 with a reduction in the proportion of players from Eastern Europe and neighbouring countries in general, while the percentage of players from the rest of (EU/EEA) Europe has temporarily more than doubled (Figure 1).[19]

After several years of liberalization, voices were increasingly raised that advocated certain counter-measures to be taken against the continuous inflow of foreign-born players that had followed the Bosman ruling. This viewpoint was accelerated by a change in government to a center-right coalition that included the right-wing populist Freedom Party of Austria (FPÖ). In 2001, the sports minister Susanne Riess-Passer (FPÖ) only conditionally gave her consent to a further extension of third-country nationals in Austrian professional football. The condition, around which a compromise was built, was the so-called '9+9 rule', agreed upon at a 'round table' meeting comprising representatives of the league, the ÖFB, the players' union, the Ministry of Economics, the leading FPÖ-politicians Jörg Haider and Peter Westenthaler, and the sports minister. The clubs voluntarily committed themselves to a 'gentlemen's agreement' –at least nine players on the match sheet had to be eligible for selection to Austrian national teams.[20] This agreement was justified by the need to advance talented young national players (in order to enhance the performance the national teams). Because EU/EEA foreigners were not treated equally to nationals in this rule, the non-conformity to EU standards of the '9+9 rule' was obvious from the beginning.[21] It was, however, never taken to the courts, not least because after a few months, the gentlemen's agreement had been undermined by Sturm Graz, a club that did not want to forgo certain foreign players in a decisive league match.

The chiefs of the professional football league (Bundesliga) clubs, however, made another arrangement, which still holds today. Although the number of third-country

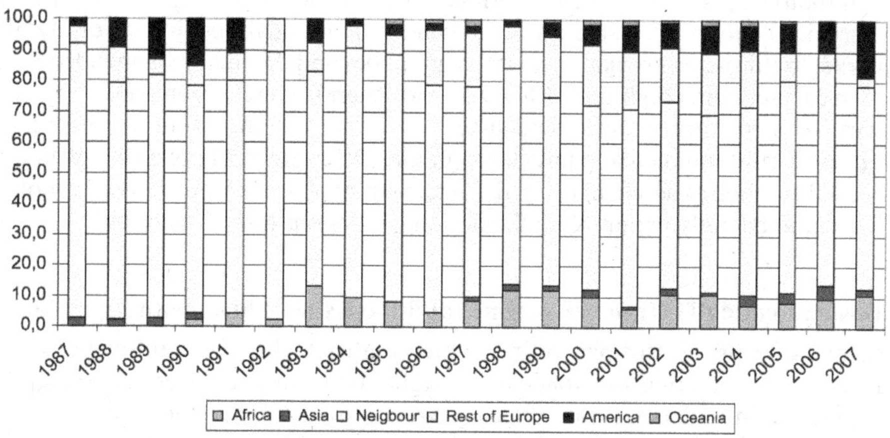

Figure 1. Development of the respective proportion of foreign-born players according to their country of origin (Africa, Asia, Neighbouring Country, Rest of Europe, America, Oceania) in Austrian football, 1987/8 to 2007/8, shown as shares of 100% of the respective numbers of foreign top league players.

players remained constant at seven until July 2003, a premium system (already part of the '9+9 rule'), which 'rewards' the use of Austrian players, was extended. With this compensatory measure, also referred to as the 'Österreicher-Topf' (the Austrians pot), money earned from broadcasting rights is distributed to clubs according to the number of minutes that players who can be selected for Austrian national teams are fielded. Legally, this arrangement seems somewhat dubious because it introduces an incentive to discriminate between Austrians and EU foreigners (potentially to the latter's disadvantage).[22] With the exception of internationally oriented clubs such as Red Bull Salzburg, most Austrian clubs seek to receive the relatively modest sums of the Austrian's pot[23] and the overall percentage of foreign players in the Austrian Bundesliga has decreased from 41% in 2003/4 to 37% in 2007/8.[24]

A number of actors have advocated measures to compensate for the consequences of liberalization since Bosman; at the forefront in this regard are prominent Austrian media outlets. They deplored the disadvantages for Austrian football of bringing (as most of the Austrian media presume, often mediocre[25]) foreign players into the Bundesliga, which was said to have increasingly prevented young national talent from playing sufficient professional football in Austria, and to have reduced the quality of the national team in the long run. The media discourse was flanked, and in some cases also further fed, by politicians, not least because the restrictions that were demanded fitted into the worldview of the right-wing populist FPÖ and their spin-off BZÖ (Alliance for the Future of Austria).

Since 2004, the admission of third-country nationals to Bundesliga clubs has been governed by the state's legislation for key professionals in certain segments of the market ('Schlüsselarbeitskräfte'), for whom a minimum wage is foreseen. A numerical restriction per club is thus no longer in place. Basically this amounts to an almost/*de facto* full liberalization, at least for the (truly) professional Premier League.[26] In the first years after the introduction of this legislation, the set quotas were not reached, although there were problems after 2006 because quotas were exhausted.

Overall, the nationality issue of the Bosman ruling set in motion, or at least substantially furthered, very significant liberalization of the nationality regime in Austrian football. As in the case of Germany, the measures accompanying the ruling were varied: mainly progressive aspects, such as the gradual opening up of the players' market to third-country nationals (thus going beyond the legally demanded deregulation measures with regard to EU/EEA foreigners), were accompanied by more conservative steps and counter-tendencies, first through the more discussed than enacted '9+9' rule and then and now through the 'Österreicher-Topf'. However, all in all, this led to enormous changes in the make-up of Austrian professional football, which seem to be aptly captured by the notion of 'system transformation'.

The Bosman ruling II (transfer regime) and the issue of broadcasting rights

The second part of the Bosman ruling, which rendered the existing transfer regime illegal, and the marketing of broadcasting rights both initiated a complex and long policy process, in which several advocacy groups tried to have their interests heard and taken care of in the context of EU institutions.[27] Austrian football had to adapt to both these changes, but the question then is: have Austrian clubs – compared, for example, with their most prominent German counterparts – or has the Austrian Football Association been involved in these struggles at the European level? Because our research has not produced any substantial result, this would seem to suggest that there has not been much activism on the part of Austrian actors. But, what accounts for this lack of activism?

Several arguments come to mind. First, Austria – as a relatively small member of the EU and a newcomer in the second half of the 1990s – has had other (more) important interests to pursue. Thus, sports policy was certainly not high on the agenda of Austrian politicians. It seems reasonable that a similar mechanism has prevented the ÖFB as the representative of Austrian football to act visibly at a European level, apart from the successful bid for EURO 2008, together with Switzerland. The ÖFB is a relatively small association,[28] whose expertise, resources and personal contacts on the European level, especially with regard to political institutions, seem to have been limited. Beyond that, its is safe to assume that the smaller national associations took part in the struggle for a new transfer regime or regarding the collective selling of broadcasting rights merely as interested spectators, monitoring (if at all) what the larger associations and the representatives of bigger clubs were trying to negotiate vis-à-vis the European Commission.[29]

Two further explanations for the lack of agency on behalf of Austrian club representatives as well as the ÖFB seem promising. On the one hand, the relationship between the (big) clubs in Austria and the national association is more harmonious and not so marked by opposition/dualism[30] as in other cases (think of Germany). Hence, the need to go to Brussles to engage EU institutions for specific interests (such as decentralized marketing) has arguably been lower. On the other hand, as shown below, the issue of broadcasting rights does not constitute such an enormous issue for the (bigger) Austrian clubs, not least since the rights are sold collectively by the league and at a relatively low rate (making the sum of money to be distributed relatively small). Currently (2007–2010) the football league receives a total of €14.33 million per year (paid by both public television ORF and Pay-TV to all clubs of the Bundesliga),[31] a sum that is easily dwarfed by the approximately €1.4 billion in the English market or the €440 million in Germany.[32] It should be obvious from this that broadcasting revenues make up a relatively small share of the average club's total annual earnings, as the average Bundesliga team spends approximately €10 million per year.[33] This does not mean that the general question of the legal permissibility of collective selling schemes is not applicable to Austria, rather it indicates that the (big) clubs – the main drivers of Europeanization in the German case, for example – have shown little activism in pursuing any interest concerning (a decentralization of) broadcasting rights via (or *vis-à-vis*) Brussels.

As has been hinted at, the revenue structure of most big clubs in Austria has been characterized throughout the last decade by a special feature, i.e. the financial backing by a large sponsor, which in turn means the establishment of structures of patronage. According to Deloitte, 60% of the football league members' revenues derive from sponsorship (season 2007/8), which represents the highest number among the 10 researched Western European leagues.[34] Thus, to reach (inter)national competitiveness, big clubs such as Sturm Graz, Austria Vienna and Red Bull Salzburg have come to rely on personal sponsors: Hannes Kartnig, Frank Stronach and Dietrich Mateschitz, who for very different reasons and with only slightly different ambitions, have pumped large sums into 'their' respective clubs.[35] This alternative source of income helps to explain why some Austrian clubs do not have the issue of broadcasting rights (and plans to generate much more from them via a decentralized system) high on their priority list.

Champions League, UEFA Cup and transnational club forums

Club competition at the European level, especially the Champions League, has been identified with regard to other leagues in Europe, such as the German Bundesliga, as a crucial dimension of Europeanization. That is because throughout the 1990s participation and success in these competitions has proven financially very lucrative and has been shown to have quite a considerable impact at the symbolic level (as regards image and reputation). In addition, one can interpret the relatively dense networks that are established through regular competition across borders as a mechanism that may alter the general patterns of orientation not only of the club's representatives, but also of the supporters/spectators, arguably leading to more Europeanized mind sets, at least a stronger focus on the 'European dimension'.

With regard to Austrian football, one has to recognize that the Champions League at least is rather like the 'exception to the rule' (of non-participation). Only three Austrian clubs have played in the group stages of the Champions League to date,[36] and only once has an Austrian team made it to the former second group stage: Sturm Graz in the 2000/1 season. For the most part, the Champions League remains a distant dream, a miracle panacea. Counting on participation in the League's group stage can be a (very) risky undertaking for Austrian clubs, as the example of FC Tirol in 2001 indicates. The club, which was burdened with a mortal debt, banked on reaching this very group stage. Shortly after it failed to get the better of Lokomotiv Moscow in the last qualifying round it had to file for bankruptcy.[37]

Even though the revenue/financing structure of Austrian clubs differs markedly from that of other European leagues, especially with regard to the substantial reliance of some of the big clubs upon the patronage system described above, participation in European football (still) substantially enhances the competitiveness of Austrian clubs. This is only reinforced by the fact that relatively low revenues emanate from broadcasting rights deals.

Thus, although the European club competitions may not form a large part of clubs' budget calculations (since reaching the financially lucrative stage of these competitions cannot be taken for granted), participiation in these tournaments is nevertheless what the more ambitious, competitive and/or traditional Austrian Bundesliga clubs, such as Red Bull Salzburg, Rapid Vienna and Austria Vienna aim for. In this regard, as stated previously, participation in the (group stage of the) Champions League would be like hitting the jackpot; the €13 million revenue generated by Sturm Graz in making it to the group stage of the Champions League in 2000/1 alone was bigger than the entire annual budget of most Austrian professional clubs at that time.[38] This gives a clear competitive advantage in national competitions, although Sturm did not profit from it due to speculative and unsuccessful transfers and higher personnel costs.

Also the UEFA Cup/Europa League can be very interesting (i.e. financially lucrative) to Austrian clubs, as the example of Austria Vienna who reached the quarter final of the UEFA Cup in 2004/5 indicates.[39] But in the former UEFA Cup, more than in the Champions League (where participation in the group stage is already rewarded with very significant revenues), the financial rewards are very much linked to how far one progresses in the competition. With the new Europa League this is supposed to change quite substantially, because appearance in the group stages (for which one still needs to qualify) would be more lucrative than was the case for the old UEFA Cup group stages, with higher guaranteed revenues. In the 2008/9 season, four Austrian clubs entered the group stage of the Europa League, thus gaining a guaranteed minimum €900,000 from UEFA, with an additional €120,000 per victory and €60,000 for a draw, in addition to considerable revenue from ticket sales and television rights. Nevertheless, participation and success in the UEFA Cup throughout recent seasons indicate that this is really an 'extra' for Austrian clubs, and not a regular and normal undertaking to be relied upon and included in regular income calculations even for the big clubs.[40]

Finally, and largely resembling the low visibility of Austrian clubs in European competition, there has been no detectable Austrian contribution to transnational club forums. No Austrian club has been a member of the G14, although now, because each European association is represented there, three Austrian clubs[41] belong to the European Club Association (ECA) which is officially recognized by UEFA. It remains, however, an open question whether the ECA will be an effective instrument, especially for 'smaller' countries/associations, let alone one characterized by frequent contact and at least partially converging expectations and mind-sets of its participants. In summary, due to the lesser involvement of Austrian clubs in European club tournaments and their marginal exposure at the transnational level, some of the Europeanization mechanisms detectable in other cases (such as the heavy involvement of big German clubs like Bayern Munich with the G14, and nowadays, the ECA[42]) simply do not 'exist' in any meaningful sense in the Austrian case.

European fan and NGO networks

In contrast to the level of clubs and sports governing bodies, a stronger and true bottom-up 'societal' or transnational dimension of Europeanization in Austrian football can be found in the field of NGOs, for example, in the work of 'FairPlay – Different colours. One game'. Based at the Vienna Institute for International Dialogue and Cooperation (vidc), FairPlay has played a considerable role in the establishment of a European anti-racism network in football in the last decade.

In 1999, the seminar 'Networking Against Racism in European Football' gathered together representatives of anti-racist football projects and fan organizations in Vienna to initiate 'a decentralized European network among anti-racist campaigns, football supporters, fan projects and football institutions across Europe with strong grass-roots orientation'.[43] This was the founding moment of the Football Against Racism in Europe (FARE) network. The delegates adopted the 'Vienna Action Plan', which included a number of demands to European sports governing bodies, for example, to 'recognize that racism and other forms of discrimination are a problem in football', to 'take responsibility by adopting and publishing anti-racist policies', 'make full use of the integrative and intercultural potentials of football' and to 'enter into a dialogue and to establish a partnership with all organizations committed to kick racism out of football, in particular with supporter groups, migrants and ethnic minorities.'[44]

From the beginning, FairPlay was a member of the FARE core administrative group. Since its foundation, the FARE network has been growing continuously. An increasing number of groups and organizations participate in FARE's activities such as the annual FARE Action Week Against Racism, which is present in 40 countries. Since 2000/1, the FARE network has established a partnership with UEFA. FARE functions as consulting partner and organizes and implements activities and initiatives financed by UEFA. This cooperation has lead to the organization of three 'Unite Against Racism' conferences with the participation of UEFA, representatives of national federations and clubs, politicians and FARE organizations. Together with

FARE, UEFA has developed a 'Ten Point Plan of Action for Professional Football Clubs', as well as two handbooks for clubs and national associations.

Together with Football Supporters International (FSI; now Football Supporters Europe, FSE), the FARE network was also involved in the establishment of Fan Embassies at international football tournaments such as the Word Cup 2006 and EURO 2008, as well as other UEFA sponsored anti-racism programs at the European Championships (see Horvath and Rosenberg in this volume).

Conclusion

In sum, if one is to speak of the Europeanization of Austrian football other than at the level of NGOs and grassroots activities, such dynamics have been most visible in two dimensions: the Central European heritage of Viennese football, which clearly predates Bosman, and the nationality issue in Austrian football, which has become the focal point of debates and policies in the wake of the Bosman ruling. In some respects, Austrian football has been more internationally oriented; in terms of the composition of teams and the transboundary contacts and alignments of clubs and football associations, it has been (Central) 'Europeanized' since the first half of the twentieth century. The Bosman ruling thus altered a nationality system that was already fairly multinational. With its mixture of progressive liberalization and countermeasures to advance national talents, advocated by media discourse and backed by right-wing populist politicians, Austrian football has nevertheless undergone a substantial transformation post-Bosman.

Its mid-1990s status as a 'new player' and a small country within the EU has contributed to the fact that Austrian actors have had rather limited interest in and impact on sports policy-making at the EU level. The absence of a marked dualism between the big Austrian clubs and the national association further hampered any influence of relevant actors going to Brussels. Broadcasting rights were never a prominent issue of debate, not least given the small amount of money to be earned in the Austrian market. Due to the evolvement of an alternative revenue structure for some of the big clubs – the patronage system – the issue of centralized versus decentralized marketing of broadcasting rights is not of paramount importance in becoming internationally competitive.

The participation of Austrian clubs in European tournaments has been sporadic in recent years, arguably contributing to the invisibility of Austrian clubs and their representatives in European club forums. Given its heritage as a founder of Central European football as a transboundary activity in the first half of the twentieth century, Austrian football has become more inward-oriented, less visible and only minimally involved in European-wide transboundary groupings. Thus, some of the Europeanizing mechanisms observable in other countries (the impact of the Champions League on club strategies; activism by club representatives in transnational club forums) is now hardly relevant in the Austrian case. Societal bottom-up processes of Europeanization can be found, however, at the level of the NGOs and fan work[45] with the participation of Austria in the FARE and FSE networks.

Acknowledgements

The authors would like to thank David Ranc and Borja Garcia for their helpful comments on first drafts of this article and Barbara Liegl (Ludwig Boltzmann Institute of Human Rights) for her expertise.

Notes

1. Brand and Niemann, 'Europeanization in the societal/transnational realm'; Niemann *et al.*, *The Transformation of European Football.*
2. Especially since the 1960s and the founding of the German Bundesliga, there is a strong interconnection between the Austrian football market and the German market. In Austria's top league (1945/46 to 2007/08), 29.8% of foreign coaches and 15% of all foreign players came from Germany, thus ranking first and second in the respective categories. Austrian players and managers have been hired by German clubs since the interwar era. Liegl and Spitaler, 'Zwischen Transnationalität und Identitätspolitik', 245–6.
3. Adrian and Schächtele, *Immer Wieder*, 81–98.
4. See, for example, Horak, 'Austrification as Modernization', 'Kaffeehaus und Vorstadt', Marschik, 'MITROPA: Representations of Central Europe', Marschik, 'Even the Parliament Interrupted its Session', Marschik and Sottopietra, *Erbfeinde und Hasslieben.*
5. Horak, 'Austrification as Modernization', 65.
6. Marschik and Sottopietra, *Erbfeinde und Hasslieben.*
7. On Meisl, see also Hafer and Hafer, *Hugo Meisl.*
8. 'Mitropa' refers to the German word for Central Europe (*Mit*teleur*opa*).
9. See on both the excellent description in Marschik, 'Even the Parliament Interrupted its Session'.
10. Ibid., 10.
11. Marschik and Sottopietra, *Erbfeinde und Hasslieben*, 297–371.
12. This paragraph and the following mainly draw on Liegl and Spitaler, 'Zwischen Transnationalität und Identitätspolitik'.
13. Nevertheless, there have been waves of foreign immigration into Austrian football, not least from neighbouring Central European states, most notably the inflow of Hungarian players in the aftermath of the 1956 failed uprising in Hungary, and the continuous migratory movement of players from former Yugoslavia, especially since the early 1960s. See: Spitaler, 'Fluchtpunkt Wien'; Radojev and Spitaler, 'From Novi Sad to Simmering'.
14. Liegl and Spitaler, 'Zwischen Transnationalität und Identitätspolitik', 240.
15. Duke, 'The Flood from the East?', 159
16. Since 1976 the employment of non-national football professionals (as of all other migrant workers) was subject to the Federal Act on the Employment of Foreigners ('Ausländerbeschäftigungsgesetz', BGBl. 218/1975). Owing to the public interest, work permits for football players were normally granted more easily by the public authorities than in some other sectors of employment.
17. Giulianotti, *Football. A Sociology of the Global Game*; Giulianotti and Robertson, 'Recovering the Social'; Lanfranchi and Taylor, *Moving with the Ball*, 222.
18. To date, research has not produced any significant result as to whether there has been some forward thinking on behalf of Austrian actors in terms of pre-empting legal action taken by non-EU players on the grounds of discrimination via further liberalization.
19. Liegl and Spitaler, 'Zwischen Transnationalität und Identitätspolitik', 247.
20. Reisinger, *Die Neuregelung der Beschäftigung von Drittstaatsangehörigen,* 73.
21. Five EU foreigners of Austria Lustenau took legal action against the (even more restrictive) new rules in the second professional league. In January 2001, the Federal Court of Justice ruled that promotion and cultivation of young talents does not justify an EU-adverse discrimination of EU citizens. Karollus, 'Gemeinschaftsrechtliche Schranken', 67. The measures in the second league were installed in the wake of a re-launch of this league as 'a young, dynamic and Austrian First League' which was supposed to be the training ground for future Austrian national players.
22. Skocek and Weisgram, *Das Spiel ist das Ernste*, 323.
23. The 'Österreicher-Topf' is disbursed each quarter year in case 11 of 18 players on the match sheets of a team have been Austrians or eligible for Austrian national teams, with an extra (amount of money is doubled) for the fielding of U21 players matching these criteria. The Bundesliga itself asserts that there has been a huge change due to this incentive, the increases shown in its business report, are however modest. Bundesliga, *Geschäftsbericht Österreichische Fußball-Bundesliga*, 18.
24. 'Zwischen Transnationalität und Identitätspolitik', 247.
25. See on that Liegl and Spitaler, *Legionäre am Ball*, 142–3.

26. The only counter-mechanism in professional football is the voluntary participation in the above described 'Österreicher-Topf'. Stricter regulations have been enacted (and are still in use) in the second professional league and the amateur section of Austrian football.
27. Parrish, *Sports Law and Policy in the EU*; Parrish and Miettinen, *The Sporting Exception*.
28. It has ~ 590,000 members, compared with 6.5 million members of the German DFB. It is small not in relation to its membership/inhabitant quota, but as a structure of representation within the European system of governance.
29. This is confirmed by the fact that Austria follows the German model in having established a system of collective selling of rights with some modifications (first- and second-use rights, Internet and mobile marketing decentralized).
30. Interview with Peter Klinglmüller, Austrian Football Association (ÖFB), May 20, 2009.
31. *Neue Kronen Zeitung*, July 4, 2007, 56.
32. The broadcasting rights issue in Austria during the last couple of years has become a 'back and forth' between public and private TV stations on a low level regarding the sum of money involved (Adrian and Schächtele, *Immer wieder*, 173). For the impact of Pay-TV on a changing landscape of Austrian football, see also Kraft, 'Kirch und die Nachkommen'.
33. Reliable data is hard to compile. The Bundesliga is not allowed to compile data on the clubs' budgets (let alone make them public), and the clubs are cautious in making them transparent. Austria Vienna has a budget of approximately €15 million annually. This seems to be the upper limit with regard to other Austrian clubs. A budget of €30–40 million– as during the heights of the sponsoring episodes at Austria Vienna or Red Bull Salzburg – clearly is exceptional in Austria, while only modest in comparison with international standards. See: Adrian and Schächtele, *Immer wieder*, 43. In the case of Austria Vienna, television revenues represent 12% of the overall budget (season 2008/09), compared with 70% from sponsor revenues and 15% from ticket sales. For clubs with higher audience numbers – such as Rapid Vienna with a turnover of €18 million in 2008/09 – the percentage of ticket sales and merchandising will be higher. *Kurier*, March 10, 2009, 29; April 11, 2009, 25.
34. Sinnreich, 'Fairplay und Folklore', 49.
35. For a good account, see Adrian and Schächtele, *Immer Wieder*, 135–60. The reasons might range from self-promotion to marketing efforts on behalf of a company, the ambitions were and are almost identical: not only to become the top Austrian team, but to be competitive at the European level (Champions League).
36. These are Sturm Graz (three times), Rapid Vienna (twice) and Austria Salzburg.
37. Adrian and Schächtele, *Immer Wieder*, 165–7.
38. *Kurier*, April 26, 2009, 32.
39. Club representatives gave estimates of four million EUR revenues for the UEFA Cup season 2004/5 (including television rights and ticket sales) before taxes. *Neue Kronen Zeitung*, April 9, 2005, 90.
40. Throughout the last 10 years (1999/2000 season to 2008/9), Austrian teams have qualified 31 times for the first round of UEFA Cup. During the first five years, without the group stage as a second round, only once a team made it to the third round (the qualification of Sturm Graz via the Champions League in 1999/2000 is not counted here). Since 2004, when the second round became a (financially potentially lucrative) group stage, this stage was only reached four times. The single, and by this exceptional, case where an Austrian team made it into the quarter finals during the last decade was Austria Vienna in the 2004/5 season.
41. As of today, these are Austria and Rapid Vienna and the Grazer AK.
42. Brand and Niemann, *The Europeanisation of German Football*.
43. FairPlay. *Report Networking against Racism*, 3.
44. Ibid, 28–32.
45. To date, no systematic studies of fans' attitudes in this regard exist. One of the exceptions concerning researching fans in Austria is the comparative study of Waddington / Malcolm / Horak, 'The Social Composition of Football Crowds'. Recently some Austrian Ultrà fan-groups have established friendships and rivalries with other Ultràs across Europe and are active in networking and campaigning for fan-interests.

References

Adrian, S., and K. Schächtele. *Immer wieder, nimmer wieder. Vom Schicksal des österreichischen Fußballs.* Cologne: Kiepenheuer & Witsch, 2008.

Brand, A., and A. Niemann. 'Europeanisation in the Societal/Trans-National Realm: What European Integration Studies Can Get Out of Analysing Football'. *Journal of Contemporary European Research* 3, 3 (2007): 182–201.

Brand, A., and A. Niemann. 'The Europeanisation of German Football: Between Modest Adjustment and System Transformation'. In *The Transformation of European Football: A Case of Europeanisation?,* ed. A. Niemann, B. Garcia and W. Grant. Manchester: Manchester University Press, 2011 (forthcoming).

Bundesliga. 'Geschäftsbericht Österreichische Fussball-Bundesliga 2007/08'. Österreichische Fussball-Bundesliga. http://www.bundesliga.at/blinfo/geschaeftsberichte/geschaeftsbericht _0708.zip.

Duke, V. 'The Flood From the East? Perestroika and the Migration of Sports Talent From Eastern Europe'. In *The Global Sports Arena: Athletic Talent Migration in an Interdependent World,* ed. J. Bale and J. Maguire, 153–67. London: Routledge, 1994.

FairPlay. Different Colours. One Game. *Report Networking against Racism in European Football (NAREF),* Vienna Seminar January 31–February 2, 1999. Vienna: vidc, 2000.

Giulianotti, R. *Football. A Sociology of the Global Game.* Oxford: Polity, 1999.

Guilianotti, R., and R. Robertson. 'Recovering the Social: Globalisation, Football and Transnationalism'. *Global Networks* 2 (2007): 144–86.

Hafer, A., and W. Hafer. *Hugo Meisl oder: Die Erfindung des modernen Fußballs.* Göttingen: Werkstatt, 2007.

Horak, R. 'Austrification as Modernization. Changes in Viennese Football Culture'. In *Game Without Frontiers. Football, Identity and Modernity,* ed. R. Giulianotti and J. Williams, 47–71. Aldershot: Ashgate, 1992.

Horak, R. 'Kaffeehaus und Vorstadt, Feuilleton und Massenvergnügen. Über die doppelte Codierung des Fußballs im Wien der Zwischenkriegszeit'. In *Global Players – Kultur, Ökonomie und Politik des Fußballs,* ed. M. Fanizadeh, G. Hödl, and W, Manzenreiter, 57–72. Frankfurt am Main: Brandes & Apsel, 2002.

Karollus, M.M. 'Gemeinschaftsrechtliche Schranken für Ausländerklauseln im Sport, insbesondere auch gegenüber Drittstaatsangehörigen'. In *Aktuelle Rechtsfragen des Fußballsports IV,* ed. A. Grundei and M. Karollus, 67–91. Vienna: Linde, 2006.

Kraft, S. 'Kirch und die Nachkommen'. *ballesterer* 15 (2004): 20–2.

Lanfranchi, P., and M. Taylor. *Moving with the Ball. The Migration of Professional Footballers.*. Oxford: Berg, 2001.

Liegl, B., and G. Spitaler. 'Zwischen Transnationalität und Identitätspolitik – Österreichische Migrationsregimes und der Profifußball (1945–2008)'. *SWS-Rundschau* 49, 1 (2009): 234–55.

Liegl, B., and G. Spitaler. *Legionäre am Ball. Migration im österreichischen Fußball nach 1945.* Vienna: Braumüller, 2008.

Marschik, M. 'MITROPA: Representations of Central Europe in Football'. *International Review for the Sociology of Sport* 36 (1998): 7–23.

Marschik, M. 'Even the Parliament Interrupted its Session… Creating Local and National Identity in Viennese Football'. *Journal of Sport and Social Issues* 22 (2001): 199–211

Marschik, M., and D. Sottopietra. *Erbfeinde und Hasslieben. Konzept und Realität Mitteleuropas im Sport.* Münster: LIT, 2000.

Niemann, A., B. Garcia, and W. Grant, ed. *The Transformation of European Football: A Case of Europeanisation?* Manchester: Manchester University Press, 2011 (forthcoming).

Parrish, R. *Sports Law and Policy in the European Union.* Manchester: Manchester University Press, 2003.

Parrish, R., and S. Miettinen. *The Sporting Exception in the European Union Law.* The Hague: Asser, 2008.

Radojev, M., and G. Spitaler. 'From Novi Sad to Simmering'. WienInternational. http://www.wieninternational.at/en/node/7952.

Reisinger, J. *Die Neuregelung der Beschäftigung von Drittstaatsangehörigen im österreichischen Fußball.* Diploma thesis, University of Graz, 2003.

Sinnreich, D. 'Fairplay und Folklore'. *ballesterer* 46 (2009): 49.

Skocek, J., and W. Weisgram. *Das Spiel ist das Ernste. Ein Jahrhundert Fußball in Österreich.* Vienna: Echomedia, 2004.

Spitaler, G. 'Fluchtpunkt Wien'. *ballesterer* 25 (2006/07): 44.

Waddington, I., D. Malcolm, and R. Horak. 'The Social Composition of Football Crowds in Western Europe'. *International Review for the Sociology of Sport* 33 (1998): 155–69.

Left off the stage: mapping inclusion and exclusion in EURO 2008

Matthias Marschik

University of Vienna, Austria

An event like EURO 2008 does not merely consist of the final round, its participants, the stadiums and the public viewing areas; it does not only consist of lucky fans who could get hold of a ticket, not-so-lucky fans who must content themselves with large screen displays, and apparent or actual hooligans. Away from the big stages, there are people and groups who are not allowed to be in attendance and there are teams or 'local heroes' for whom qualification or even every point scored in the qualification is already a sensation. In this article, I present examples of how an event like EURO 2008 also constructs identities, provides structures and defines inclusions and exclusions beyond the aforementioned powerful discourses and demonstrate that it is not a matter of consequences of one-sided normative power, but of hegemonic processes of negotiation in which open or subtle acts of resistances materialize. I exemplify this with the case of the small football country Malta.

Introduction

Discourses on major football events, whether it is the World Cup or the European Championships, predominantly consist of – potential – favourites, contenders and champions, or of present and future stars. One speaks and writes primarily of countries such as Italy, Spain, France or Brazil, of Beckham, Kuranyi and Cristiano Ronaldo, of athletic, national and economic successes and their consequences at the highest level. During the run-up, one also speaks of politics and economics, from the national reputation of the organizer and the participant countries, to the politicians (every now and then the female politicians as well) who hope for an image transfer from the successful sport onto their person or party; from an indirect economic return on advertising budgets, to the victory purses of the favoured teams. A European Football Championship develops from and consists of a complex interaction of the production of a sports spectacle with the genuine interests of politics and economics – in addition to millions of football fans.

None of this is included in what follows. An event like EURO 2008 does not merely consist of the final round, its participants, the stadiums and public viewing areas, the advertising agencies, or the number of rooms booked; it does not only consist of lucky fans who could get hold of a ticket, not-so-lucky fans who must content themselves with large screen displays, and apparent or actual hooligans who – every now and then, justifiably – cause anxieties. Away from these big stages, there are people and groups who are not allowed to be in attendance, there are teams or 'local heroes' for whom qualification is already a sensation, and federations for which even this goal is illusory and every point scored in qualification represents a victory. There are regions that would be happy to be there, and others that participate despite their lack of membership.

In what follows, I would like to bring examples of how an event like EURO 2008 (including the qualifying rounds) also constructs identities, provides structures and defines inclusions and exclusions beyond the aforementioned powerful discourses. I would also like to demonstrate that it is not a matter of the consequences of a one-sided normative power, but of hegemonic processes of negotiation in which open or subtle acts of resistance materialize, and struggles 'to articulate the relations between social and economic power, political forms of agency, and modes of discursive practices'[1] take place. In other words, in the discourses of football hegemony and normative power, power analyses can, in terms of cultural studies, be organized 'by means of popular–cultural phenomena and formations'.[2] This will be exemplified with the case of the small football country Malta.

Premises

That international football organizations pursue strategies of inclusion and exclusion, particularly in execution of major events, would not be culturally significant but only of interest in relation to sport were it not that football produces and transports social norms and values far beyond the realm of sports due to its enormous popularity and popularization. World or continental championships of national teams, for example EURO 2008, as well as international club competitions like the Champions League, reach a multitude of people who have little to no interest in football. Not coincidentally, Louis Althusser[3] ranked sports among the most important components of the (cultural) ideological apparatus of state, and he therefore attributes to it direct effective power concerning social values and standards.

Sport, and in particular global football in its medialized manifestation, is an extremely popular social formation in constant exchange with other social fields and for that reason creates in no way only a snapshot or a microcosm of society. However, sport and football form neither autonomous nor semiautonomous spheres – as the discourse on an 'apolitical' or even 'neutral' sphere of sport implies[4] – which would then exist uncoupled from the remaining social terrain, as suggested, for example, by the positioning of sports broadcasts in the media apart from 'serious stuff' like political or economic reporting.

As the use of football terms in everyday speech makes clear, sport provides measures of value for other areas, going far beyond the importance of sport-related decisions and the practices developing from them. The influence of sport on the formation, alteration or consolidation of individual identities, as well as national and regional affiliations, is evident and well-documented. In addition, in sporting events, general meanings of achievement, struggle and victory, masculinity, youth or community are constructed or at least clarified. These define the political and economic conditions for success, which are transferred from sport, and most especially from football, into society and as popular 'common sense' form the basis for political and economic views.[5]

There is no doubt that sport, and especially football, is creating certain pictures of and gazes on Europe. If the organizational structures of an event such as EURO 2008 explicitly or implicitly exclude certain units, groups or individuals from participation, if they thereby legitimize the meanings and practices of sports,[6] then this is by no means only a sport-political decision with sport-related consequences. Rather the organizational structures of the event set as fact which concrete arrangements exist and/or are noticed, how individuals define themselves, how they integrate in communities and what the potential places and framework data of these collectives are. On the one hand, sports political inclusion and exclusion give parameters of where and how cultural (and that is, just as sporting as political and economic) participation or exclusion are to be interpreted and, on the other hand, form a substantial nominative power for the standards and values that prevail within such 'communities', representing the conditions for membership or even exclusion that define a cultural community.[7]

Both organizational inclusion and exclusion, as well as discursive creations of parameters of meaning, social associations and cultural standards and values, never function in the form of enforced regulations, but are always subject to processes of negotiation, even if under unequal conditions. So as individuals and groups of fans set themselves against the construction of all-seating stadiums, and thus achieve at least small concessions, they are also representatives of marginalized or excluded groups that are not completely without chance compared with the sports organizations, their points of view are represented in and outside the organization, they conclude alliances or search for more potent support. This applies even more so when topographic – but also symbolic boundaries are kept far from the central positions of power, but at the same time have a substantial function supporting and safeguarding the central positions, because their existence elevates the greats, because they provide the new players, merchandising customers and potential supporters, and in addition, because (only) they guarantee the cultural meaning of the sport of football. Power is 'never in the position to totalize itself'.[8]

One struggles, therefore, not only in the sport, but also for it – that is, for its meanings. Everyday cultures are, like culture generally, always shaped by one 'way of struggle' between competitive power fields, and also between the moral attitudes that they produce, represent and mediate. Popular culture is a place where the fight for or against a culture of the powerful is played out, and an arena of agreement and resistance. The 'real' structures are not the result of a one-sided normative power, but outcomes of struggles for conditions and meanings, of negotiations between completely unequal partners.[9]

Within those everyday cultures, sport takes on a special position, not or not only because of its enormous popularity, but in particular because of its physical materiality: sport is experienced as unmediated, as authentic. Its structures of inclusion and exclusion, its norms and values are received particularly unmediated. On the one hand, it concerns the connection of human performance with the body, with sudden achievement that manifests itself in visible effort, in sweat and exhaustion. On the other hand, it concerns the direct emotionality of sports, on the side of the participants as well as the public. Via physis, therefore, the messages of sport – the discourses arranged by it as well as the discourses on it – are experienced particularly authentically.

To summarize, on the one hand, sport possesses and constructs eminent cultural meanings right there, where enormous funds are spent on the production of global events, as, for example, at EURO 2008. On the other hand, athletic practices are sites of negotiation; they are struggles both on the unmediated terrain of the match, and also on the field of meanings. They are places of both discursive conflicts over power and completely concrete physical competition and physical representation. This is shown in the following two examples; first, by the structures of inclusion and exclusion with regards to the 2008 European Football Championship, and second, by the struggles of a participating, yet nevertheless excluded, competitor in this (discursive as well as real) game.

The 'little' absence: inclusion and exclusion at EURO 2008

'Football' and 'Europe' formed the basic parameters of EURO 2008, and a cursory glance will make it clear that these two seemingly simple categories are not, under any circumstances, congruent with the 'football' and 'Europe' that were represented in Switzerland and Austria. A differentiated system of structures of inclusion and exclusion should see to it that, in principle equality is proclaimed and maximum success can be guaranteed. Success naturally means primarily economic profit, but by no means only that. Because success also promises indirect non-commercial profitability from the preservation of the enormous fascination with the sport of football, which is increasingly being undermined by postmodern trends of physical culture, to the preservation of the standards and values of a white, male, bourgeois and ultimately 'western'[10] meritocracy, which in the global economic crisis is no longer unconditionally accepted by any means. Thus we consider the most important selection criteria that formed the basis for participation in EURO 2008.

Nation/nationalism

The European Football Championship is based on an anachronistic concept. It presents, in an extreme form, the modern idea of the nation-state and its bourgeois ideals of belonging and community. It introduces a Europe that is based on political decisions of togetherness and difference. The European Football Championship is based on a map of the national–political structure of Greater Europe; therefore it includes Russia and Turkey. In this way, it triumphs over current intercontinental barriers such as the European Union (EU), or the Eurozone, just as it had over the 'Iron Curtain' for 30 years, but due to safety reasons not over Schengen.

Above all, however, the European Football Championship stands in contrast to other major sporting events in which individual athletes compete against each other and overlay the national and individual levels. And it differs from team sports events in which clubs compete (such as the football Champions League), which attests to far more capitalistic–postmodern multiculturalism.[11]

The European Championship concept is marked by extreme unfairness, such as when Team Russia (area: 17,000,000 km^2; population: 142,000,000) plays against San Marino (area: 60 km^2; population: 31,000): thus, from an athletic standpoint, the small country is almost (but not completely) without chance. However, an average semi-professional from Andorra has the chance to become a national player, just as the fans are able to see each home game without expense. The EURO not only represents the liberal national idea of the equality postulate, but it also contributes important facets to the definition of nationalism: the characterization of styles of play and the behaviour of fans, as well as the special matches that often form important facets of national identity and self-reassurance, are causes of national conflicts as well as international understanding.

The national and nationality discourse underlying a European Football Championship is confronted, however, with the consequences of gradual dissolution: although it still stages itself as a Europe of nation-states with (neo-)colonialist features, this is increasingly undermined by the naturalization of good players or different interpretations of citizenship and nation.

Economic weighting

The clash of national teams creates geopolitical, not purely economic, bases of competition. In the sense of success and profit maximization, that is why UEFA have intervened ever more strongly, in order to bring the most attractive and most lucrative teams into the final round. In both of the first two competitions, 17 (1960) and 29 (1964) participating teams had to qualify for the final round in knockout games. From 1968 onwards, qualification was completed in a group phase formed on the basis of a seeding list. Wherever the paring was still left to chance – such as with the qualification for the 1964 European Championship, where France eliminated England in the preliminary round while Ireland advanced against Iceland – such coincidences were gradually made impossible. Only since 1980 has the host country or countries been automatically advanced to the final round.

That the small can win against the large, as in many other sports, constitutes no small part of the fascination of the football. This can be seen very clearly on the basis of national selections. But economic premises – from the invested sponsor and advertising money, to TV revenues, to the number of football supporters – suggest not eliminating the sporting surprises inherent in the system, but minimizing their number. UEFA and the national federations are also anxious to support and strengthen the existing economic and sport-political inequalities in order to improve the chances of the larger and more lucrative teams.

This happens through conscious control of the pairings, rather than by a random principle. Thus in club football, the UEFA five-year ranking considerably favours clubs from major football nations. In addition, the UEFA Coefficient – the basis for the seeding lists for national team events – sets narrow boundaries for surprises.

This is due to a fear of financial losses from sponsors, TV rights and ratings, ticket sales or overnight stays if the major football nations are missing from the final round. Qualification for the 2004 European Championships failed with Romania, Ireland, Belgium and Turkey among the top-ranked teams; according to the method used for EURO 2008, only England could not qualify. If the gap between the large and small federations and national teams is constantly increased by organizational interference, this has important economic and cultural consequences. Further deviation from the fine line between ensuring the chance of surprises and forcing and/or preferential treatment of the favourites may lead to a massive loss of interest in football in smaller football nations and thus endanger European football culture.

Gender

In contrast to the Olympic Games, in which women are under-represented and discriminated against through organizational measures as well as cultural structures, at the (men's) European Football Championship (as also with the World Cup) more than half of Europe is not present at all: therefore, it is crucial how uncontradicted this absence of women is and remains. Even though football federations prognosticate a 'feminine' future and clubs have long recognized women as an important market segment of the public – locally, for example, with TV consumption – a parallel event for both the women's and men's European Championships is not under discussion, although even the World Championships in Nordic ski sports have added the long-proscribed women's ski jump to the regular programme of included events since 2009.

EURO 2008 stages a masculine and male-structured Europe, which is arranged and coordinated by men, admired (or also condemned) by men and accepts women only in limited places: as feminine ornamentation in stadiums and on fan miles, as a contribution to security, as consumers of tourism and advertising offerings or as candidates for the official 'Miss Euro 2008': 'What is more beautiful to watch than football and one or more beautiful women'.[12]

Thus the Vienna Tourist Board started the 'enjoy life, enjoy sports' campaign in the summer of 2007, in which it hoped that the Viennese footballer Nicola Watzinger, as spokeswoman, would lure women to the European Championships. Admittedly, advertising directed at women was already part of the concept, 'where there is less about the games, but more about the "action" in the city around the event'.[13] In a project for the sustainability of the EURO, between sustainable waste prevention and barrier-free access for the disabled, there was a section on women and football, concerning girls' football, prostitution and female stewards. However, the aim was to integrate women 'into the event' through 'side events' like public viewings or neighbourhood parties. 'Even those not interested in football' – and by that they likely meant women per se – 'should also have an opportunity to celebrate'.[14]

Fit, young, mobile

A European Football Championship is a (masculine) festival of youth and youthfulness, in which the facets of achievement, strength, stamina, technique and creativity are celebrated. Older men are in demand only as supervisors and as tacticians. Ultimately, at the core of the events, are young adult men, who celebrate themselves because the fan culture is also drawn from this subpopulation. No matter who really participates in the concrete events, images of the EURO demonstrate that only the fit, the young and the mobile can and should participate actively or as spectators, because the EURO stages itself as a mobile Europe of the free movement of goods and persons, and this includes officials, players and fans.

Excluded or substantially hindered from participation are all whose citizenship lacks mobility or flexibility in any form, such as refugees, the stateless or the undocumented. The physically and mentally disabled, blind, deaf, homeless or people below the poverty line are excluded as players,[15] and as spectators are often limited only to television consumption. Those who do not bow to the civil order are also kept away, above all, those fans (this includes not only hooligans) covered by the Austrian State Police Act amended for EURO 2008, along with 'hooligan data' and mobile phone tracking.[16]

Moreover, there were also restrictions distorting economic fairness, for example, an extremely slim sport-political social network, when the majority of the fans – in contrast to the beneficiaries of specific VIP offers – had hardly any possibility of seeing a match and were dependent on fan miles, because they proved to be not fit enough for the Internet ticket auctions and thus lacked the necessary 'connections' for the acquisition of tickets. The EURO is an event for a young, mobile, fit Europe.

Structural politics

The EURO is a sporting competition between teams from nation-states. But this definition lacks clarity; in some cases, such as the example of Great Britain, however, national autonomy means sporting autonomy. In this understanding of participation, several dependent territories or provinces are not affiliated as members of the European association, partly at the urge of the national federations, partly at the decision of UEFA, and are not admitted into the European Championship qualification.

This includes, for example, the Spanish autonomous communities of Euskadi (Basque Country), Navarre and Catalonia, but also the Balearic and Canary Islands, which have their own federations and have held unofficial international matches for nearly 100 years, yet whose UEFA entry is blocked by the Spanish federation. The same is true for Gibraltar, whose football association has existed since 1895 and who has held its own championship since 1907. Their 1997 application for membership of UEFA was finally rejected in 2007.[17] Even the Southern French Occitania has had a football federation since 1901 and in 2006 proved successful as an organizer of the 'VIVA World Cup', a tournament for 'unwanted' national teams.

In such competitions, the regional teams from territories that have little interest in UEFA membership (such as Rijeka, Wallonia, a team of Roma, the autonomous Moldovan province of Gagauzia or Malta's small sister island Gozo) take part, but so too do those who have fought to be included in the association for years without success, such as Greenland, Monaco, the Channel Islands and Lapland (Sámpi). Teams from Kurdistan, North Cyprus and Transnistria have even less chance of recognition. There are a few regions whose political status would not permit a membership application to be entirely unsuccessful, yet they refrain from applying, for example, the Azores and Madeira, in addition to the Vatican City. The chance of seeing one's inward regional/national identity represented outwardly via football seems so obviously attractive, yet these wishes are dealt with restrictively by UEFA and the national federations.

Internal inclusion

Since the founding of FIFA in May 1904, there have been discussions about the possibility of membership, because, on the one hand, federations and not nations acquire it and, on the other hand, only one federation was certified per nation. The first 'victim' of this regulation was the Bohemian federation, which was accepted in 1906, but was excluded again two years later on Austria's intervention, whereas the 'British solution' of participation was retained by England, Scotland, Wales and (Northern) Ireland, and to this day forms the model for some requests of regional federations with FIFA and UEFA, created in 1954.

After 10 years of negotiations, the football federation of the Faeroe Islands has succeeded only in so far as it has reached an exception analogous to that of the British countries from Article 5 of the UEFA Statutes, which provides that member federations must have their seat in a territory recognized by the UN as an independent state and must be responsible for the for the organization and implementation of the sport of football in the region of their country. Only a two-thirds majority of the UEFA Congress can allow further exceptions. At present, however, only Greenland, whose admission has long failed because of the absence of a lawn pitch, has a concrete chance of that. For the remaining applicants, the nation-state hegemony currently forms an insurmountable hurdle.

External inclusion

Article 5 of the UEFA Statutes states furthermore that in exceptional cases – and with the consent of FIFA – national federations from other continents can also become members, provided that they are not members of another continental confederation. The approval of such an application – with the support of Greece – has been granted to Cyprus, independent since 1960 (which, despite EU membership, belongs geographically to Asia). After the collapse of the USSR, applications from Armenia and Georgia (1992), Azerbaijan (1994) and Kazakhstan (2002) have also been accepted. Israel's football federation has been a UEFA member since 1994 – analogous to developments in almost every other sport.

It is therefore not only the examples of Russia and Turkey that point to a European expansionist policy on the part of UEFA and the collective football representations. Rather, despite constant assertions of an 'apolitical' sporting event, massive sport, as well as general, politics operate within UEFA. During the course of the European Championships – much as NATO undertakes reconstruction of the world order – the future structures and affiliations of a new Europe are formulated and tested.

This is much clearer at the personal level, where the question of citizenship in the hegemonic European sense is dealt with, when it serves the national reputation. There arise, however, collisions between genuine national consciousness and the quest for national athletic success, as the different practices of player eligibility show: while in some countries these have been restrictively administered, Ireland owes the rise of its national team in the 1990s in particular to the fact that every player who had Irish ancestors in the second generation was eligible to play. Moreover, there is a strong post-colonial component, as when for example in Portugal, players primarily from the former colonies of Mozambique and Angola (e.g. Abel Xavier), but also from Brazil (e.g. Deco) were naturalized.

Inclusive exclusion

In the last places in the UEFA rankings, whether it is the five-year ranking of clubs or the UEFA National Team Coefficient, there are almost always the same countries. As of April 2008, places 47 to 53 are occupied by Azerbaijan, the Faroe Islands, Luxembourg, Malta, Andorra, Montenegro and San Marino. Not coincidentally, these countries (except Montenegro) also found themselves in last place in their qualifying groups, because it is not only athletic performance, but also the sport-political environment that has assigned them to the fringes of European football. If the gap has already become nearly unbridgeable in the large events in club football, then the international team level is the last chance to stir up attention. If Internazionale Milano or Chelsea never again perform at Camp d'Esports d'Aixovall in Andorra or in the Stadio Olimpico di Serravalle San Marino, the big national teams still have to play countries in the 'underdog' position and thus provide public interest, and advertising and TV revenue.

Even if they are never represented in the finals, and achieve only modest success in the preliminary rounds, participation in the European Championships is of enormous sporting, economic and political importance for the small countries. Particularly, if modest successes are seen as tremendous achievements from a national perspective, for example, the five points achieved by Malta or the seven points by Liechtenstein in qualification for EURO 2008. The Liechtenstein football federation declared 2007 to have been a year with 'great successes, fascinating perspectives and strengthening of the economic base (…). 2007 was the most successful year in the history of the Liechtenstein national team.' The country had 'once more earned respect and recognition in Europe and will recall themselves positively in memory'.[18]

The lack of international success does not preclude national football euphoria by any means. The assumption is that contact with the world of European or global football will not end. This may be achieved through the transfer of players to major clubs or be secured by regular games against the 'greats'. At the club level, however, this comparison is almost completely invalid when the league champions and cup winners from the small football nations eliminate one another in the preliminary rounds. The qualification rounds of the European Championships and the World Cup are therefore the only regularly occurring events in which this contact is maintained.

The 'little' struggle: the example of Malta

As initially stated, the aforementioned structures of inclusion and exclusion are not the results of a dictatorial European association that does not tolerate dissent, but of a negotiation process in which excluded particpants or those without chance also possess a voice – although often a faint one. Ultimately, UEFA is, according to its own definition, 'a representative democracy, comprised of 53 national football associations' and the leitmotif of its structure is called 'subsidiarity', which is why it only intervenes as an international institution in the affairs of national sports federations 'if international, or in some cases, worldwide action is required'.[19]

The faint voices in and outside UEFA, moreover, usually do not articulate any protests or appeals, but give their at least halfhearted approval and consent in hegemonic negotiation processes if they expect to benefit in other areas and/or conform to the basal values and standards of the 'greats', as laid down in the structure of European football events. This should be apparent in what follows, in the example of the sport and football politics of the European 'football dwarf' Malta. It must first be said that even in those football countries that have had little success at the international level, the sport contributes substantially, although most differently, to the construction, preservation of or change in national cultures and identities, its values not, or not substantially, differing from those of the 'great powers' of football.

In Malta, football has been played since the end of the nineteenth century,[20] and the concrete practices of the sport have been characterized, on the one hand, by the British colonial power and, on the other hand, by the Italophile bourgeois middle class.[21] As early as the 1930s, semi-professional football events[22] were held which achieved enormous popularity, and the legendary Empire Stadium in Gzira, where all the major games took place, was often too small: in this context, at least, football meant Malta's presence on the international stage. As part of the British Empire, Malta admittedly had no official national teams and the team selected from the football association (MFA XI) held only mostly meaningless friendly matches. The major football events were therefore first, the national championships, second, matches against English teams and the military and third, tournaments with international participation, because especially in the winter, English as well as Central European clubs liked to accept invitations to Malta's mild climate. These football events, however, were hardly suited to promoting a Maltese national identity.

Instead, football contributed substantially to the arrangement of regional and local consciousness in Malta. Controversies ran along political dividing lines (National vs. Constitutional Party, later National vs. Labour Party), as well as along national orientations towards Italy and/or England, and the middle classes verus workers (both of which were good for party politics).[23] Football rivalries were often based on local patriotism along provincial and local borders, or on the parishes of extremely Catholic

Malta. Football games encouraged traditional local rivalries, but also went beyond that in the type of ceremonies.

National identity in Malta is characterized not only by its late independence (1964), but also by the smallness of the country. It seems less 'imagined', but rather shaped through personal contacts and relationships.[24] In 1957, Malta held official international matches, the first of which against Austria triggered a great deal of enthusiasm due to a close 2–3 defeat in Malta. But since then, the Maltese team has barely been successful in meaningful games: in the qualifying rounds of the European Championship and World Cup, it has never been higher than last place and victories are seldom. In the qualifying rounds of the European Championships, Malta has recorded three victories against Greece (1976), Iceland (1984) and Hungary (2007), and in World Cup qualifying games it has managed only one victory (1993 against Estonia). A much-discussed low point was the two 1–2 defeats against the Faroe Islands in 1997, whereas qualification for the European Championship in 2008, with the victory against Hungary in the fall of 2006 and two draws against Turkey and Moldova, was celebrated as a high point of national football.

If football in Malta (and that means, despite the introduction of a women's league in the mid-1990s onward, in the male population) enjoys tremendous popularity, then this applies to the national team only in exceptional cases. More likely, this popularity is attributed to the intranational meetings and their associated rivalries. Important international matches may attract around 4000–5000 spectators in the stadium, whereas other games may have fewer than 1000. A low point was the 300 spectators for Malta's last match in the 1997 World Cup qualifier against Yugoslavia, whereas the rest of the nation watched the game between Italy and England on TV and thousands of fans celebrated England's qualification for the World Cup later in the evening with a motorcade. The top games of the local Premier League, however, consistently draw > 10,000 fans at the National Stadium at Ta'Qali, and the atmosphere and support, as well as the jubilant celebrations that follow, are incomparably louder than for the international matches.

It is not the international matches, but the great duels between Floriana, Hamrun, Sliema Wanderers, Valletta City and Hibernians Paola, as well as the new challengers Birkirkara and Marsaxlokk, that have turned football in Malta into a 'national obsession'. This obsession leads to weddings and family celebrations, but also political events and even parliamentary debates being postponed or cancelled if they coincide with an important game. The same is also true for TV broadcasts of the Champions League games or international matches in which English or Italian teams are involved. For this reason, Malta is home to a large number of fan clubs devoted to the top Italian and English teams, often with more than 1000 members. Active participation in football is also enormous: the Malta Football Association is the largest sports organization in the country; there are 11,400 players (including 200 women) in 65 clubs vying for seven championships (including two in Gozo). The sums of money changing hands in football are also enormous – in comparison with the size of the country – both in terms of bets, which were long forbidden and have only recently been legalized, as well as in the fiercely debated but hardly ever detected cases of corruption.

Equally oversized is the association budget, which comes partly from the sponsorship of global firms, and partly from an already traditional local patronage system: there is barely a well-known politician or businessman who does not either sponsor 'his' club indirectly or finance it directly. The president of one of the big clubs is linked to enormous social capital and island-wide fame.[25]

Malta still has to struggle with its history as an island often conquered and occupied by various powers. The consequences of its 160-year status as a British colony have not yet been addressed, nor has the idea of unification with Italy, which was repeatedly advocated until the 1950s. Thus, since the end of the 1980s, a veritable 'industry of identity' has been established, although one characterized more by continuous discussions and struggles for self-positioning than by solutions or self-characterizations.[26] Football has a critical function in the identity of the 'in-between': between Italian, English, and not least religious influences, particularly since it forces its supporters to take a clear position.

Since the 1960s, Malta has been a fixed part of European football culture at both the club and national team levels. But whereas in many countries, sport – and especially football – may be expected to make a massive contribution to the establishment and strengthening of national identity, in the case of Malta, this relationship creates a paradox, because 'the exchange is far from egalitarian, and the Maltese are all too aware that they are at the poor end of the relationship'.[27] The situation in Malta is therefore not comparable with either those larger countries in which football represents a fixed component of the national positioning struggles in Europe and at the global level, or with the micro-states, for which a football presence on this level alone is already tantamount to success. Football, therefore, forms one of the key elements of Malta's identity as a 'nationless state',[28] as both a product and source 'of the schizophrenic identity politics of Malta'.[29] It manifests itself in the fact that Maltese football fans install expensive satellite equipment to receive foreign games and celebrate the successes of their favourite – mostly Italian or English – teams in the same way that they fete the victory of their local club, but they pay little attention to the matches of their own national team.

The dual position is also seen in the expression of sports politics. Thus, on the one hand, UEFA promotes Maltese football, for example, by allowing international games on the sandy ground of Gzira – contrary to regulations – or by distributing generous subsidies to junior clubs. On the other hand, Malta is clearly at a disadvantage if the rankings make athletic success almost impossible. Even the national federation, the MFA, tries, on the one hand, to strengthen national identity, for example by bypassing the Bosman ruling to stipulate that only three non-Maltese, whether from the EU or not, may be active in clubs. On the other hand, the federation is working against the national interest if its income is invested particularly into prestige projects like the construction of a conference centre. A prime example of ambiguous sports policy is the long-time president of the MFA, Joseph Mifsud, who worked in UEFA in a variety of offices and is currently a member of the UEFA Executive Committee. Mifsud has increasingly proclaimed that his job is to work for European – not Maltese – football. In particular, he goes to the big clubs, which are mostly violently hostile to him, on a confrontational course and at the same time promotes the prevalent 'foreign-ness as a gauge of value'.[30]

Maltese sports politics, therefore, coincide with the general political strategy to derive authority from the experience of permanent deprivation, to always have one's own advantage in sight. This can be seen, for example, if claims for international support arise, in the case of the grant being judged critically or as too low; it can be seen in changing national, as well as international, alliances and even in strategic threats to withdraw from European football events. Through Mifsud, the MFA has cultivated good relations with Günther Netzer and Franz Beckenbauer, and has obtained Horst Heese and Sigi Held as national coaches, who, after they were deemed unfit for their positions, were soon dismissed and replaced by local coaches, albeit not without a further search for foreign advisers. (Rumors persist that Germany acquired Malta's support for their bid for the 2006 World Cup in this way. Maltese delegate Joe Mifsud actually adopted a pro-German line only at the last moment. In response, despite more lucrative offers, the broadcast rights for the Maltese Premier League went only in 2000 to the CWL Telesport AG of the Kirch group. Also Franz Beckenbauer organized an appearance of Bayern Munich in Malta, which benefitted the MFA's income at the same time.)

Armstrong and Mitchell[31] define Maltese football practice at the intersection of globality and locality, thus excluding or neglecting the national. Enthusiasm arises, on the one hand, for local clubs and games and, on the other hand, for global sporting events, which have always been perceived as superior, and manifests itself as 'regard for the foreign' and as 'cultural intimacy between coloniser and colonised'. At the same time, the 'foreign', which is recognized as superior, is vehemently rejected. If Malta's football is thus located between regionalism and transnationalism, Maltese identity is defined as that of a nation defined from the outside, but the role of victim has increasingly changed to an active positioning with growing negotiation options in a process of cultural decolonization.

Hegemonic football staging

In the presentation of the exclusion mechanisms of sport using the example of EURO 2008 and in the paradigmatic sketch of the struggles for hegemony with the case of football politics in Malta, the point is not that sport is the most important, but rather it as an essential, element of the construction of individual and collective identities, the creation, preservation and changing of value systems and the locations of their validity. Its effectiveness involves, on the one hand, discourses constructed and represented within football by their physicality and immediate physical presence, as manifest in major events such as EURO 2008, on the playing field, on the sidelines and in the fan zones, where the television both needs and strengthens this physical and emotional density. On the other hand, the special effect of an event such as the European Championship is based on its apparent equality and neutrality, because 'the appearance of neutrality and balance' is 'necessary to provide certain exclusions with legitimacy'.[32]

UEFA combines solid strategies of exclusion with a – on the occasion of EURO 2008, sustainably operated – 'respect' campaign, according to which, UEFA uses football and its popularity 'to help in combating social ills, promoting civic commitments and defending major humanitarian causes'.[33]

This proves that football federations are aware of social responsibility. Thus the umbrella organization of European team sports wrote in a 2008 structural paper with a digression on 'good governance': 'Team sports also have the ability and desire to deliver wider public benefits, in particular, to advance the fight against racism and corruption and to promote the principles of fairplay'. It similarly addressed 'societal issues which are linked to, or somehow highly visible through sport, including: violence; corruption; money-laundering; trafficking/smuggling of minors; stadia and security; illegal betting; xenophobia, racism and other forms of discrimination; match-fixing and doping'.[34]

Thus it is necessary to state that sport, and especially football, must be understood as active authorities for socialization and education, and by no means as images of society, as happens in many places. The gap between some anti-racist campaigns and the exclusion of those who, as shown, are of little use at football's highest level, appears all the more striking. This brings together the intentions of the large and small, the promising members and those without chance of the European football community, who can absolutely agree on a homogeneous picture of Europe. These common, rarely discussed norms and values also form the basis of what is possible in other, less congruent areas of negotiation, especially since, as the example of Malta makes clear, such small federations inwardly, that is, in opposition to their members, act in a fashion very similar to UEFA.

This gives UEFA a very important position – only mentioned here and not elaborated – within FIFA and its sports politics, with the possibility of great influence on world football events, and thus on global or globalized (sport) cultures in general. UEFA also has a hegemonic sports political position within Europe, one that extends far beyond sport to encompass political, economic and cultural effects, and includes a direct normative power as well as an indirect construction of meaning in different areas, which even concerns Europe itself. UEFA avails of both of its possibilities for direct influence, and the major continental competitions should be increasingly seen as stages for collective self-production: with the Champions League and other competitions at the club level, the European football federation constructs a new late- or postmodern Europe, based on unchecked mobility (of participants as well as fans), extreme commercialization and the transnational integration of markets. In this way, football is an essential forerunner or pioneer of a Europeanization that causes nation-states to appear increasingly obsolete. With the European Championships and other competitions at the international level, however, football continues to impart the functions of a socialization authority in relation to the modern traditional nation-state.[35]

UEFA rests (just as, on a smaller scale, the MFA does) largely on a traditional concept of the nation that does not take on the late-modern extensions of nation – or takes them up to only a limited extent – and emphasizes neither the primacy of 'justice', referring back to civil nationalism, nor elements of cosmopolitanism. Thus, UEFA increasingly argues on the basis of 'human rights',[36] but admittedly acts only afterwards, when benefits beckon. The differentiation in a late-modern Champions League and an actually quite nationalistic and national confrontation-promoting European Championship serves, in terms of profit maximization, two different, albeit overlapping, target audiences.

The overview of strategies of inclusion and exclusion in the football practices of Europe, of the manners of the small or potential partners, demonstrates clearly the extent to which neo-colonialist and hegemonic Europe produces itself in football events, and how powerfully it is able to implement this positioning. Pout bluntly, as on the political and economic terrain, in football, Europe defines itself inwards as well as outwards, and actively determines who may feel welcome, and in what form, and who may be counted as the 'big players' in this game. A parallel to the Maltese situation can be seen here in the form of patronage and the meaning of personal contacts, which makes it understandable why small federations with few advantages played in and supported the big EURO 2008 game.

In this sense, strategies of inclusion and exclusion and hegemonic discourses with the agreement of the excluded themselves can still come together in the common goal of a white, male, bourgeois and western discourse, in which achievement manifests itself in terms of successes and victories. The excluded are by no means outside this discourse or the authority it constructs, but will only produce through it the central norms and values with which to establish and strengthen the image of others. Even alternative competitions like the VIVA World Cup or football events in 'dwarf states' such as Malta are ultimately defined by the hegemonic structures of European high-level football and, based on similar structures and premises, they belong to the same discourses. If their accomplishment is 'to create order and introduce into a field of phenomena distinctions such as true/false, meaningful/nonsensical, masculine/feminine and the like, then it seems likely that this is to be understood not only as a purely textual, but as a very violent, physical operation'.[37] This is what EURO 2008 achieved in a specifically European context.

Notes

1. Grossberg, *Dancing in Spite of Myself*, 7.
2. Marchart, *Cultural Studies*, 251.
3. Althusser, *Ideologie und Ideologische Staatsapparate*, 120
4. Marschik, 'Sport als "leerer Signifikant"'.
5. Whannel, *Media Sport Stars*.
6. Hargreaves and McDonald, 'Cultural Studies and the Sociology of Sport', 53.
7. Miller, *Cultural Citizenship*.
8. Grossberg, *Bringing it All Back Home*, 256.
9. Hall, 'Erneuerung des Marxismus'.
10. Hall, 'Der Westen und der Rest'.
11. Markovits and Rensmann, *Querpass*, 231.
12. EM-Blogger, 'Miss EM 2008'.
13. WienTourismus, 'Wein'.
14. ÖFB, *Nachhaltige Fußball-EM*, 59.
15. Although there was a UEFA-Social Responsibility Project: 'Football for All', where disabled persons played matches in the host cities of EURO 2008.
16. SPG, 'Bundesgesetz'.
17. Salzburger, 'Mittendrin'.
18. LFV, 'Ein bewegtes Jahr'.
19. UEFA, Overview.
20. For a detailed history of Maltese football, see the work that has since reached eight volumes, *Goals, Cups and Tears* by Carmel Baldacchino, which completely documents the time between 1886 and 1999.
21. Baldacchino, *Goals, Cups and Tears*.
22. Marschik, 'They Lived Like Heroes'.
23. Armstrong and Mitchell, *Global and Local Football*, 52–66.
24. Armstrong and Mitchell, 'Players, Patrons and Politicians', 140.
25. Armstrong and Mitchell, *Global and Local Football*, 67–92.
26. Vella, 'The Favourite Dream of the Colonies'.
27. Armstrong and Mitchell, *Global and Local Football*, 130.
28. Baldacchino, 'The Nationless State?'.
29. Armstrong and Mitchell, *Global and Local Football*, 37.
30. Ibid., 70.
31. Ibid., 22.
32. Marchart, *Cultural Studies*, 151.
33. UEFA, 'Introduction'.
34. European Team Sports Federations, 'Safeguarding the Heritage', 13.
35. Sonntag, *Gefühlsausbrüche*.
36. cf. Nash, 'Cultural Studies und Menschenrechte', 241.
37. Sarasin, *Geschichtswissenschaft*, 40.

References

Althusser, L. *Ideologie und Ideologische Staatsapparate.* Hamburg: VSA, 1977.

Armstrong, G., and J.P. Mitchell. *Global and Local Football. Politics and Europeanisation on the fringes of the EU.* London: Routledge, 2008.

Armstrong, G., and J.P. Mitchell. 'Players, Patrons and Politicians: Oppositional Cultures in Maltese Football'. In *Fear and Loathing in World Football,* ed. G. Armstrong and R. Giulianotti, 137–58. Oxford: Berg, 2001.

Baldacchino, C. *Goals, Cups and Tears. A History of Maltese Football. Volume One: 1886–1919. The Golden Age of Maltese Football.* Valletta: Bugelli, 1989.

Baldacchino, G. 'The Nationless State? Malta, National Identity and the European Union'. *West European Politics* 25, 4 (2002): 191–206.

EM-Blogger. 'Miss EM 2008'. http://www.em-blogger.at/index.php/2008/03/18/miss-em-2008/

European Team Sport Federations. 'Safeguarding the Heritage and Future of Team Sport in Europe'. http://www.uefa.com/multimediafiles/download/uefa/others/73/43/98/734398_download.pdf.

Grossberg, L. *Dancing in Spite of Myself.* Durham, NC: Duke University Press, 1997.

Grossberg, L. *Bringing it All Back Home.* Durham, NC: Duke University Press, 1997.

Hall, S. 'Gramscis Erneuerung des Marxismus und ihre Bedeutung für die Erforschung von "Rasse" und "Ethnizität"'. In *Ideologie, Kultur, Rassismus. Ausgewählte Schriften 1,* ed. N. Räthzel, 56–91. Hamburg: Argument, 1989.

Hall, S. 'Der Westen und der Rest: Diskurs und Macht'. In *Rassismus und kulturelle Identität. Ausgewählte Schriften 2,* ed. U. Mehlem *et al.,* 137–79. Hamburg: Argument, 1994.

Hargreaves, J., and I. McDonald. 'Cultural Studies and the Sociology of Sport'. In *Handbook of Sports Studies,* ed. J. Coakley and E. Dunning, 48–60. London: Sage, 2000.

LFV. 'Ein bewegtes Jahr. LFV Geschäftsbericht 2007.' *LFV,* Vaduz 2008.

Marchart, O. *Cultural Studies.* Konstanz: UVK, 2008.

Markovits, A.S., and L. Rensmann. *Querpass. Sport und Politik in Europa und den USA.* Göttingen: Werkstatt, 2007.

Marschik, M. 'They Lived Like Heroes. Arbeitsemigration im österreichischen Fußball der dreißiger Jahre'. *Spectrum der Sportwissenschaften* 7, 2 (1995): 14–29.

Marschik, M. 'Sport als "leerer Signifikant" – Die Neutralisierung des Sportes als Bedingung seiner kulturellen Bedeutungen'. *Kurswechsel* 10, 2 (2004): 35–43.

Miller, T. *Cultural Citizenship. Cosmopolitanism, Consumerism, and Television in a Neoliberal Age.* Philadelphia: Temple University Press, 2007.

Nash, K. 'Cultural Studies und Menschenrechte'. In *Die Politik der Cultural Studies. Cultural Studies der Politik,* ed. K. Harrasser, S. Riedmann, and A. Scott, 221–47. Wien: Turia+Kant, 2007

ÖFB. *Nachhaltige Fußball-EM 2008. Nachhaltigkeitskonzept UEFA EURO 2008. Endbericht August 2006.* Im Auftrag des Österreichischen Fußball-Bundes.' http://www.umweltamball.at/article/articleview/60493/1/20697.

Sarasin, P. *Geschichtswissenschaft und Diskursanalyse.* Frankfurt am Main: Suhrkamp, 2003.

Salzburger N. 'Mittendrin und nicht dabei'. http://blogs.salzburg.com/euro2008/hintergrund/index.html.

Sonntag, A. *Gefühlsausbrüche. Europas Fußball zwischen Tradition und Postmoderne.* Wiesbaden: VS Verlag für Sozialwissenschaften, 2008.

SPG. 'Bundesgesetz, mit dem das Sicherheitspolizeigesetz geändert wird'. http://www.parlament.gv.at/PG/DE/XXIII/I/I_00158/fname_081068.pdf.

UEFA. 'UEFA. Overview'. http://www.uefa.com/uefa/aboutuefa/index.html. 2009

UEFA. 'UEFA. Introduction: Assistance Programmes: Respect'. http://www.uefa.com/uefa/keytopics/kind=8/index.html. 2009

Vella, M. '"That Favourite Dream of the Colonies": Industrialization, Dependence and the Limits of Development Discourse in Malta'. In *Maltese Society. A Sociological Inquiry,* ed. R.G. Sultana and G. Baldacchino, 55–78. Msida: Mireva Publications, 1994.

Whannel, G. *Media Sport Stars. Masculinities and Moralities.* London: Routledge, 2002.

Wien Tourismus. 'Wien: Wo sich die EM 2008 entscheidet. Lebenslust & Sportgenuss in der Fanzone Europas'. http://b2b.wien.info/data/marketing2008/em2008.pdf.

Europe divided, or Europe united? German and British press coverage of the 2008 European Championship

Sanna Inthorn

School of Political, Social and International Studies, University of East Anglia, UK

This article explores the dialogue of national and pan-European identities in German and British press coverage of EURO 2008. Its findings suggest that in media coverage of international football tournaments we may find traces of a common European identity. However, the concept of Europe that emerges is one of unity in diversity. Rather than an image of pan-European harmony, it is the concept of the nation which dominates press discourse.

Introduction

Since the 1980s, regulatory, economic and technological shifts have reconfigured traditional communication spaces and industries, creating 'new spaces of identity' in which global and local meet.[1] As media markets have become increasingly denationalized and commercialized, global media empires headed by transnational corporations have emerged.[2] With its historically entrenched popular appeal, the unexpectedness of outcomes and comparatively low production costs,[3] sport has become a key product in this competitive market.[4] Reaching audiences across the globe, televised international sport events, such as the Olympics or the football World Cup have become 'mega-events'.[5] These mega-events are 'especially dramatic presentiments of a fully developed global culture of the future, in which the "whole world is watching" … the same thing at the same time'.[6] Yet the emergence of a global sports culture is not limited to mega-events that occur with calendric regularity. The sports industries themselves are actively seeking to expand their markets. Football clubs such as Real Madrid have developed themselves into a product consumers all over the world can identify with.[7] Athletes too are part of and contribute to this globalizing sports culture as their geographic origin often is no longer the same as that of the team they are meant to represent.[8] Identities have become de-territorialized[9] and through both real, 'imaginative' and 'virtual' travel, consumers may access a wealth of information from across the globe.[10] There are now 'self-invented virtual diasporas', communities of fans 'forged from the global dispersal of club-focused images and products, and from the voluntaristic identification of individuals'.[11] Sport is thus an intrinsic part of a globalizing world in which flows of information, commodities and people 'have intensified to the extent that the sense of spatial distance which separated and insulated people from the need to take into account all the other people which make up what has become known as humanity has become eroded'.[12] Sport therefore is a cultural sphere with the potential to foster supranational, or even global identities.

However, as Rowe observes 'this picture may be deceptive, and sport seen as stubbornly resistant to the "harder" forms of globalization because of its dependency on the robustness of the *idea* of the sporting nation'.[13] National identities remain central to sport culture because 'its affective force derives directly from the connotative attachment of competition to identity' and 'at the heart of sport's ethos is the idea of competition'.[14] Numerous studies document the persistence of the nation as a reference point in sports and sports media in particular. Media coverage of international sports events draws on national stereotypes[15] and suggests the existence of national characters through references to style of play and fan behaviour.[16] References to a golden past of sporting victories,[17] but also wars fought between the countries represented by opposing teams,[18] suggest a common national past. Together with military language,[19] these discursive themes amplify national identities and accentuate a dichotomy of national 'self' and 'other'. Personal pronouns suggest unity of the 'self' and distance it from the 'other'.[20] Media coverage, but also the organization of international sports events, often encourages audiences to read these events through a nation-based grid. Athletes are labelled by nationality[21] and in public discourse sport stars often become symbols of the nation and its characteristics.[22] Global sport events, such as the football World Cup, are made sense of in national terms as evidenced in discussions of national players or issues and culturally specific techniques of production, commentating conventions and camera angles.[23] Such media practices suggest that sports media industries are marked by a process of glocalization, whereby 'local cultures adapt and redefine any global cultural product to suit their particular needs, beliefs and customs'.[24] There is thus an interplay between supranational and national identity politics in sport. The national here is not necessarily a reaction against globalization processes, but nationalism and globalization are best understood as intertwined. Local and national identities are strengthened, but at the same time there is an increasing awareness of the growing integration of the world.[25]

Taking the lead from these previous studies which suggest that in sports culture we may see a dialogue of the global and the local, this article explores the negotiation of the national with the supranational in press coverage of the 2008 European Football Championship. Previous studies have acknowledged the potential of intercontinental competitions, such as the Ryder or Solheim Cups, but also of intracontinental European competitions, such as the UEFA Champions League, to foster a supranational European identity. With reference to intercontinental golf competitions, Lee and Maguire suggest that such a pan-European identity 'is weaker than a single nation's identity'.[26] Similarly, King argues that that even though fans who follow their team through the Champions League competition may express an interest in European culture and identify with the local before the national, it may be too much of a leap to interpret these expressions as evidence of a European cultural consciousness.[27] The dialogue of the local and the European may be one in which the nation remains the loudest voice after all. Based on an analysis of British and German press coverage of EURO 2008, this artcile asks if the media are a platform for a dialogue of European and national identities and explores to what extent the nation may remain a key point of identification. Previous studies suggest that both German and British newspapers construct concepts of national identities in their reporting of international football tournaments.[28] Where media discourse in the two countries might differ is in the extent to which a concept of European identity is imagined in the first place and how it is framed. Whereas Germany has made European integration an integral part of its post-war identity, Britain has repeatedly expressed concerns over its loss of national sovereignty to Brussels. The construction of European identities in press discourse of these two countries therefore may be shaped by their different cultural frames.[29]

The argument is based on a both quantitative and qualitative analysis of a random sample of newspaper articles (n = 400), containing the keywords 'European Championship/Europameisterschaft' or 'EURO 2008/EM 2008', published between June 6 and 30, 2008 in *The Times*, *The Guardian*, the *Frankfurter Rundschau* and *Die Welt*. Although this is a small sample, it is balanced in terms of political outlooks and contains newspapers which have national reach. Further, the choice of broadsheet papers allows the study to look at a lesser explored section of the media market. Tabloid papers are well known for their use of national stereotypes.[30] Their's is a genre in which the boundaries of entertainment and information are blurred[31] and ethnocultural 'othering' is often part of humorous discourse.[32] Yet if we want to explore the full extent to which media discourse draws on concepts of national self and other, it is important not to ignore the genre of broadsheet news. Although they may adopt a discourse of sobriety, broadsheet papers too reinforce myths of national identity.[33] In this study, a basic quantitative analysis was used to explore the extent to which key themes of national and European identity discourse appear in the broadsheet press. Based on the findings of previous studies,[34] the frequencies of the following themes were established:

(1) use of war rhetoric;
(2) use of personal pronouns that constitute a national or European 'us' and 'them';
(3) references to national and European styles of play;
(4) references to national and European cultural practices, national past and national corpus; and
(5) references to national proximity and relevance.

In order to establish how these themes are constructed at the sentence level and to allow the study to explore possible discursive struggles over meaning within an article, references to the above themes were studied with the help of a qualitative discourse analysis.

How the press imagines the nation

Personal pronouns are a 'banal'[35] and everyday feature of media language through which the nation can be imagined as a united collectivity. They invite audiences to position themselves along a dichotomy of a national 'us' and its 'other'. *The Times*, for example, refers to football as 'our national game'.[36]

War rhetoric too emphasizes the competitive nature of tournaments and helps to suggest a dichotomy of nations. Thirteen per cent of articles in the British press and 14% of articles in the German press make use of this linguistic feature. *The Times*, for example, refers to a match between Portugal and Germany as a 'fascinating battle'[37] and *Die Welt*[38] describes the game of Turkey versus Croatia as a 'duel'.

The language of war and personal pronouns divide the European football map into nations and help to emphasize the divisions between them. References to collective cultural practices, the national past and the national corpus help to flesh out these concepts. Together they imply that the members of a nation share a national character, cultural traditions and a collective memory and suggest that they call a specific geographic area their homeland. Twenty-three per cent of British newspaper articles and 15% of German newspaper articles suggest either the national 'other' or the national 'self in this way. The following paragraphs look at these themes of the ethno-cultural nation in more detail.

National culture and national styles of play

The migration of players but also football managers today makes it difficult to speak of styles of play that are distinct to a nation. Yet despite the globalization of the game, references to seemingly unchanging national styles of play remain a common feature in football reporting. They correspond to stereotyped images, 'vested in tradition that communities give themselves and wish to show to others'.[39] By suggesting the existence of a national style, media discourse not only imagines a cultural practice unique to a national collectivity, but also alludes to traits of a seemingly innate national character.[40] Examples include the French as having flair and the Germans as being a team of hard-working, slightly dull but efficient 'panzer'[41] players. The myth of French flair, based on the appreciations of Gallic culture, cuisine and lifestyle,[42] has been observed in British press coverage of international football tournaments for some time, but it also crops up in German newspapers.[43] In football reporting, the appreciation of Gallic culture finds expression in the suggestion that French football displays high levels of style and technique.[44] *The Times*, for example, spots 'occasional glimpses of French flair'[45] in the play of Franck Ribery 'who demonstrated that the fact that he plays in the Bundesliga should not be used to malign his talents'.[46] This snapshot of British press discourse, of course, does more than construct a concept of French national culture. It also alludes to a lack of quality in German football culture. The suggestion that the Bundesliga is a national league with few players of Ribery's calibre is more than a statement about football talent. It taps into a discourse which makes hard work and willpower national character traits.[47] The German press too evokes this theme and makes it part of the imagery of the 'self'. *Die Welt*, for example, although critical of the German team for lacking creativity and being predictable, nevertheless suggests that other teams might 'be a little bit afraid of a German eleven which at the moment might play badly and without beauty, but which relies on its luck during tournaments and it old virtues'.[48] The theme of the so-called 'German virtues' is not new to German football reporting in 2008, but has been a common feature of reporting for some time. Alluding to qualities such as willpower and self-discipline, they are often criticized for being unattractive and boring to watch, but they are nevertheless placed at the heart of an ethno-cultural concept of German national identity.[49] In the German press, they are often contrasted to the stereotypes of southern teams and the Brazilians in particular, who are deemed to play with imagination, rhythm and style.[50] During a European tournament, the stereotype of the Brazilian 'samba players' is of course less readily available, yet references to teams from Spain, Portugal and Italy sustain the discourse which imagines southern nations as temperamental, emotional and full of Latin flair. This is a feature common to both the German and the British press, and similar to the national stereotypes of the hard-working Germans and French flair they have been documented by research studies over the years.[51] In 2008, the *Frankfurter Rundschau*, for example, suggests that fashion know-how comes naturally to the Italian team:

> Of course, the Italians – no other team dresses this fashionably during the European Championship. It starts with coach Roberto Donadoni, who dressed in a dark suit, white

> shirt and slim tie stands like a model at the side of the pitch, and it continues with the players. For the playing of the national anthem they wear elegant white training jackets with stand-up collars. These [jackets] have such a fashionable cut that these men could get past any bouncer of an in-club.[52]

The Times, even in the absence of the Brazilian team, manages to fit in a stereotype of this nation, by recalling how during EURO 2004 the Brazilian coach of the Portugese team lashed out against a Serbian player:

> His fierce temper – he also has a charming side – was illustrated in September last year at the end of Portugal's European Championship qualifying match against Serbia, a 1–1 draw. When Ivica Dragutinovic, the Serbia defender, slapped Scolari on the hand, the Brazilian-born coach grazed him in the face with a left hook.[53]

Such heterotypification, whereby playing style and behaviour are linked with supposed national characteristics,[54] is a particularly powerful discursive theme which suggests the nation to be ethno-cultural in nature. It suggests that it is possible to identify internally homogenous collectivities of people who share characteristics that are distinct from those of others and thereby gives rise to the assumption that nations are natural and not socio-political and cultural constructs.

This discourse of the ethno-cultural nation is further strengthened by references to cultural practices that are supposedly typical for the population of a nation-state. In particular, cultures of language and cuisine are referred to and help to suggest the distinctiveness and difference of nations. *The Guardian*, for example, citing Italian player Daniele De Rossi, combines a word from the Italian original with a translation, thereby signalling to readers that Italian is the 'other' and English the natural 'self':

> Daniele De Rossi said: "The biscotto (fix) is a worry and will be in our heads because, even during the game, you are always thinking a little bit about the other result."[55]

Similarly, the *Frankfurter Rundschau* inserts Italian words into a report on the replacement of Roberto Donadoni by Marcello Lippi as manager of the Italian team:

> "Arrivederci" Roberto Donadoni, "Bienvenuto" Marcello Lippi: the expected change of leadership at the top of the Italian national team is complete.[56]

References to food have a similar function to such markers of linguistic difference in that they help to suggest shared cultural practices that are specific to a nation. In the following example *The Guardian*'s chief sports writer Richard Williams reminisces about his visit to Turkey and its cultural, including culinary, delights:

> Forty years ago I was fortunate to be staying with my uncle, a professor at Istanbul University. ... He showed me the rare tomato-coloured faience in the little mosque by the Spice Market; he took me to eat swordfish at a restaurant on the Galata bridge; he drove me along the Bosphorus to the Black Sea, past the ancient palaces and forts; he played me his recordings of Asik Veysel, the old blind troubadour of Anatolia; he pointed me in the direction of Troy; and he took me to a football match.[57]

The national landscape

Not only does press discourse suggest the internal unity of nations and their distinctiveness from others through references to national character and culture, it also imagines these nations to have a geographically marked homeland. References to landscapes, but also buildings construct the national corpus. In 2008, the identities of the host nations Austria and Switzerland as alpine regions are emphasized. Austria is called an 'alpine republic'[58] and the mountain range is used as a metaphor for the Championship itself:

> Henrythenavigator may have been the toast of Royal Ascot yesterday, but his namesake, and his team-mates, have lost their way in the Alps and will return home chastened, with Domenech's talk of a bright future filled with more holes than a Swiss cheese.[59]

Yet markers of the 'homeland' supposedly known to the target audience of newspapers are also referred to. *Die Welt*, for example, reports on demands for a 'Fanmeile'[60] at the Brandenburg Gate in Berlin[61] and fan celebrations at Reeperbahn and Schanzenviertel in Hamburg.[62]

The national past

The final key theme which sustains the idea of the naturalness and distinctiveness of nations is that of the national past. The memory of a golden football past may even become central to a concept of the national 'self'. In Germany, the winning World Cup team of 1954 around Fritz Walter is repeatedly celebrated in popular culture and has entered cultural memory as a moment of national rebirth post 1945.[63] In 2008, the German press taps into this particular memory of 1954 through small references, such as comparisons of the weather forecast with the so-called 'Fritz Walter weather', a combination of 'rain and soft ground'[64] favoured by the star. Yet the 2006 World Cup, hosted by Germany, also functions as a symbol of past national success and a reference point for positive self-identification; 2006 features as symbol of a successful and attractively playing German team, but also as a turning point for Germany's image as a nation. World Cup 2006 is said to have 'changed Germany's image to the positive across the world'.[65] Yet not only are the successes of the 'home nation' mentioned. Press discourse also refers to the past successes of 'other' teams, such as Spain's 'sole success at international level, the 1964 European Championship'[66] or in the run-up to a game gives readers an overview of a team's past history and general performance levels, as does *The Guardian* in its television listings for the Championship:

> ITV1m 4.30 pm
>
> If you support Romania – and still want to look forward to the game – please look away now. Italy have lost only twice against Romania in 14 games. Last Romanian success? 1989. Last goal? 1989. What's more: Romania do not tend to do well in their second game at Euro tournaments (three games, three defeats).[67]

In the first instance, such information about past teams, past victories and successes seem to refer to the history of football only. Football is not necessarily a cultural sphere which easily embraces all members of a nation-state. Women, for example, may feel excluded as their participation in sport culture may be limited to very specific roles, including sexualized objects of the male gaze or heterosexual mothers.[68] Yet press discourse glosses over such internal divisions and places the football past at the heart of a supposedly collectively shared national culture. *The Times*, for example, by suggesting that the final could bring 'a night to savour for a success-starved nation'[69] implies that the people of Spain had been collectively suffering from decades of football defeats. Similar to references of style of play, the national past is a discursive theme which suggests that nations can be easily identified and distinguished from one another. Instead of inviting readers to feel part of a wider European collectivity, it suggests a Europe of individual nations and implies that shared cultural practices and experiences will 'naturally' lead citizens to identify with a particular national collectivity.

Cultural relevance

In press reporting of international football tournaments, the concept of the nation is going strong. The nation seems to be the main frame through which press discourse makes sense of the world and interprets it for its readers. The selection of news and the framing of stories are processes informed by concepts of national culture. Stories have to make sense in terms of journalists' knowledge and experience.[70] Economic criteria, such as the considerations of sponsors and advertisers and media competitors play a role, but so too do concepts of news values, which have become part of journalistic routines. In order to make sense of the persistent strength of national discourse in the sports media, the news values of relevance and proximity[71] are of particular interest. Stories are selected and written with a concept of a geographically and culturally defined collectivity in mind. The press constructs the imagined national community through its discourse.[72] Yet at the same time, press discourse itself is shaped by a concept of the very same community. International news events, for example, may be given a national or local angle.[73] In the reporting of EURO 2008 the same practice can be observed. Stories that are about the teams or fans of other nations are often made relevant to the audience of either Germany or Britain by insertions of national reference points. A story on the linguistic and cultural diversity within the Spanish team in *Die Welt*, for example, includes a reference to a German airline which refused to make in-flight announcements in Catalan.[74] In the British press, stories often include a reference to players who 'off international duty' work in the British Premier League as in the following example from *The Guardian*:

> Spain's supporting cast did not look like they were treating the match with utter seriousness, the one exception being Alonso, captaining the side and displaying the passing range and perceptive qualities that demonstrate why Juventus are willing to pay £15m for him. The Liverpool midfielder also came close to scoring the goal of the tournament from inside his own half of the pitch.[75]

Entailed in these small, almost passing references to the nation, but also in stories that have national events as the main story are assumptions about what is of interest and what is known to the audience at home, again sustaining the concept of a nationally shared culture. A particularly interesting finding is that *The Times* and *The Guardian* opt for this national angle almost as often as the *Frankfurter Rundschau* and *Die Welt*. None of the British home nations qualified for EURO 2008. Despite this lack of obvious reference points for the nation, the British press reported on this international tournament through the lens of the national community. Sixty-two per cent of British newspaper articles, compared with 68% of German newspaper articles report on EURO 2008 with a focus on the national 'self'.

European identities

Press discourse in both Germany and Britain presents its readers with a concept of a Europe marked by diversity, rather than unity. Ten per cent of British newspaper articles and only 2% of German newspaper articles construct Europe as a homogenous collectivity with a particular, distinctively European culture. In the British press, Europe appears both as continental 'other' and as a cultural space in which citizens are united by their appreciation of popular culture, including English football and music:

> A popular chant outside the stadiums was "Wo sind die Englander" (set to the tune of La donna e mobile) and it was usually accompanied by a good laugh all round. A few songs were pretty much all the English contributed to this tournament. Still, a tube train full of drunken Germans singing "Ve luff United, ve do" was an illuminating sight, as was the fact that pretty much every nation seems to have a song to the tune of Yellow Submarine.[76]

> Liverpool fans should be proud of Fernando Torres's goalscoring performance yesterday, but they may not be pleased. The last thing the club need is for a giant continental side to turn his head, as is happening with Cristiano Ronaldo. But Torres is so good, it's a danger.[77]

Thus, even though references to European culture are more frequent in the British than in the German press, British newspapers offer a complex concept of pan-European identity. Europe is both 'other' and 'self'. Yet notably, Europe is only imagined as 'self' once it is dominated by English culture and fits into the framework of the English nation.

In the German press, we can find the occasional reference to a Europe united in its enthusiasm for the tournament and its sport. It is interesting to see how this concept of Europe as the 'self' of which the German national community is imagined to be a part, ties in with the concept of Europe as the 'other' as we can find it in the British press. The continent of European nations that qualified stands against 'the island',[78] which did not:

> Noone talks about the English. It is simply not fair. Just because they did not qualify and are not allowed to play during the European Championship. At least on Thursday they had reason to be happy – after all, not only did the Croats kick England out of the qualifiers, but dramatically beat unloved Germany. And this on the same day the England striker chose to marry his childhood sweetheart. The date for this wedding was not only a clever choice, but also a little bit mean, just like we expect it from one of the naughtiest of footballers. According to the motto: Let the whole of Europe talk about football, I'm getting married. In one of the most beautiful places of Italy, Portofino, I'm showing you all who's boss. Well, the plan did not quite work out; it was raining. Italy is no longer what it once was.[79]

The British press in its cautious approach to the concept of a united Europe and the German press in its attempts to place the German 'self' within this supranational collectivity reflect and sustain wider political and cultural discourse in the two countries. Whereas Germany is constructed as 'good European', Britain is positioned as hovering on the doorstep to Europe. What does not emerge strongly from this discourse of European identities is a challenge to the concept of the nation. In both the German and the British press such references are relatively rare. The concept of a pan-European identity appears in conjunction with references to the nation, as the last example illustrates. Even though Germany is imagined to be part of a (continental) Europe united through football, the article stresses the divisions of Germany and England and imagines a concept of Italian national identity through references to climate and landscape. There is a dialogue of the national with the European, yet it seems that, as suggested by Lee and Maguire, a single nation's identity remains stronger than a pan-European one.[80]

Conclusion

At the beginning of EURO 2004, British journalist Rod Liddle writes in *The Times*:

> I am aware that this is a juvenile and unpleasant character trait of mine – and irrational, too. ... But all this notwithstanding, my enjoyment of Euro 2004 will reach a zenith when I can truly loathe the opposition for their real or imagined character traits of arrogance, deviousness, sexual rapacity, cowardice and duplicity. Yes, obviously, I'm talking about the French.[81]

In 2008, the discourse of the nation has not lost its attraction. One of the ten reasons *The Guardian* gives to its readers to explain 'why EURO 2008 will be well worth tuning in to' are 'national stereotypes'.[82] There are several reasons why the concept of the nation remains central to the sports media industries. International sport tournaments are built around the idea that the world can and should be mapped into nations, and the grammar of competitive sports such as football relies on the idea of a national 'us' and 'them'.[83] Not only sports media, but also sports institutions and governments refer to national teams as a symbol of the nation, or use sports to construct concepts of nationhood.[84] The nation also is a key concept of lived fan cultures and popular culture surrounding the game. National stereotypes in particular are central to humour in football culture.[85] They are often reproduced in a playful and knowing way, as illustrated by the last two examples. Such postmodern irony has been celebrated for making it possible to 'speak *to* a discourse from *within* it, but without being totally recuperated by it'.[86] So while stereotypes are evoked, they may even invite readers to critically reflect on the place of the nation in sport culture. Yet not all discursive constructions of the nation are subversive. They may even be expression of 'everyday chauvinism' which takes as norm the cultural practices and institutions of the national self.[87] Although humour may challenge the emotive depth of the nation, it does not necessarily challenge the centrality of the national self in sport.

Yet while we chart the continuing presence of national identity discourse in the media, it is important not to ignore the potential of other collective identities. Globalized sports media industries offer consumers de-territorialized identities. This article suggests that press coverage of a European football tournament does offer a platform for the negotiation of pan-European identities. Both British and German newspapers suggest a unity of Europeans who share a geographic territory and aspects of culture. However, it is doubtful whether these references present a challenge to the concept of the nation as the main point of identification. Europe emerges as a collectivity united in national diversity. While all Europeans seemingly celebrate football and know the same songs, they are nevertheless divided into different national collectivities. The Germans may love Manchester United, but they remain the 'other' to the English and the Italians. England, although integral to Europe through its popular culture, is positioned as 'other' to the European continent. Just as global sporting competitions do not deliver on the promise of promoting a sense of internationalization,[88] a European competition does not promote a strong sense of European identity. The European Football Championships remain an international event, which is why we can find nationalism and not pan-European harmony.

Notes

1. Falcous and Maguire, 'Imagining "America"', 60.
2. Murdock, 'Concentration and Ownership in the Era of Privatization'.
3. Andrews, 'Sport in the Late Capitalist Movement'.
4. Falcous and Maguire, 'Imagining "America"', 61.
5. Roche, 'Mega-events and Modernity Revisited', 31.
6. Rowe, 'Sport and the Repudiation of the Global', 284.
7. Houlihan and Parkes, *Football Money League*.
8. Poli, 'The Denationalization of Sport'.
9. Ibid.
10. Szerzynski and Urry, 'Visuality, Mobility and the Cosmopolitan', 116–17.
11. Giulianotti and Robertson, 'The Globalization of Football', 551.
12. Featherstone 1993, cited in Szerzynski and Urry, 'Visuality, Mobility and the Cosmopolitan', 117.
13. Rowe, 'Sport and the Repudiation of the Global', 285.
14. Ibid.
15. Maguire and Poulton, 'European Identity Politics in Euro 96'; Crolley, Hand, and Jutter, 'Playing the Identity Card'; Garland, 'The Same Old Story?'.
16. Blain, Boyle, and O'Donnell, *Sport and National Identity in the European Media*.
17. Poulton, 'Mediated Patriot Games'.
18. Crolley, Hand, and Jutter, 'Playing the Identity Card'.
19. Tuck, 'The Men in White'.
20. Tuck, 'The Men in White'; Poulton, 'Mediated Patriot Games'.
21. Poli, 'The Denationalization of Sport', 651.
22. Jackson and Ponic, 'Pride and Prejudice'.
23. Giulianotti and Robertson, 'The Globalization of Football', 549.
24. Ibid., 546.
25. Lee and Maguire, 'Global Festivals Through a National Prism', 8.
26. Ibid.
27. King, 'Football Fandom and Post-National Idenity in the New Europe'.
28. Crolley, Hand, and Jutter, 'Playing the Identity Card'; Inthorn, 'A Game of Nations?'; Inthorn, *German Media and National Identity*.
29. Inthorn, 'What Does it Mean to be an EU Citizen?'.
30. See, for example, Garland, 'The Same Old Story?'.
31. van Zoonen, 'The Ethics of Making Private Life Public'.
32. Garland, 'The Same Old Story?', 86.
33. Crolley, Hand, and Jutter, 'Playing the Identity Card'.
34. Billig, *Banal Nationalism*; Blain, Boyle, and O'Donnell, *Sport and National Identity in the European Media*; Crolley, Hand, and Jutter, 'Playing the Identity Card'; Garland, 'The Same Old Story?'; Maguire and Poulton, 'European Identity Politics in Euro 96'; O'Donnell, 'Mapping the Mythical'; Poulton, 'Mediated Patriot Games'; Poli, 'The Denationalization of Sport'; Tuck, 'The Men in White'.
35. Billig, *Banal Nationalism*.
36. Hughes, 'Abramovich Shows Up to Put the Heat on Scolari', 6.
37. Samuel, 'Fabregas Finally Puts Italy Out of Their Misery'.
38. 'Türken nach Elfmeterschießen'.
39. Bromberger 1994, cited in Lanfranchi and Taylor, *Moving with the Ball*, 191.
40. Garland, 'The Same Old Story?', 82.
41. Own quotation marks.
42. Crolley, Hand, and Jutter, 'Playing the Identity Card', 112.
43. Ibid., 112–24.
44. Ibid.
45. Hughes, 'Henry Sulks, Anelka Labours and France Stumble at First Hurdle'.

46. Ibid.
47. Crolley, Hand, and Jutter, 'Playing the Identity Card', 110; Blain, Boyle, and O'Donnell, *Sport and National Identity in the European Media*, 78.
48. Köttker, 'Mangel an Kreativität'.
49. Inthorn, *German Media and National Identity*, 109–10.
50. Ibid., 107.
51. Crolley, Hand, and Jutter, 'Playing the Identity card', 114; O'Donnell, 'Mapping the Mythical', 351.
52. Danicke, 'Die Angst vor Ballonseide'.
53. Kempson, 'Chelsea Plump for Pragmatist Who can Bring Palyers to Heel'.
54. Garland, 'The Same Old Story?', 82.
55. Fifield, 'Azzurri beg for a favour'.
56. 'Donadoni geht, Lippi kommt'.
57. Williams, 'Adrenaline-fuelled Turks Sense Greatness in Their Grasp'.
58. Schwertfeger, 'Countdown für Löws Schützlinge'.
59. Samuel, 'Pirlo Ensures Italy Fight on as Group of Death Claims France'.
60. This term, loosely translated into 'fan zone' describes a usually traffic-free area where public viewing screens and other entertainment are on offer.
61. Frommann, 'Platz frei für König Fußball'.
62. Schirg and Zand-Vakili, 'Hamburg – ein Freudenhaus'.
63. Cooke and Young, 'Selling Sex with History?', 188–9.
64. 'Gute Nachricht für das Finale'.
65. Frommann, 'Und wieder Freude'.
66. Hunter, 'Alonso Desperate to End a Tradition of Failure'.
67. 'Football: Euro 2008: Day 7'.
68. Carrington '"Football's Coming Home" But Whose Home?'; Choi, *Femininity and the Physically Active Woman.*
69. Kay, 'Torres Fame on Wane While Fabregas Star Rises'.
70. Manning, *News and News Sources*, 61.
71. Ibid., 62.
72. Billig, *'anal Nationalism.*
73. Manning, *News and News Sources*, 62.
74. Haubrich, 'Mit Katalanen ins Finale'.
75. Taylor, 'Second-string Alonso Displays Class of Spanish Squad'.
76. Ronay, 'Triffids in Defence and the Return of the Macho Manager'.
77. Cascarino, 'Torres has Stomach for Big Stage and a Battle'.
78. Own quotation marks.
79. Fischer, 'Die Spiele und ein Hochzeitsfall'.
80. Lee and Maguire, 'Global Festivals Through a National Prism', 8.
81. Liddle, 'The Beautiful Game of Hatred'.
82. Pearson, 'Jazz Up Your Viewing with Big Phil's Rants and an Orange Papal Blessing''.
83. Rowe, 'Sport and the Repudiation of the Global'
84. Gemmell, 'South African Cricket'; Grundlingh, 'From Redemption to Recidivism?'; McDevitt, 'Muscular Catholicism'; Nauright, 'Global Games'.
85. Brooks, '"More Than a Game"'; Carrington '"Football's Coming Home" But Whose Home'; Millward, 'Rivalries and Racisms'.
86. Hutcheon 1988, cited in Ryan, 'Postmodern Parody', 59.
87. Ross and York, '"First, They're Foreigners"', 368.
88. Lee and Maguire, 'Global Festivals Through a National Prism', 7.

References

Andrews, D.L. 'Sport in the Late Capitalist Movement'. In *The Commercialisation of Sport,* ed. T. Slack, 3–28. Abingdon: Routledge, 2004.

Billig, M. *Banal Nationalism.* London: Sage, 1995.

Blain, N., R. Boyle, and H. O'Donnell. *Sport and National Identity in the European Media.* Leicester: Leicester University Press, 1993.

Brooks, K. '"More Than a Game": *The Footy Show,* Fandom and the Construction of Football Celebrities'. *Football Studies* 3 (2000): 27–48.

Carrington, B. '"Football's Coming Home" But Whose Home? And do We Want It?: Nation, Football and the Politics of Exclusion'. In *FANATICS! Power, Identity and Fandom in Football,* ed. A. Brown, 101–23. London: Routledge, 1998.

Cascarino, T. 'Torres has Stomach for Big Stage and a Battle', *The Times,* June 30, 2008, 6.

Choi, P.Y.L. *Femininity and the Physically Active Woman.* London: Routledge, 2000.

Cooke, P., and C. Young. 'Selling Sex with History? German Football in Literature and Film and the Quest to Normalise the Nation'. In *German Football: History, Culture, Society,* ed. A. Tomlinson and C. Young, 181–203. London: Routledge, 2006.

Crolley, L., D. Hand, and R. Jeutter. 'Playing the Identity Card: Stereotypes in European Football'. *Soccer & Society* 1 (2000): 107–28.

Danicke, S. 'Die Angst vor Ballonseide', *Frankfurter Rundschau,* June 21, 2008, 37.

'Donadoni geht, Lippi kommt', *Frankfurter Rundschau,* June 27, 2008, 4.

Falcous, M., and J. Maguire. 'Imagining "America": the NBA and Local–Global Mediaspaces'. *International Review for the Sociology of Sport* 41 (2006): 59–78.

Fifield, D. 'Azzurri Beg for a Favour from Van Basten', *Guardian,* June 17, 2008, 4.

Fischer, A. 'Die Spiele und ein Hochzeitsfall', *Frankfurter Rundschau,* June 14, 2008, 11.

Football: Euro 2008: Day 7', *Guardian,* June 13, 2008, 4.

Frommann, S. 'Platz frei für König Fußball', *Die Welt,* June 7, 2008, 2.

Frommann, S. 'Und wieder Freude', *Die Welt,* June 7, 2008, 1.

Garland, J. 'The Same Old Story? Englishness, The Tabloid Press and the 2000 Football World Cup'. *Leisure Studies* 23 (2004): 79–92.

Gemmell, J. 'South African Cricket: "The Rainbow Nation Must Have a Rainbow Team"'. *Sport in Society* 10 (2007): 49–70.

Giulianotti, R., and R. Robertson. 'The Globalization of Football: A Study in the Glocalization of the 'Serious Life'. *The British Journal of Sociology* 55 (2004): 545–68.

Grundlingh, A. 'From Redemption to Recidivism? Rugby and Change in South Africa During the 1995 Rugby World Cup and its Aftermath'. *Sporting Traditions* 14 (1998): 67–86.

'Gute Nachricht für das Finale', *Die Welt,* June 28, 2008, 18.

Haubrich, R. 'Mit Katalanen ins Finale', *Die Welt,*June 28, 2008, 29.

Houlihan, A., and R. Parkes. *Football Money League: Changing of the Guard.* Manchester: Sports Business Group at Deloitte, 2006.

Hughes, M. 'Abramovich Shows Up to Put Heat on Scolari', *The Times,* June 16, 2008, 6.

Hughes, M. 'Henry Sulks, Anelka Labours and France Stumble at First Hurdle', *The Times,* June 10 2008, 69.

Hunter, A. 'Alonso Desperate to End a Tradition of Failure', *Guardian,* June 6, 2008, 6.

Inthorn, S. 'A Game of Nations? Football and National identities'. In *German Football: History, Culture, Society,* ed. A. Tomlinson and C. Young, 155–67. London: Routledge, 2006.

Inthorn, S. 'What Does it Mean to Be an EU Citizen? How News Media Construct Civic and Cultural Concepts of Europe'. *Westminster Papers in Communication and Culture* 3 (2006): 71–90.

Inthorn, S. *German Media and National Identity.* Youngston, NY: Cambria Press, 2008.

Jackson, S.J., and P. Ponic. 'Pride and Prejudice: Reflecting on Sport Heroes, National Identity, and Crisis in Canada'. *Sport in Society* 4 (2001): 43–62.

Kay, O. 'Torres Fame on Wane While Fabregas Star Rises', *The Times,* June 27, 2008, 88.

Kempson, R. 'Chelsea Plump for Pragmatist Who Can Bring Players to Heel', *The Times,* June 12 2008, 84.

King, A. 'Football Fandom and Post-National Identity in the New Europe'. *British Journal of Sociology* 51 (2000): 419–42.

Köttker, R. 'Mangel an Kreativität', *Die Welt,* June 18, 2008, 17.

Lanfranchi, P., and M. Taylor. *Moving with the Ball: The Migration of Professional Footballers.* Oxford: Berg, 2001.

Lee, J.W., and J. Maguire. 'Global Festivals Through a National Prism: The Global National Nexus in South Korean Media Coverage of the 2004 Athens Olympic Games'. *International Review for the Sociology of Sport* 44 (2009): 5–24.

Liddle, R. 'The Beautiful Game of Hatred', *The Times,* June 12, 2004, 8.

Maguire, J., and E. Poulton. 'European Identity Politics in Euro 96: Invented Traditions and National Habitus Codes'. *International Review for the Sociology of Sport* 34 (1999): 17–29.

Manning, P. *News and News Sources: A Critical Introduction.* London: Sage, 2001.
McDevitt, P.F. 'Muscular Catholicism: Nationalism, Masculinity and Gaelic Team Sports, 1884–1916'. *Gender & History* 9 (1997): 262–84.
Millward, P. 'Rivalries and Racisms: "Closed" and "Open" Islamophobic Dispositions Amongst Football Supporters'. *Sociological Research Online* 13 (2008). http://www.socresonline.org.uk/13/6/5.html.
Murdock, G. 'Concentration and Ownership in the Era of Privatization'. In *Media Studies: A Reader,* edited by P. Marris and S. Thornham, 142–55. New York: New York University Press, 2000.
Nauright, J. 'Global Games: Culture, Political Economy and Sport in the Globalised World of the 21st Century'. *Third World Quarterly* 25 (2004): 1325–36.
O'Donnell, H. 'Mapping the Mythical: A Geopolitics of National Sporting Stereotypes'. *Discourse & Society* 5 (1994): 345–80.
Pearson, H. 'Jazz Up Your Viewing with Big Phil's Rants and an Orange Papal Blessing', *Guardian,* June 7, 2008, 3.
Poli, R. 'The Denationalization of Sport: De-Ethnicization of the Nation and Identity Deterritorialization'. *Sport in* Society, 10 (2007): 646–61.
Poulton, E. 'Mediated Patriot Games: The Construction and Representation of National Identities in the British Television Production of Euro '96'. *International Review for the Sociology of Sport* 39 (2004): 437–55.
Ronay, B. 'Triffids in Defence and the Return of the Macho Manager', *Guardian,* June 30, 2008, 5.
Roche, M. 'Mega-Events and Modernity Revisited: Globalization and the Case of the Olympics'. *Sociological Review* 5 (2006): 25–40.
Ross, M., and L. York. '"First, They're Foreigners": "The Daily Show" with Jon Stewart and the Limits of Dissdent Laughter'. *Canadian Review of American Studies* 37 (2007): 351–70.
Rowe, D. 'Sport and the Repudiation of the Global', *International Review for the Sociology of Sport* 38 (2003): 281–94.
Ryan, A.J. 'Postmodern Parody: A Political Strategy in Contemporary Canadian Native Art', *Art Journal,* 51 (1992): 59–65.
Samuel, M. 'Fabregas Finally Puts Italy Out of Their Misery', *The Times,* June 23, 2008, 6.
Samuel, M. 'Pirlo Ensures Italy Fight on as Group of Death Claims France', *The Times,* June 18, 2008, 78.
Schirg, O., and A. Zand-Vakili. 'Hamburg – ein Freudenhaus', *Die* Welt, June 27, 2008, 35.
Schwertfeger, T. 'Countdown für Löws Schützlinge', *Die Welt,* June 16, 2008, 17.
Szerzynski, B., and J. Urry. 'Visuality, Mobility and the Cosmopolitan: Inhabiting the World from Afar'. *The British Journal of Sociology* 57 (2006): 113–31.
Taylor, D. 'Second-string Alonso Displays Class of Spanish Squad', *Guardian,* June 19, 2008, 3.
Tuck, J. 'The Men in White: Reflections on Rugby Union, the Media and Englishness'. *International Review for the Sociology of Sport* 38 (2003): 177–99.
'Türken nach Elfmeterschießen im Halbfinale'. *Die Welt,* June 21, 2008, 18.
Williams, R. 'Adrenaline-fuelled Turks Sense Greatness in their Grasp', *Guardian,* June 25, 2008, 8.
Zoonen, L. van. 'The Ethics of Making Private Life Public'. In *The Media in Question: Popular Cultures and Public Interests,* edited by K. Brants, J. Hermes and L. van Zoonen, 113–23. London: Sage.

(En-)gendering the European football family: the changing discourse on women and gender at EURO 2008

Nicole Selmer[a] and Almut Sülzle[b]

[a]*F_in Women in Football, Germany;* [b]*Department of Gender Studies, Philipps-University-Marburg, Germany*

The World Cup 2006 and EURO 2008 have produced widespread images of mostly peaceful, colourful and international public crowds with both actual women and female elements being a constitutive part of these images. This combination of female roles and requisites with the traditional male positioning of football events, however, is not without inconsistencies. In our article, we take a closer look at the way this, as we see it, new symbolic European football family is shaped, in particular we look at the precarious positions given to women in this construction. Our analysis of relevant modes of inclusion and exclusion points at transgressions of national and sexual identity on certain levels, which might offer further possibilities of change. For the present, however, we argue that the (en-) gendered football family remains locked within the boundaries of ethnical and sexual culture stereotypes and is inextricably linked to the commercial interests of the football industry.

Introduction

A year before EURO 2008 kicked off, the Austrian government's cultural tournament coordinator, Heinz Palme, set a very high benchmark. To become a success, Palme claimed, the EURO must reach out to appeal to everyone. Under the caption 'EURO 2008 to be a family event: Palme counts on women's enthusiasm', the Austrian news portal news.at quoted Palme as saying, 'Only as a family event can all groups of society be reached.' The 'passion of women and the enthusiasm of children' were regarded as guarantees of success similar to that of the World Cup in Germany.[1] Photographs of crowds of EURO fans in Austria and Switzerland indicate that Palme's vision came true. Although the enthusiasm present at the World Cup in Germany may not have been surpassed, the overall changes in fan outlook and behaviour were decidedly positive.

Let us turn back the clock a few years. In 2000, the European Championships were held in Belgium and the Netherlands under the slogan 'Football Without Frontiers', a reference to the co-hosting of the event and to the transnational power of football as such. However, that slogan was undermined when, due to fear of hooliganism, the Schengen agreement was suspended and border controls were temporarily re-imposed. These concerns were not wholly unfounded, as at the Word Cup in France only two years earlier a police officer was nearly beaten to death by German hooligans.[2] At the 2000 tournament, two people were seriously injured in a fight between

Turkish and English fans, and at the England–Germany game in Charleroi, English fans started throwing chairs around while a waiting crowd of international journalists and television teams stood by and observed. Football fans were depicted as being dangerous and exclusively male, making travelling to the tournament and staying in the host cities on match days come across as an unappealing activity for the whole family.

In this article, we use a cultural studies analysis of media articles on EURO 2008 to discuss the question of how gendered symbols and images of major football events have changed, particularly in regard to the fans.[3] How did the image of international football fans turn from red-faced, pot-bellied, chair-throwing English men into Heinz Palme's passionate women and enthusiastic children within the space of only a few years? We ask how families came to be involved and take a closer look at the ways that female family members, i.e. wives, girlfriends, female fans and victims of football violence, were portrayed in the media, and also investigate the evolvement of football players into family men. We then discuss how the 'carnevalization' of football is tied to gender questions and the positive and negative consequences of this for female fans.

A family of old men discovers its golden heart

When UEFA and the other football bodies describe themselves, the notion of the 'football family' is often invoked. Generally, the term refers to an assembly of member associations, i.e. the football governing bodies in the different countries, and thus depicts a family of not-so-young men. This monosexual group of (mostly white) fathers and sons is relatively incompatible with an everyday family life concept and, even though it can be regarded as an asset in terms of maintaining power within the 'family', it emerges as a drawback when looking at match sales. If the EURO and the World Cup are going to be family events that appeal to everyone, their predominating representative image cannot be that of aged and maybe even overweight men sitting around conference tables. However, it is also not possible for the images to consist solely of agile young men playing the game, and it is least desirable of all for the game to be embodied by football hooligans laying waste to inner cities. Obviously, from a marketing perspective, a softer approach is needed, a … let's say 'female' touch.

We have mentioned the security measures that were taken during EURO 2000. These same measures were also seen in Portugal in 2004, including the temporary suspension of the Schengen agreement. That tournament also saw the concerted establishment[4] of the fitting trademark 'EURO' to designate what was in the beginning simply the 'European Championships.' Another remarkable aspect of the 2004 tournament was the scarcity of bold headlines about violence among fans; instead, a more relaxed, party-orientated image was the order of the day. This image was consistent with the tournament's logo, which differed noticeably from its predecessors:[5] EURO 2004 was symbolized by a golden football surrounded by a glowing golden heart.

We think that, interestingly enough, this 'change of heart' originated on a far-away continent. When the World Cup 2002 took place in South Korea and Japan, it not only met with a totally different kind of fan culture – which included a huge percentage of women[6] – but also with what is now known as 'public viewing.' In 2002, the collective open-air viewing of football on giant TV screens began its success story in the tournament's Asian host countries, gradually making its way back to football's home continent of Europe.[7]

The establishment of fan parks, fan fests or fan zones, as the areas for collectively watching TV were dubbed in 2004, 2006 and 2008 respectively, marked the discovery of a new sales niche: the corporate, commercial and social integration of inner city areas into football events. This step resulted in the paradoxical dual effect of making the tournaments both more open and more closed: more open because the events now take place not only in stadiums, but also in public inner city spaces, and more closed because this same public space is submitted to the same rigorous security and crowd management measures as the stadiums. András Szigetvari and Anke Hagemann describe and discuss the effects of this new security concept, juridical concerns and spatial organization in their contributions to this issue. As we see it, the emergence of these huge enclosed fan areas in city centres has turned football into a party event and family affair; and as such it now both requires and produces new roles, new images and even new ways of talking about football for those attending the event, especially women and children.[8]

Fans have always gathered in city centres before matches, but now parts of the city have been converted into fortresses replete with visitation rights, fences and strict regulations. However, the fences are gaily painted, inside the fortresses you'll find bouncing castles and the strictest regulation of all is: have fun! Within these fan zones, EURO football really becomes what Palme envisioned: a custom-made event for everyone, with playground activities during the day,[9] concerts and parties in the evening and a few games of football in-between.

'Fans of today': the new European football family

How does this new type of family public relate to the old ideas about football and football fans? For one, the allegedly 'new' female fans[10] are cast in roles that complement, contradict or even displace the old male fans:

> Sexy curves, hot outfits and daring acts – the fan of today goes to any lengths to draw attention. The times of smelly undershirts, sweaty TV evenings and men with big bellies are over![11]

This is how the Austrian magazine *NEWS* portrayed contemporary female fans. Despite being blatantly sexualized, women are nevertheless categorized as 'fans' or even as 'the fans of today.' They are not placed on the fringes and regarded merely as decoration, but are instead an integral part of the fan party. They are even said to have put an end to the reign of the likewise scantily clad but rather unattractive male fan – which may be true in terms of media images, but out in the streets and at stadiums, paunchy men are still alive and kicking. However this may be, the media discourse on female fans is more complex and eventful than one would ever suspect just from looking at the pictures of 'sexy curves' and 'hot outfits.'

Image is everything: female fans and WAGs

Photographs are the preferred mode of communicating about women at men's football and can be sorted into two categories: pictures of players' 'wives and girlfriends' (cleverly dubbed WAGs by the British press) and pictures of female fans. With the WAGs, society talk edges into the sports section and football into the tabloid press. Celebrity WAGs cooperate with the press and are presented just like pop stars or models – which some of them in fact are, even when not accompanied by their footballer. Some go to great lengths to get top ranking on the list of sexiest WAGs, like Alena Seredova posing in a goal dressed in lingerie and high heels.[12] With the player and his WAG everything fits: sports event and the world of glamour profit from each other and increase their respective value with the dream team of athletics and sexy people.

Similar to the WAGs, female fans are mostly represented by 'picture footage',[13] with the difference that the caption does not provide a name and the person is not assigned to a player, instead carrying comments about the body or nationality like 'Happy in Belly-top and Black-Red-Gold' or 'Swedish Beauties.'[14] Both WAGs and fans are portrayed mostly by pictures with little text and the similarity between the representations is striking. Both are shown with skimpy clothing, often only wearing underwear or a bikini, showing off smiles and bodies for the camera, made-up and painted with flags, with a zoom on the cleavage. Female fans are often captured posing for the camera and 'Our Prettiest Fans' pictures are especially popular in online newspaper editions and Internet portals. Such images made their first appearance in huge numbers at the World Cup 2002 in Japan and South Korea, and since EURO 2004 they have dominated the media presentation of female fans.[15] It is always the same postures, and sometimes even the same pictures, which are used in abundance, often to illustrate articles that are neither about women nor even about fans. Even quality publications like Germany's *Spiegel* or *Süddeutsche Zeitung* have fan pictures on the Internet whose imagery belongs to that of the yellow press. It is not astonishing, therefore, that these pictures can be found years later still posted on pornographic boards.[16] Some especially successful images appear again and again, like that of a Brazilian dancer whose bikini has slipped aside to offer her breasts and nipples for view. This imagery ascribes female fans and WAGs alike with the role of the sexy accessory. For WAGs, the role is clearly defined: she supplements the player, her sexiness complementing his athletic power. Pictures of female fans are also sorted into this established pattern, thus turning them into attractive complements to male fans, at least on the Internet.

Part of the party family

'Women and Football – the party never ends' headlines the German weekly *Focus'* online gallery of female fans.[17] At the EURO party event, women are more than just accessories, they are part of the party family, which does not work without them. 'Today football is one big party and a party needs women, without them it just isn't a party.'[18] One could paraphrase this statement as 'today women are a part of football.' So, has football stopped being a male affair? WAGs, for one, have never been a threat to the masculine reputation of football. Quite the contrary, real men are expected to take an interest in beautiful women. Apart from that though, wives are still not allowed on the pitch or in the locker room, but remain on the fringe and in the stands. With the fans things get dicey. The fan zones are not exclusively male spaces where women are relegated to bringing beer and watching the fight. That's not the way these parties work. Women are not relegated to catering but are in the midst of things. They not only make up approximately half of the public, but they are also an elementary and non-negotiable part of the event.

Women belong to fan zone parties, but it would be a mistake to draw the conclusion that football no longer is construed as male. One has only to think of league football in the stadiums where male dominance remains uncontested. It is not a case of football becoming unmanly, but rather this new type of party bringing in its wake its own gender role casting. The EURO differs from similar street events such as techno or carnival parades only in that its audience dresses up in national colours. The main thing about a fan party is to party along, with or without an expert knowledge of football, no matter if you are a boy or a girl. This means that women with high expertise or men without any at all can each find their spot in the goings on. And, of course, the traditional male fan can mix with the crowds, single or with his buddies, or bearing a woman on his shoulders through the party masses.

Female gazes, male bodies

In addition to reports about women being part of the fan zone parties, there is a strong sector of media coverage that remains faithful to the cliché of female ignorance about football. During EURO 2008, for the very first time more women than men watched a football match on German TV: 55% of viewers watching the semi-final between Germany and Turkey were women.[19] This fact stirred up a lot of attention and seemed to demand an explanation. 'Men's bums' was the reason given in reflex, i.e. women are not interested in football so much as in athletic male bodies, which permits the belief in the exclusively male love of football to be upheld, in spite of the alarming statistics. The BBC sees German national coach Joachim Löw as a draw for women to watch football –'He is a huge hit with the ladies in Germany.'[20] A German newspaper explains the basic gender differences, 'Women do watch games a bit differently from men. They admire not only the players' commitment and passion but also their trained calves, muscular upper bodies and luscious bums, and like to wag their tongues about it among the girls.'[21]

Women's magazines, in particular, favour this sexist cliché, sometimes with an ironic wink of the eye but mostly quite seriously. They repeatedly ponder the issue of how SHE can become the perfect complement to the football-addicted man. The point here is not to make football interesting for women (the assumption being that it simply is not), but rather to dwell on the side effects of the event: party snacks in the colours of the participating teams, well-trained male bodies on TV around the clock, and hints on how to cope with a boyfriend who loses all interest in conversation and sex. The German magazine *Freundin*'s EURO 2008 special section included topics like 'Fashion, Accessories, Perfume. The perfect dress code for the EURO 2008'; 'EURO Flirtation' (providing football knowledge for the clueless 'to score with the man of your dreams'), cooking tips and, of course, 'the most attractive players of the EURO 08: 21 good arguments to turn you into a fan on the spot', along with a picture gallery of players very similar to the erotic presentation of the WAGs.

Those reports can be summed up in one statement: Women don't take part in the EURO event because of the football game but because of the male bodies. For men who like football fandom to be an exclusively male space this is initially reassuring, although it may not be in the long run. The undeniable female presence may lead to concern with the male fans' own appearance and behaviour. After all, women might get bored with watching and evaluating the players and start taking votes on the sexiest male fan.

Real fans

While the assertion of a specifically female approach to the game still takes up the majority of coverage on the topic of women and football, and seems to be most compatible with the established male way of being a fan, at times other voices can be heard. In Germany, a poll conducted by the Allensbach Institute shortly before EURO 2008 supplied evidence against the theory of a sudden female love for football. Fifty-three per cent of women interviewed claimed to be not very interested in the games or undecided about it (as opposed to 19% of the men). Those women who were going to watch the matches of the German team were reported as being just as much 'into it' as the men.[22]

Another good example is a German dating agency that published a study on 'how couples survive the EURO', in which they looked at the topic of women with a knowledge of football. The conclusion, legitimized by the institute's psychological expert, was that '34% of men think it's sexy when a woman has a clue about football.'[23] Thus, even the combination of (male) fan and (female) fan seems possible.

Our point is neither to confirm nor contest these 'studies', but rather to point out that they are obviously deemed fit to enter the discourse on women and football. According to the (unwritten) rules of this discourse, it is not totally inappropriate to admit that women and men may have the same knowledge and enthusiasm. Women are also allowed a say in the matter as experts: At the 'Press Club' on German TV prior to the EURO 2008 finals, two male and two female journalists discussed the topic '80 Million National Coaches – How can we win today?'[24] Even if football-competent female fans are still regarded as the exception, they are nonetheless part of the repertoire of female roles in the context of the EURO. As for male fans, this possibly results in the feeling of losing a field of competence. In an article for German women's magazine *Brigitte*, a male football journalist ponders the question 'Why are women taking football away from men?' and ends with the desperate cry 'Does no woman want to know what offside is anymore?'[25]

The Klagenfurt case: women in danger

In addition to the aforementioned roles ascribed to women in the modelling of the new public at major football events, there are also those that diverge from the party (and family) line: 'women in danger' were featured highly in security debates before and during EURO 2008. In the small Austrian host town Klagenfurt, a media panic pushed strongly by domestic right-wing politics, resulted in the widespread absence of locals in the fan zones and inner city. Football fans, especially those from Croatia, Germany and Poland, were portrayed as being a dangerous and predominantly male out-of-control mass – a clear threat to women in particular. As part of the German embassy fan team, Nicole Selmer was able observe first-hand the reactions of local women, employers and institutions to the EURO event in their city. The reactions were noticeably shaped by the fears and rumours going round before and during the first few days of the tournament. For example, one pub closed at 6 pm so that female staff members would not have to be out on the streets in the evening, a saleswoman at a bakery kept pepper spray on the sales counter for safety, and one local woman out on the town during a match day was obviously having fun but told us that her girlfriends all thought she must be crazy to be there.[26]

Far from making light of the very real risk that women face from male violence, our point here is that the situation in Klagenfurt was symptomatic of a policy focused upon keeping people in fear; more precisely, in fear of threats coming from outside their own experience, in this case from foreign football fans. The danger of rape is thus externalized, despite it being a well-known fact that sexual violence against women is first and foremost an 'internal' problem that occurs above all within the family. The idea of ominous foreign men endangering women has become a common feature in media coverage before major football events. Susanne Kimm and Birgit Sauer describe in detail (in this issue) the situation preceding the World Cup in Germany, where the debate surrounding an alleged increase in prostitution and the trafficking of women because of the tournament was the foundation for constructing an external threat that in turn served to distract from the actual facts and conditions of female oppression.[27]

Vienna 2008 gave us an example of how security issues that specifically affect women at football events could be handled differently. Before the tournament began, Sandra Frauenberger, Executive City Councillor for Women's Issues in Vienna, enacted measures intended to heighten safety for women during the EURO. These included additional lighting around the stadium and fan zone, an emergency hotline and a so-called 'security package' with safety tips and whistles.[28] These provisions assumed that women would be present at the stadium and in the fan zones and were intended to protect them not to keep them away. They corresponded to quite common and sensible demands from women's organizations about security in public space. However, it is important to mention that the basis for linking the EURO and concerns about violence against women was formed by a study on the correlation of major sport events and increased domestic violence.[29]

Sandra Frauenberger's initiative in Vienna aimed to keep the issue of possible threats during public events separate from the more definite threats women experience inside their own family and demanded 'half of the football field' for women.[30] In Klagenfurt, the equation 'football event = danger for women' stigmatized fan zones and stadiums as being most dangerous places and women were admonished to stay at home and not participate in the event. In other words, to stay in the place that, according to the above-mentioned British study, actually poses the greatest threat to them. This cautioning added to the subdued party spirit of the locals, garnered sneers from the rest of Austria and led to the invention of the epitaph 'Ghost City' for Klagenfurt.

Playing house: father, mother and child

If the EURO is meant to be a family event then children as well as women are going to be part of it. This includes the players' offspring as well, bringing the mothering qualities of WAGs and fatherly footballers into the focus of attention. At EURO 2008, this was most prominent with the Dutch team, whose children made a rather spectacular appearance on the pitch after the game. The German tabloid *Bild* reported their victory over France with the headline 'The Dutch Fathers of Success. [...] After the match the players celebrated by going to the Dutch section of the stadium and enjoying the victory with their biggest fans' – their children.[31]

But players are also sons themselves, a fact we learned more about in press reports like the one on the Beckham household's mother-and-son tiff over erotic photos, 'The daughter-in-law may get away with it, but the son doesn't. His mother didn't like the ads showing pictures of David Beckham in skimpy briefs at all.'[32] Dolores Aveiro, Cristiano Ronaldo's mum, also reported publicly about his time as a youth player, 'He cried when he played a pass and his mates didn't score. He was easily upset and was given nicknames like "whiner" or "little bee" because nobody could catch up with him.'[33]

Children without celebrity status can also get out on the pitch and be presented on television across the world. In 2002, McDonald's started its 'Player Escort' campaign, recruiting kids to accompany players onto the field and stand before them during the national anthems. The selection process for this very successful campaign differs in the participating countries: children and parents fill in application forms at McDonald's restaurants, send in photos or videos that show their love of football, or play football in mini tournaments to win a place in the programme. During EURO 2008, the winning children accompanied by one parent received a package tour complete with travel, accommodation, sightseeing and a match ticket. These children became celebrities in their own way – through an article in the local newspaper or coverage on McDonalds products and the company website. For UEFA, the sponsor campaign is a welcome initiative. The head of UEFA marketing in 2004 – EURO of the Golden Heart – stated that, 'These children represent the future of football, and the unique and very special opportunity to be a Player Escort will live within them for the rest of their lives.' 'And they didn't even have to eat at McDonalds', said the father of one EURO 2008 escort child during their stay in Basel.

Celebrity or not, related or not – these images and stories of children and fathers on the pitch and of parents in the grandstands are also part of the football family. They are the mirror image of the crowd watching the big screens: happy kids on men's shoulders, women in tears of joy or sadness. To quote from the McDonald's Player Escort video spot these are the 'once in a lifetime experiences that modern football is all about'.[34] The role of women and children in this setting is, as we have shown, a crucial one. Their inclusion promotes football as the 'game of the people' and strengthens the heterosexual family model by moving it into the once monosexual male world of football. In addition, women and children function as guarantees for security because, where they are, danger and violence have no place.

Football goes carnival: (im-)possibility of subversion

'Football goes carnival', penned German football journalist and author Christoph Biermann during the summer of EURO 2008, not without a hint of regret.[35] A primary characteristic of the carnival fan, of course, is that he or she dresses up and parties in the city. This can be detrimental to the stadium atmosphere as the carnivalesque fans are often not familiar with the art of supporting their team and the football carnival itself becomes the draw for thousands of people who do not come to see the games but just to be part of the party.

At EURO 2008, fan zone sponsor Carlsberg picked up on the importance of dressing up at events and began giving away wigs: a green headband printed with 'Carlsberg' and an attached hairpiece in the respective colours of each participating team. This, together with other fan merchandise products ranging from face paint and flags to silly hats, are symbolic of an interesting aspect of the football carnival: the relevance of nation-specific characteristics of fan costumes is diminished by everyone wearing basically the same things but in different colours,[36] an observation supported by Christoph Biermann's statements. It is both possible and popular to dress up as a football fan, decked out in all the essential accessories regardless of your own nationality or ethnic background. Shirts printed with 'Brasil' or 'Italia' are regarded more as a fashion statement than a patriotic message. At the EURO, locals in Switzerland dressed up in the team colours of the nations their city was hosting on a particular day,

'In the case of Spain, Italy, Portugal, Turkey or Croatia that might just be explained with family relations. But how do you explain someone in a Dutch or Swedish jersey talking flawless *Schwyzerdütsch*? Apparently you dress up as fan from another nation to join their carnival.'[37]

Not only national boundaries are being blurred by the carnival spirit, but also gender categories. A very striking feature of the football carnival is the ubiquity of elements otherwise reserved for women or, actually, drag queens. Painting your face, wearing fake hair, donning flags as skirts or even dressing up as 'real' women with traditional national accessories like clogs and white hats for the Dutch or a mantilla for the Spanish – all these modes of dress have become acceptable for men at the football carnival. In fact, when looking at online fan galleries it appears that this kind of effemination is almost a requirement for a picture of a man to find its way into these galleries. While female fans are most popular undressed, the male fans have to dress up.

Rather than arising from a transitory effeminate identity, this gender-bending dressing up seems to stem from the perception of the football carnival as a state of exception. For a short time, a destabilization of the dress codes and thus a feminization of maleness is not only allowed but even encouraged, e.g. by photographers, on the premise that this spectacle is restricted to the event culture of major tournaments. As of yet, these carnival elements do not seem to have invaded club football to any great extent.

Conclusion: (en-)gendering the football family

For many club supporters, 'football as a family event' is nothing more than a fitting epitaph for their favourite sport. However, for UEFA, FIFA and the sponsors of major tournaments it is a measure of success. We have already described how the concept of football as a family event has become reality and looked at the ways in which the new members of the football family, women and children, are fitted into existing patterns (like the sexy female fan shaped along the image of the WAG) and new ones (such as players as fathers or the party family). This is what we call the *(en-)gendering* of the football family.

In our view, the mingling of the football party with other forms of celebration in the streets in particular has caused changes. To a much greater extent than before, football events are occurring in public spaces and thus encompass a broader part of the population. This can also be regarded as a good thing because it offers the possibility of participation to those who were previously excluded.[38] We have mentioned that carnival elements bring along transgressions both in terms of gender and of national identity, but that, at the same time, the carnival itself can be regarded as a calculated moment of temporary destabilization. Likewise, the attention paid to women and children, the diversification of roles for female fans in the media and the general opening up of the previously closed boys' club of football, both in public and in private, can be regarded as a positive development. Unfortunately, the attention paid to female fans is very sexualized and sexist, with a clear focus on female attractiveness and the alleged interest of female fans in the attractiveness of the players instead of in the game.

Furthermore, the participation opportunities provided by the new football family are unfailingly incorporated in the economic system of football from the very start. Seen in this context, the ostensible shopping power of women is a perfect combination with carnival merchandising. A study conducted by EURO 2008 sponsor MasterCard predicted a sales figure of more than €4 million per game due to the female economic boos alone, consisting of money spent on merchandise, food and beverages, travel and accomodations, television sets, etc. Sports business expert and researcher Simon Chadwick comments, 'This research clearly demonstrates the rising financial significance of females in the football industry. Whether women are committed fans or spending elsewhere around the big games this summer, the fairer sex is making an important economic contribution. The football industry is waking up to the spending power of female supporters.'[39] Thus, the new football family's main *raison d'être* is that it can be capitalized on. Family is, as we have shown, a cipher for safety and as such it is also a cipher for threefold profit – father, mother and child.

Notes

1. apa/red. 'EURO 2008 soll zum Familienevent werden: Palme baut auf Leidenschaft der Frauen.' May 30, 2007. news.at. http://www.news.at/articles/0721/207/182062_s4/euro-2008-familienevent-palme-leidenschaft-frauen.
2. For a view of the tournament from the perspective of a German social pedagogic fan project, see Schneider and Gabriel, *Fußball ohne Grenzen*.
3. Our article relies on participant observation during the EURO, done by Nicole Selmer as a journalist and a member of the German fan embassy team and upon research by Almut Sülzle on spectator behaviour and fan participation in her role as an evaluator for the EU project 'AGIS Eurotour 2008.'
4. The term EURO was also used for the previous two events but measures against so-called 'ambush marketing' were more strictly enforced during Portugal 2004.
5. The logos of the EURO tournaments as found on uefa.com began as a uniform flag with the colours of the respective host country, the UEFA name and the year. The real break with that approach came with the 1996 tournament when England used its own logo – a ball with colourful inserts – that was less cold and more inviting. In 2000, the Championship was represented by an asexual figure silhouetted against the national colours of the two host countries.
6. Tagsold, 'Mittendrin'.
7. For example, in 2002 city authorities organized 'public viewing' in Hamburg, Germany. In Portugal 2004, there was an official UEFA 'fan park' in Lisbon with a capacity of more than 10,000 people. The big tournaments in 2006 and 2008 saw official fan areas in every host city.
8. Wolfram Manzenreiter sees the metaphor of the football family as 'domestic symbolism that hardly evokes the empowerment of women' (Manzenreiter, 'Her Place in the "House of Football"', 216). We emphasize the point that, as undeniably domestic as it may be, the concept of football as family event at least provides women who were never before part of the game, metaphorically or otherwise, the possibility of inclusion.
9. Perfectly illustrated by the advertisement for the Vienna fan zone by stadt wien marketing, 'Football for all. Between 9am and 1pm the Fan Zone is devoted to children and teenagers.' (June 4, 2008) stadt wien marketing. http://www.fanzone-vienna.at/index.php?id=20&tx_ttnews[tt_news]=11&tx_ttnews[backPid]=19&cHash=ef5bc123cf.
10. For a discussion about the unwritten history of female fandom and the discovery of the female target group see also Selmer, 'Frauen auf den Tribünen' and Selmer, 'Neue Zielgruppe'.
11. News.at. http://www.news.at/nw1/gen/slideshows/slide/show;sport/fussball/euro_2008/sexy_fans/;kid;270?flags=nopop;1.
12. Mirror.co.uk. 'Euro 2008: Top 10 Euro WAGs in pictures.' (June 3, 2008) Mirror.co.uk. http://www.mirror.co.uk/sport/euro2008/2008/06/03/euro-2008-top-10-euro-wags-in-pictures-115875-20593832/. Another example in the British press: bbc.co.uk. 'Euro WAGs 2008'. May 31, 2008. bbc.co.uk. http://news.bbc.co.uk/sport2/hi/football/euro_2008/7405376.stm.
13. Brüggemann and Riehle, *'Wir' und 'die Anderen'*, 72.
14. Focus.de. 'Frauen und Fußball – Party ohne Ende'. Focus.de. http://www.focus.de/sport/fussball/em2008/tid-10227/frauen-und-fussball-party-ohne-ende_did_19244.html?special=4448.

15. See Schediwy, *Sommermärchen im Blätterwald*; Brüggemann and Riehle, *'Wir' und 'die Anderen'*.
16. See Sülzle, 'Girlisierung des Fußballs'.
17. Focus.de. 'Frauen und Fußball - Party ohne Ende'. Focus.de. http://www.focus.de/sport/fussball/em2008/tid-10227/frauen-und-fussball-party-ohne-ende_did_19244.html?special=4448.
18. Köhler, N. 'Sag niemals: Der ist aber süß!' *Stuttgarter Zeitung*, June 7, 2008, Weekend supplement.
19. RPO. 'TV-Quoten beim Spiel Deutschland – Türkei'. RP Online. June 26, 2008. http://www.rp-online.de/public/article/gesellschaft/medien/583298/33-Millionen-vor-der-Glotze.html.
20. Fletcher, P. 'Final expectations at fever pitch.' bbc.co.uk. June 19, 2008. http://www.bbc.co.uk/blogs/euro2008/2008/06/final_expectations_at_fever_pi.html
21. 'Modische Abseits-Fallen und der spezielle weibliche Blick auf die Fußballer-Waden.' *Frankfurter Neue Presse*, June 6, 2008.
22. Institut für Demoskopie Allensbach. 'Fußball-EM 2008. 21 Prozent: "Deutschland holt den Titel.? 'Auch Frauen kennen Fußballfieber.' Allensbacher Berichte Nr. 8/2008.
23. Elitepartner. 'Studie: "Süße, ich erklär Dir Abseits – so überstehen Paare die EM."' Press release, June 3, 2008.
24. ARD Presseclub. '80 Millionen Bundestrainer – Wie schaffen wir den Sieg?.' June 29, 2008. wdr.de. http://www.wdr.de/tv/presseclub/2008/0629/gaeste.phtml.
25. Brichzi, D. 'Frauenversteher: Frauen und Fußball. Warum Frauen den Männern den Fußball wegnehmen.' Brigitte.de. http://www.brigitte.de/liebe/beziehung/frauen-und-fussball/index.html
26. The German press also commented on the Klagenfurt situation and the fear of foreign football men. 'Angst statt Euphorie in Klagenfurt – vor allem bei Frauen.' Tagesspiegel.de, June 6, 2008. http://www.tagesspiegel.de/sport/EM-2008-Oesterreich;art17482,2548752, and the interview with Michael Gabriel, head of the German fan work team, at Spiegel Online. 'EM-Bilanz aus Fansicht. "Angst vor Hooligans beim Brotkauf"' (Interview with Michael Gabriel by Christoph Ruf). Spiegel-Online, June 22, 2008. http://www.spiegel.de/sport/fussball/0,1518,561004,00.html.
27. The debate on 'forced prostitution' that had been irresponsibly fuelled before the World Cup 2006 was not taken up in Austria. In Switzerland, however, the topic was pushed by the campaign 'Euro 08 against trafficking of women' (www.frauenhandeleuro08.ch). See also Schuster and Sülzle, *Zwangsprostitution*.
28. ene. 'Euro 2008 without fear.' wieninternational.at. http://www.wieninternational.at/en/node/9115.
29. Ibid.
30. Ibid.
31. Bild.de. 'Das sind Hollands Väter des Erfolges.' Bild.de. http://www.bild.de/BILD/sport/fussball/EM-2008/2008/06/14/holland-vaeter-des-erfolges/bild-de-erklaert-die-toranjes.html.
32. CB/AP. 'Mama Beckham: Empört wegen Unterwäschefotos.' Focus Online. April 2, 2008. http://www.focus.de/panorama/boulevard/mama-beckham-empoert-wegen-unterwaeschefotos_aid_268076.html.
33. Rhyner, S. 'Von der "Heulsuse? zum Weltfussballer.' sportalplus.com. June 6, 2008. http://www.sportalplus.com/sportch/generated/article/fussball/2008/06/18/4925700000.html.
34. McDonald's. 'Cases: McDonald's Players Escort.' branded-entertainment-circle.ch. http://www.branded-entertainment-circle.ch/content/view/23/9/.
35. Biermann, C. 'Fußball wird Karneval.' Spiegel-Online, June 25, 2008. http://www.spiegel.de/sport/fussball/0,1518,561741,00.html.
36. Dressing up with much more that just a jersey and a flag or scarf seems to be an innovation arising from Dutch fans and, as such, is definitely older than fan zone parties themselves. The fan culture most resistant to the carnival element is possibly the English one, where males seem likely to stick with baring their chests instead of donning face paint and a wig. See also Giulianotti, who describes how carnival fans have existed since the early 1980s in northern Europe (Scotland, Norway, Holland), 'wearing their national costume [and] open friendliness rather than hostility towards rival fans and local hosts' Giulianotti, *Football*, 59. On dress codes, fan uniforms and the sports spectacle in Japan see also Manzenreiter, 'Sport Spectacles'.

37. Biermann, C. 'Fußball wird Karneval.' Spiegel-Online, June 25, 2008. http://www.spiegel.de/sport/fussball/0,1518,561741,00.html. These observations can also be linked to the concept of transitory identification in commercialized football as proposed by Knoch, 'Gemeinschaft auf Zeit.'
38. Our observations seem to indicate that this development, i.e. the interest in female fans and their specific role in the family event, is not restricted to the host countries of the last two tournaments, but can also be observed in other (at least Western) European countries. It will be most interesting to see, if the 'branding' of the EURO 2012 in Poland and Ukraine will also take up these points.
39. SportBusiness. 'Women Spending €140m on UEFA EURO 2008™, Says MasterCard Study'. SportBusiness Group. http://www.sportbusiness.com/news/167014/women-spending-140m-on-uefa-euro-2008-says-mastercard-study. Interestingly, this 'female contribution' to the football industry amounts to no more than 10% of the total economic impact, and in some countries like Germany or Sweden up to 30%. This leaves open the question whether the female economic boost is real, or just another myth about women and football.

References

Brüggemann, B., and R. Riehle. *'Wir' und 'die Anderen'. Eine Pressedokumentation zu Integrations- und Ausgrenzungsprozessen während der Fußball-WM 2006.* Berlin: Friedrich Ebert Stiftung, 2006.

Gabriel, M. 'In der Falle – Die Konstruktion von Fußballfans als gefährliche Gruppe'. In *"Fußball ohne Grenzen". Die Euro 2000 in Belgien und den Niederlanden,* ed. T. Schneider and M. Gabriel, 25–34. Frankfurt am Main: KOS, 2001.

Giulianotti, R. *Football. A Sociology of the Global Game.* Cambridge: Polity Press, 1999.

Knoch, H. 'Gemeinschaft auf Zeit. Fußball und die Transformation des Nationalen in Deutschland und England'. In *Fußballwelten. Zum Verhältnis von Sport, Politik, Ökonomie und Gesellschaft,* ed. P. Lösche, U. Ruge, and K. Stolz, 117–53. Opladen: Leske + Budrich, 2002.

Manzenreiter, W. 'Her Place in the "House of Football". Globalisation, Cultural Sexism and Women's Football in East Asian Societies'. In *Football Goes East: Business, Culture and the People's Game in China, Japan and Korea,* ed. W. Manzenreiter and J. Horne, 197–221. London: Routledge, 2004.

Manzenreiter, W. 'Sport Spectacles, Uniformities and the Search for Identity in Late Modern Japan'. *Sociological Review* 54, S2 (2006): 144–59.

Schediwy, D. *Sommermärchen im Blätterwald. Die Fußball-WM 2006 im Spiegel der Presse.* Marburg: Tectum, 2008.

Schneider, T., and M. Gabriel, ed. *"Fußball ohne Grenzen". Die Euro 2000 in Belgien und den Niederlanden.* Frankfurt am Main: KOS, 2001.

Schuster, M., and A. Sülzle. *Zwangsprostitution, Sexarbeit, Menschenhandel und die WM 2006. Gutachten zu Kampagnen zu Prostitution und Menschenhandel in Deutschland im Umfeld der Fußballweltmeisterschaft der Männer 2006.* Wien: Wiener Institut für Entwicklungsfragen und Zusammenarbeit (vidc), 2006.

Selmer, N. 'Die Frauen auf den Tribünen – Ein ungeschriebenes Kapitel der Fußballgeschichte'. In *Wo das Fußballherz schlägt. Fußball-Land Nordrhein-Westfalen,* ed. S. Goch and R. Piorr, 185–94. Essen: Klartext, 2006.

Selmer, N. 'Neue Zielgruppe oder ideologische Verschiebemasse – Vom Umgang der Fußballindustrie mit weiblichen Fans'. In *kicken. Ein Buch voller Erinnerungen an die bekanntlich wichtigste Nebensache der Welt,* ed. Büro der Erinnerungen Landesmuseum Johanneum, 294–99. Graz: publication pn, 2007.

Sülzle, A. 'Die Girlisierung des Fußballs. Fallstudie zu Fußball, Medien und Geschlecht im Kontext der WM-Berichterstattung'. In *Bilder – Bücher – Bytes. Zur Medialität des Alltags,* ed. M. Simon and T. Hengartner, 480–90. Münster: Waxmann, 2009.

Tagsold, C. 'Mittendrin und doch abseits. Frauen in japanischen Fußballstadien'. In *gender kicks. Texte zu Fußball und Geschlecht,* ed. A. Hagel, N., Selmer and A. Sülzle, 89–98. Frankfurt: Koordinationsstelle Fanprojekte Schriftenreihe Band 10, 2005.

Discourses on forced prostitution, trafficking in women, and football: a comparison of anti-trafficking campaigns during the World Cup 2006 and the European Championship 2008

Susanne Kimm and Birgit Sauer

Department of Political Science, University of Vienna, Austria

Compared with the massive campaigns against trafficking in women during the 2006 men's football World Cup in Germany, the issue was not taken up very much in Austria, which hosted the European Championships in 2008. Except for some smaller initiatives, the public debates were not as strong as two years before. In Germany, not only were fears of an increased demand for sexual services due to the number of male football fans and 'a flood' of foreign prostitutes expressed, but so too was the concern that they would not come voluntarily. It was assumed that many of the women would be trafficked and forced into prostitution. Quite a number of women's organizations in Germany thus campaigned against trafficking in women during the 2006 championship. This article compares the discourses in Germany and Austria and sheds light on the reasons for their similarities and differences. In particular, we explain the modest public debates and the lack of explicit mobilization against trafficking in women by Austrian feminist organizations. In doing so, the article sketches the most important strands in the argumentation of anti-trafficking campaigns and their entanglement with other social fields, such as migration and gender relations. The focus of this article lies in the problematic mixing of concepts such as trafficking, forced prostitution, sex work and migration, and on the effects this might have.

'Expect emotions'
(Slogan of EURO 2008)

Introduction

The FIFA World Cup in Germany in 2006 served as a role model for the organization of the EURO, the European Football Championship held in June 2008 in Austria and Switzerland. The summer event in 2006 was promoted by the German organizers as 'a time to make friends.' But not everyone who arrived for the World Cup was welcome: politicians, and particularly women's organizations, were concerned above all about (forced) prostitutes and trafficking in women. When rumours arose about the setting up of containers for sexual services (*Verrichtungsboxen*) in the city of Cologne, numerous women's organizations began to mobilize against forced prostitution during the World Cup. They feared that many of the prostitutes offering their services were trafficked to Germany and forced to work in the sex industry. The number of 40,000 trafficked women appeared in the media – although figures about trafficking are always estimates and the phenomenon is hardly quantifiable. Thus, although neither the demand for nor the supply of sex work could be estimated 'realistically', the German media jumped at the topic.

Also, politicians and women's organizations assumed a close relationship between football, masculinity and prostitution. Fantasies about the demand for sex work during the World Cup blossomed: where men are in sports euphoria, where emotionalized masculinity unfolds, there must be a demand for sex work – be it in a male-bonded 'joint adventure' or be it to relieve frustration after the football match.

Compared with Germany, Austrian activists and politicians remained rather silent concerning a possible relationship between the football event, masculinity, prostitution and trafficking in women. Although in Switzerland, three campaigns against trafficking in women were organized, few newspaper articles appeared and some smaller campaigns were launched in Austrian host cities such as Klagenfurt.[1] No large nationwide campaign mobilized against prostitution and trafficking in women before and during the football event. Austrian non-governmental organizations (NGOs) working in the field of trafficking in women ultimately decided not to launch a campaign against trafficking that connected the issue with football. Instead, Austrian women's organizations took up a former campaign from 2007, focusing on the (social) rights of sex workers more generally.

Thus, the key question of this article is why we could not observe a mobilization around the Austrian football event like in Germany. We hypothesize, first, that Austrian NGOs refrained from an anti-trafficking campaign because they had learned from the effects of the German campaigns and the discourse that emerged around the campaigns, namely the anti-sex work and anti-immigration frames. Another explaining factor, which forms our second hypothesis, might be found in the differing governance of prostitution in the compared countries.

An underlying assumption of our argument is that in campaigns such as those during the World Cup and the European Championship, not only is trafficking in women combated, but the discourse around trafficking becomes a struggle over the more general fields of governing prostitution and migration.[2] Thus, European borders are constructed as selective: open for peaceful sport fans, but closed for illegal migrants. Moreover, we argue, that the anti-trafficking campaigns instrumentalize football events to construct a specific type of masculinity in order to attract attention for their issue. Analysis of anti-trafficking campaigns shows that the economy of attention is part of the football industry and that football events are therefore open to the strategic framing of issues discursively attached to these events, such as masculinity and forced prostitution.

In a first step, we outline the discourse over connecting football with masculinity and sex (work), which emerged as subtext of public debates during the football events in both countries. Then we sketch the regulations regarding trafficking in women and prostitution in Austria and Germany. In the next step, we present the aims and frames of major German campaigns, and finally we explain the differences in the Austrian campaign, in order to make our argument that the campaigns during both events contributed to the discourse on the formation of the rights not only of trafficked women, but also of (migrant) sex workers, about sports masculinities and European borders in both countries.

Football, masculinity and sex (work)

Media debates, but also feminist discussions, in Austria and Germany connect football to masculinity and sex. These ideas nourish the assumption that the 'male' event football prompts a special demand for sex. 'The equation is simple', stated the German feminist magazine *EMMA*, 'where football is played, there are men, and where men are, there are also prostitutes'.[3] Also, the Austrian daily *Kleine Zeitung* in Graz quoted the Austrian journalist Corinna Milborn, author of a book about trafficking African women into prostitution:[4] 'Sport for the masses and the "oldest profession" are two sides of the same coin. (...) It would be an illusion to believe that, where ten thousands of men gather, illegal prostitution does not increase.'[5] The framing of the football-macho gained public attention when the German team did not want to join the anti-trafficking campaign.

Also sex workers assumed that the German World Cup would result in a special demand for sexual services. They expected more customers, and some sex workers even travelled to Germany especially for this event.[6] Thus, it might be argued, the connection between football events and a demand for sexual service is not necessarily unsubstantiated – as gender critical sports studies have shown. Sport tournaments have been connected to constructions of masculinities: endurance, combativeness and aggressiveness are ascriptions to male identities.[7] Football in Europe has been constructed for a long time as *the* male form of sport: men play against men and are cheered predominantly by male fans. And if masculinity is (re)produced through sport and football, it is not unreasonable to assume that sport events are major loci to display sexual potency, male power and dominance by purchasing sexual services from women.

However, the connection between male dominance and purchased sexual services has been put into question in a recent study on the clients of sex workers. The study, based on interviews with customers, rejects the automatism and simplicity of the image of a male 'perpetrator' and a female 'victim'.[8] Furthermore, it may be questioned whether a suppressive masculinity wants to reproduce itself in an 'après match' of an exploitative sexual act, because the football match itself is perceived more and more as a sexually laden event. Moreover, unambiguous gender-specific male ascriptions to football have been eroded for some time: more and more women are among the public at former exclusively male football matches. The fan community is not homo-social anymore. Women also attain increasing attention on the pitch – which is even more true for the USA, that for the old continent of football.[9] These transformations were also visible at the German World Cup in 2006: prostitutes travelling to Germany left the football event early, disappointed by the bad business.[10]

Moreover, this framing by feminist organizations de-thematized the weak links in the football chain: the European football industry is profiting from trafficked young men. Thus, men are also victims of the football economy and not only perpetrators. Another aspect is remarkable: although every big conference or fair attracts sex workers, it is the football events, which are open to deploy fantasies about masculinity and forced prostitution. Thus, to construct a connection between football, masculinity and prostitution is a discursive political strategy, which might be pursued by rather different actors – one of them being anti-trafficking organizations.

'Governing trafficking in persons': competing frames and regulations

Trafficking in women and persons is a pressing global issue. It has become a profitable business in the last two decades. Estimates of the numbers of trafficked persons range from 700,000 to 2,000,000 per year, the vast majority of them women and children. Reasons for trafficking are often explained by push and pull factors. Push factors, concerning the economic situation and socio-economic opportunities in poorer countries, are accompanied by the pull factors of migration: neo-liberal restructuring in the countries of Western Europe and the deregulation of labour markets led to an increasing demand for cheap and unsecured labour. The market integration of the European Union (EU), however, led to new barriers, i.e. the closing of the Schengen borders and to a reduction of work migration to EU–Europe. The possibilities to immigrate to the EU are therefore declining. Thus, the crossing of borders to EU–Europe is often only possible in non-legal ways, for example, through the medium of smugglers. This dependence on smugglers and the illegality of crossing EU borders, however, builds a structure that fosters people trafficking.

It is often overlooked that trafficking not only results in forced prostitution. Women are also trafficked into marriage or other forms of precarious labour such as household work, jobs in the tourism industry or begging. Furthermore, the roles in the process of trafficking in women are not distributed as clearly as might be assumed. To consider women only as victims and men in criminal networks as perpetrators is a simplified and polarizing view that does not take into account the 'grey areas'. It goes without saying that the inhuman conditions of work and the violence experienced by trafficked women are not voluntarily chosen. But the trafficking process is much more complex and ambiguous than suggested by the image of the seduced girl forced into slavery-like conditions under false pretences by a male trafficker. Many women (also those trafficked later on) cooperate with smugglers 'voluntarily', because for them, this is the only possibility of migrating to the 'West'. Also, migration into sex work is chosen consciously by some women. Thus, trafficking might be best understood as exploitation in the process of migration – a process in which force and voluntariness are intertwined. Trafficking might begin as a voluntary decision to migrate with the help of smugglers and might end in a slavery-like kuli-system of forced labour.[11]

We would like to point to the fact that 'trafficking' is also a phenomenon that has gained attention in connection with football,[12] particularly concerning African players.[13] Even with a superficial comparison, parallels between both forms of trafficking can be discovered. Just as with the typical fields of work for trafficked women, football is a way to migrate to Europe. In both cases, middlemen (or middlewomen) are involved who make a profit out of this business. Trafficked women and traded players work for (comparably) little money and under precarious conditions. And in both cases, tighter immigration laws are handled as a 'solution'.[14] Also concerning football, some authors criticize a one-sided view on trafficking and emphasize the ambivalence of trafficking players. Following their argumentation, agents who procure players are, of course, businessmen who, above all, have profit in mind. But as long as this is a way for some African players to escape hardship and hopelessness, it is a channel for advancement that Africans use consciously and deliberately. Therefore, they warn against biased reports from a victim perspective.[15]

With regard to trafficking in women, only little by little did a policy change take place, in which the protection of national borders against illegally immigrating women was completed by the idea of victim protection. In 2000, the UN Palermo *Protocol to Prevent, Suppress and Punish Trafficking in Persons, especially Women and Children* was passed. The 'Palermo Protocol' provides a legal definition of trafficking which reflects changes in the framing of the issue. Trafficking in persons means 'the recruitment, transportation, transfer, harboring or receipt of persons, by means of the threat or use of force' or 'of the abuse of power'. The purpose of trafficking is seen as 'control over another person' and 'exploitation' of this person. Exploitation is then defined in a broad way as 'exploitation of the prostitution of others', 'other forms of sexual exploitation', and 'forced labor or services', as well as the 'removal of organs'.[16]

In 2002, the European Council harmonized fines for people trafficking. The Council of Europe passed a convention against trafficking in human beings in 2005. This document also took up the new understanding of trafficking in women: the connection between trafficking in women and prostitution was loosened, by explicitly mentioning other precarious labour markets into which people are trafficked. The crime is now seen not only as a form of illegal border crossing, but also as trafficking into any form of dependant, unsecured and exploitative labour, also within national borders. Victim protection is, thus, placed central. Austria and Germany have changed their criminal laws, based on these international regulations and have adopted the new definitions of trafficking.

Prostitution regimes in Austria and Germany

Although both counties have quite similar policies on trafficking in women, they differ in their prostitution regimes and policies. The Austrian prostitution regime can be characterized as reglementaristic: prostitution is not subject to criminal prosecution. However, this system has large gaps regarding labour legislation and social security. Registered sex workers (and pimps) have to pay taxes, although the contract between customer and sex worker is still considered as immoral and unenforceable (*sittenwidrig*). This weakens the legal situation of sex workers towards their customers, as they have no possibility of suing those who are unwilling to pay for the service. Therefore, sex work is still residing on the margins of legality.

Since the late 1990s, the situation of – in the first place registered – sex workers improved a little. For example, they have been able to participate in the state pension insurance system since 1998.[17] Unlike in Germany, the – albeit slow – reform process in Austria stopped at the turn of the century, and the public discourse changed. The focus on the improvement of work conditions and the legal situation of prostitutes shifted (again) towards more control, containment and penalization mainly of so-called illegal, non-registered prostitutes. Since then, a law-and-order debate and a discussion about public security have gained importance at the national and regional level.

The success of NGOs in scandalizing trafficking in women and persons since the mid-1990s entailed an unintended and ambivalent 'failure', i.e. the discursive subsumption of any sex work under trafficking in women. The intensifying international and national debates on trafficking in women virtually superseded the debate on empowering women in sex work.[18] Thus, in 2006, the foreigners' law was tightened again and the legal situation of migrant sex workers worsened. Now they receive a visa that is restricted to six months, cannot be renewed and must be applied for from abroad.[19]

As in Austria, for a long time the German prostitution regime could be classified as reglementaristic:[20] prostitution was legal within limits, namely the contract was immoral and thus unenforceable. Since 2002, Germany has a new federal prostitution law, which may be seen as a shift towards a semi-sex work regime. The most important change compared with the old law – and also the most important difference from the Austrian legal situation – is that prostitution is no longer regarded as immoral. Now the agreement on the payment for sexual service establishes a legally effective claim. Thus, the price a sex worker and a customer agree upon can be sued for and sex work became a sort of normal service. An expertise commissioned by the Federal Ministry for Family, Seniors, Women and Youth speaks of a shift in the legal policy approach from 'protection from prostitution' towards 'protection in prostitution'.[21]

A point of criticism concerning the new law is that it does not carry any advantages for migrant sex workers without legal residence status. They have no residence permit and are therefore without any rights. According to estimations, the new law has no effect for at least half of the persons working in prostitution in Germany. The laws regulating sex work are only of secondary importance for migrants in the sex industry.[22]

Actors, styles and frames of the German anti-trafficking campaigns

Prior to and during the World Cup 2006, numerous campaigns focusing on trafficking in women and (forced) prostitution were organized. The following section describes some of them, introduces their leading actors and analyses the underlying concepts and frames of (forced) prostitution, football, trafficking in women and migration.

Deutscher Frauenrat:[23] *final whistle*[24]

The largest campaign, 'final whistle – end forced prostitution', was initiated by the *Deutscher Frauenrat*, financed by state resources and widely supported by NGOs and the public. The president of the German Football Association, Theo Zwanziger, as well as the mayor of Berlin, Klaus Wowereit (SPD[25]), supported the campaign. The *Deutscher Frauenrat* unites 54 women's associations and organizations with different backgrounds, ranging from confessional through professional associations to the women's groups of political parties, trade unions and the German Olympic Sport Federation. Its general goal is equal opportunities for women and men. Sex work is not among its most central issues but the council has formulated a specific position and frame in the debate: (voluntary) prostitution and forced prostitution should be considered separately; this also includes the demand for far-reaching legal protection for prostitutes. Furthermore, improved measures for the protection of victims of trafficking are claimed.

The campaign's demands addressed the state and concerned three fields: the countries of origin of trafficked women, the victims of trafficking and forced prostitution in Germany, and the German authorities. Regarding the countries of origin, the living conditions should be improved; for Germany, the *Frauenrat* demanded an improvement in victim protection.

In the campaign documentation, the goal is described as follows:

> The campaign 'final whistle' used the World Cup as a tribune, in order to raise awareness on the issue in a wide public both at home and abroad and to push it on the socio-political agenda, also beyond the football tournament. (…) The campaign did not turn against football fans, clients, prostitutes, or prostitution in general. Rather, the initiators and supporters of the campaign stood behind the prostitution law passed in 2002 in Germany, that legalises the purchase and selling of sexual services under certain preconditions.[26]

Question and answer booklets were compiled for activists at the information booths of the football event. This material made the distinction between voluntary and forced prostitution explicit.[27] However, conveying these positions was not always easy, as the campaign's résumé showed.[28] It was hard to prevent the fight against trafficking in persons for the purpose of sexual exploitation being mixed up with a debate about legal prostitution:

> Political groups exist (...) who criticise or reject the prostitution law. The pressure is particularly strong from abroad: from women's and human rights organisations that don't accept a difference between voluntary and forced prostitution and that consider every form of commercial sex as coercion and violence; and from politicians of different political orientation and provenance who want to prohibit prostitution for religious or gender political reasons.[29]

Evangelische Diakonie: *Act against forced prostitution*[30]

The campaign 'Act against forced prostitution' by the protestant organization *Diakonie* appealed to the wider public as well as to customers of prostitutes, who were asked to contact the police or a counselling centre if they suspected forced prostitution.

The *Diakonie* mentions 'help, support, care for and accompanying people at the margins of society' as its major tasks; the campaign particularly addressed the responsibility of clients:[31]

> Men in Germany can make use of the services of prostitutes who are independent and work self-determined. However, modern men surely do not want consciously to exploit the services of women who are victims of this flagrant human rights violation. (...) A responsible man rejects every form of violence against women and children.[32]

Thus, the *Diakonie's* campaign differentiated between voluntary/self-determined and forced prostitution.[33] The argument used by the *Diakonie* follows an economic logic of supply and demand and is directed at an informed consumer that is able to take informed buying decisions.

FiM: stop forced prostitution

The campaign by the NGO FiM (*Frauenrecht ist Menschenrecht*; Women's Right is Human Right) headed in a similar direction and addressed customer responsibility. In the first place, it used the Internet to spread information. More than 40,000 people visited the campaign website, many of whom were redirected by links from sex sites whose owners supported the campaign.[34] The campaign was developed by the advertising agency Saatchi & Saatchi; Heide Simonis, chair of the German committee for UNICEF, held the patronage of the campaign, which was supported by a very heterogeneous spectrum of counselling centres.[35]

The campaign distinguished legal and voluntary prostitution from services that are rendered involuntarily. The organizers emphasized that the campaign was not directed against prostitution or against men who buy sexual services. But it wanted to raise awareness of forced prostitutes with the following slogans: 'You can choose, the women have no choice' and 'look – recognize – act'. Also, a market argument was used: 'Forced prostitution is also a fraud of men who get into the grey area of organized crime. As a customer you are betrayed because the service is not provided voluntarily.'[36] The argumentation, like the campaign by the *Diakonie*, refers to the responsibility and the consciousness of men about a criminal market, which is created and therefore might be changed by them.

Solwodi: *red card for sexual exploitation and forced prostitution*[37]

The campaign of the Catholic counselling agency *Solwodi*[38] encompassed three stages:[39] together with *Renovabis*, a Catholic initiative focused on Eastern Europe, the agency organized a campaign in countries of origin entitled 'yellow card.' It was aimed at women in their home countries and informed them about the practices of traffickers. The 'red card' was used in Germany to raise public awareness and to advertise an emergency phone number, the third element of the campaign.

Solwodi did not emphasize any difference between voluntary and forced prostitution, but considered prostitution in general to be an effect of gender-specific inequalities and a consequence of female poverty. However, trafficking in women was not always clearly separated from prostitution, as is illustrated in the following quote. Many women see:

> (t)heir only chance to escape miserable living conditions and to earn enough money in order to feed their family (…) in the following ways out: marriage with a 'rich' foreigner, employment abroad or prostitution. This way they get into the hands of traffickers, smugglers or criminal marriage brokers. These women are often sold to brothel owners and forced to prostitution with brutal violence, or they become dependent on husbands that exploit them physically and emotionally.[40]

context e. V.[41]*: freiersein*[42]

The focus of the campaign 'freiersein' was not restricted to forced prostitution and women as victims, but was conceptualized in a broader sense. 'freiersein'

> informed about topics around prostitution with all its facets. It was addressed to all men, not particularly football fans, and to the public. Men were not targeted as potential perpetrators but as potential customers. The aims of the campaign were health prevention (…), establishing basic rules for the contact with sex workers and taking taboo off prostitution.[43]

The brochure 'Fair Play: Don't shoot an own goal', which was distributed at football matches, set up 10 rules for the contact with sex workers. Only one rule dealt with how to act in the case of suspecting force or violence. On the campaign's website information about 'punishability of the facilitation of prostitution' and 'penalization of johns' was available. At first, the argumentation reads similar to that used by *Solwodi* – trafficking as a consequence of the feminization of poverty. However, it is clearly stated that 'prostitution cannot simply be equated with trafficking in persons/women, force, organized crime and illegal immigration'.[44]

Ban Ying: *prostitution without force and violence*[45]

The Berlin-based counselling centre *Ban Ying* (Thai: 'house of women') focuses on the violence women experience in the process of migration. To combat people trafficking, the organization demands the right of migrants to work legally and less-restrictive immigration regulations. It advocates an improvement of witness protection for the victims of trafficking as well as for their social security. In particular, it demands residence and work permits that are independent of a testimony in criminal proceedings, the so-called 'Italian model.'[46]

Ban Ying's campaign addressed customers and gave information on what to do in the case of suspected force. The activists got involved into the media debate[47] and made it explicit that their aim was to combat trafficking, but not prostitution. Arrow-shaped posters were affixed on the walls on men's restrooms. These contained a short message: 'Prostitution without force and violence'.

The Austrian campaign

Austrian NGOs also considered campaigning against trafficking in women during EURO 2008. In February 2007, the project *FairPlay* at the Vienna Institute for International Dialogue and Cooperation (vidc), an organization that works with football fans, hosted a round table, entitled 'Trafficking in women for the purpose of prostitution during the EURO 2008.' The round table critically discussed the evaluation of the German campaigns.

'Why at all a campaign on the occasion of the EURO?' was one of the major questions arising in another preparation group, organized by LEFÖ, a Vienna-based NGO counselling migrants and trafficked women. According to the discussions – with reference to the earlier German campaigns – such a campaign might run the risk of being picked up in a way that ran counter to the goal of sensitizing clients and the wider public to the human rights violation of trafficking. However, they were aware that media interest in Austria could be used in a campaign on sex work. In these first considerations one point was made quite clear: any campaign in Austria should not refer to trafficking in women but concentrate on the rights of sex workers. This frame should avoid the problematic discourse in Germany two years earlier.[48]

In June 2007, LEFÖ presented a rough concept with the title 'Keen on emotions? Keen on rights!' (*Lust auf Emotionen? Lust auf Rechte!*) – referring to the official slogan of the EURO. This concept emphasized the focus of the Austrian campaign not to concentrate on female sex workers as victims of sexually aggressive male football fans, 'red-light bosses' and traffickers.

Obviously, Austrian groups had learned from the experiences of the German campaigns. They were aware of the dangers of using the football event for their political strategy. The campaign, supported by LEFÖ and the Linz-based organization MAIZ, did not aim at scandalizing – possible – forced prostitution during the EURO, but rather focused on the long-term improvement in human and working rights of sex workers in Austria. The aim was to abolish the concept that the contract between customer and sex worker is immoral and unenforceable, i.e. the recognition of prostitution as work. Furthermore, the campaign wanted to call attention to gender-specific violence, exploitation and force connected to trafficking in women, but not just trafficking into prostitution.[49] The campaign, moreover, referred to an improvement in the legal situation of migrant sex workers, to a reform of the foreigners' law package of 2005 and to protection from violence, discrimination, sexism and racism.[50]

Similar to the German case in 2006, other Austrian initiatives were started by, for example, the Carinthian Green Party and Johanna Mikl-Leitner from the ÖVP,[51] at that time member of the Lower Austrian government. Via a petition, the Greens demanded, among other issues, the establishing of a point of contact for victims of trafficking and forced prostitution in Carinthia, prevention measures in the countries of origin and a ban on containers for sexual services (*Verrichtungsboxen*). The *Land* Lower Austria hosted a round table, which dealt with media rumours that brothels had been 'upgrading' in view of the football event and 20–50% more prostitutes had been engaged. Together with the EU parliament, the Austrian social democrat MEP Christa

Prets started the campaign 'Red Card for Forced Prostitution'.[52] However, these campaigns did not gain huge media and public attention.

How to fight trafficking in women? Lessons from the football campaigns

The German campaigns were aware of the huge attention the football event would attract and they therefore mobilized the event for their aims by using a simplified image of 'football masculinity'. At the same time, they neglected the complex connection between men, masculinity, sport and sexual service. This turned out to be problematic for the aim of the campaigns, namely fighting trafficking and forced prostitution.

According to media reports, Ban Ying stated that no increase of trafficking cases was observed during the championship.[53] Evaluations also showed that the assumed number of prostitutes did not have any firm foundation. Although the issue of trafficking attracted a great deal of media attention, the campaigns failed to a great extent to scandalize precarious and exploitative working conditions or the role of repressive migration restrictions, and therefore rather repressive positions towards prostitution and migration were strengthened.

Although most of the organizations and activists pointed out the necessity of differentiating between voluntary sex work and forced prostitution in trafficked women, this did not work out. Rather, by mobilizing the discursive connection of 'forced prostitution' and 'trafficking in women' – not least by media reports – a hegemonic interpretation was set: prostitution is always coercion. Eventually, this discredited all sex workers, discursively victimizing them. Because of the mixing and often-interchangeable use of the notions 'trafficking in women', 'smuggling' and 'forced prostitution', prostitution was represented as mostly connected to crime, and migrant sex workers were equated with the victims of trafficking.[54] Thus, prostitution continues to be stigmatized by using the prefix 'forced'.

Austrian NGOs decided – against the background of the German experiences – not to organize a campaign against forced prostitution, in order to not strengthen the, already existing, immorality discourse. Austrian NGOs in the field used different framings, trying to establish a counter discourse to other political actors, which copied the German campaign and jumped on the framing of forced prostitution. However, these Austrian campaigns against forced prostitution did not provoke much public or media debate on tightening prostitution legislation. How can we now understand the differences between the debates in Germany and Austria?

On the one hand, the differences be explained by policy learning. Although Austrian NGOs had for a long time been mobilizing and sensitizing successfully on the issue of trafficking in women, they were aware of the pitfalls of such a campaign. Instrumentalizing masculinity and football with the aim of combating trafficking in women was not considered to be successful. Thus, they reframed the football event and focused on sex workers' rights.

The German campaigns must be contextualized in abolitionist attempts that, not least after the liberalization of the German prostitution regime and the partial establishment of a sex work regime, tried to attain attention and legitimization in order to change the existing legislation again. Conservative German actors saw a window of opportunity during which to tighten the German prostitution law. The linking of trafficking in women and prostitution in the campaigns evoked a discursive chaining of conservative law and order norms and abolitionist demands vis-à-vis prostitution that wanted to attack the liberalized German prostitution law with feminist anti-patriarchal ideas. This alliance aims to limit prostitution, either by punishing customers or by encouraging women to leave their jobs in the sex industry. The client was labelled as a 'hooligan', as violent and therefore as someone who has to be punished. This was picked up by the Bavarian CSU[55] which demanded an amendment to the German prostitution law – along the lines of the Swedish model of punishing johns; that is, not only johns of coerced prostitutes, but all johns. This, however, results in the criminalization of sex work.

Austrian NGOs had already experienced this since the late 1990s. By the end of the last century, scandalizing trafficking had led to a backlash against the rights of prostitutes in Austria and against establishing a sex work regime. Fighting trafficking in women might contribute to ongoing struggles over governing prostitution and migration. Framing the issue of trafficking is therefore an important aspect of governing morally charged policy issues.

In Austria, by contrast, abolitionist forces have not been predominant in trafficking debates. This might be because Austria, different from Germany, still has a reglementaristic prostitution regime with only poor rights for prostitutes. Moreover, in Austria the debate on prostitution had shifted towards de-liberalization by the end of the 1990s. Thus, the major factors to explain differences in the campaigns during the two football events might be the differing governance of prostitution, or prostitution regimes, in Austria and Germany.

Another law-and-order discourse may connect the campaigns against forced prostitution – a discourse about the general threat to public security, not only by emotionally uninhibited football fans, but also by prostitutes. Moreover, a racist discourse was evoked: the way in which the media took up the issue insinuated that the trafficked prostitutes came from the 'East' and disturbed the 'friendly encounter of the nations' in the West. Thus, the German campaigns deployed a xenophobic subtext with reference to trafficking networks and prostitutes from 'the East',[56] contributing to the ongoing struggle over a more restrictive immigration law. *Ban Ying* stated that during the championship raids in brothels were intensified nationwide, with the result that prostitutes without residence documents were deported. Schuster and Sülzle summarize the problematic consequences as follows:[57] because of the discursive unification of all migrant sex workers as victims of forced prostitution, the view of their specific needs is obstructed and the advocacy for better working conditions and residence rights is impeded, as only the salvation of the victims remains in the foreground.

We have also argued that the framing of the sex industry and trafficking in women during the football championships was important for the effects of the campaigns as well as for the different strategies of NGOs in both countries. Thus, we have analysed the messages conveyed in the German and Austrian campaigns, and the frames and discourses referred to. Crucial for our analysis was the consideration that the German campaigns narrowed the focus on trafficking in women to trafficking into prostitution. Other exploitative labour markets in which women are trafficked were not taken into account. In doing so, prostitution was framed as violence against women and often equated with 'forced prostitution'. This framing runs the risk of ignoring the needs of migrant sex workers,[58] and a racist momentum creeps into the discourse of victim protection by blaming criminal individuals or networks from 'the East'. Thereby, the role of restrictive regulations on immigration, residence and work, the economic divide between countries of origin and destination countries, and the demand for sexual services are eclipsed. At the same time, restrictive measures, in particular regarding immigration controls can be justified. Thus, 'fortress Europe' was legitimized.

Notes

1. Beer-Odebrecht, *Sex in Boxen*.
2. Rutvica Andrijašević makes a similar point in her analysis of IOM campaigns. She argues that 'IOM's trafficking imaginary discloses as well as addresses the anxiety about the transformation of European political community and its boundaries.' Andrijašević, *Trafficking in Women*, 150.
3. Quoted from Ihme, *Zu Gast bei Freunden*, 253; all translations by the authors.
4. Milborn and Kreutzer, *Ware Frau*.
5. Winkler, *Für den Frauenhandel*.
6. Interview with the German political scientist Silvia Kontos.
7. Diketmüller, *SportMachtFrauen(Bewegung)Raum*.
8. Grenz, *Prostitution*.
9. Of course – and this must be noted as a restriction – in the USA the importance of 'soccer' is not comparable with that of (American) football.
10. Schuster and Sülzle, *Zwangsprostitution*, 11.
11. De Vries, *An Image of Sexual Danger*, 24–5.
12. Lindberg, *Soccer Slaves*, 3.
13. Poli, *Africans' Status*; Poli, *Migrations and Trade*.
14. Lindberg, *Soccer Slaves*, 3.
15. Mehler and Njoya, *Fußball in Afrika*, 6.
16. United Nations 2000: Art. 3; also Council of Europe 2005: Art. 4.
17. Sauer, *Taxes, Rights and Regimentation*.
18. Sauer, *An der Front*.
19. Patulova and Blum, *Das NAG(t)*.
20. For detailed information see Mitrovic, *Der gesellschaftliche Umgang*, and Schewe-Gerigk, *Das deutsche Prostitutionsgesetz*.
21. Renzikowski, *Reglementierung von Prostitution*, 38.
22. Munk, *Migration und Sexarbeit*, 59–60.
23. The translation of the organization's name is 'German women's council'. As they provide no English translation for their name even in the English version of their website, we use the German expression here.
24. Abpfiff.
25. Social Democratic Party
26. Deutscher Frauenrat, *abpfiff*, 9.
27. Deutscher Frauenrat, *Frage- und Antwortkatalog*.
28. Deutscher Frauenrat, *abpfiff*, 35.
29. Ibid.
30. *Handeln gegen Zwangsprostitution*; The *Diakonie* is a protestant welfare organization.
31. http://www.diakonie.de (accessed April 1, 2008).
32. http://www.diakonie.de/2168.htm (accessed March 25, 2008).
33. However, the website contains passages in which the notions prostitution, trafficking in persons and forced prostitution are distinguished not very sharply or not at all.
34. Künkel, *Sex, Crime und 'richtige Männer'*, 272.
35. Ibid.
36. http://www.stoppt-zwangsprostitution.de/html/freier.html (accessed March 25, 2008).
37. Rote Karte für sexuelle Ausbeutung und Zwangsprostitution.
38. Solidarity with women in distress.
39. http://www.solwodi.de/406.0.html (accessed March 27, 2008).
40. http://www.solwodi.de/148.0.html (accessed April 24, 2009).
41. context e.V., Centrum für Prostitutionsstudien, (Centre for Prostitution Studies) was the initiator of the campaign; it was realized by numerous allied organizations: http://www.freiersein.de/aktuell/freiersein-WM2006-Partner.php (accessed March 27, 2008).
42. The title is a word-play: 'Freier' means 'john' as well as 'more free'; so it can be read as 'being a john' or 'being more free'.

43. Schuster and Sülzle, *Zwangsprostitution*, 10.
44. http://www.freiersein.de/information/strafbarkeit-foerderung.php (accessed July 27, 2009).
45. 'Prostitution ohne Zwang und Gewalt'. For a description/analysis of the campaign see Künkel *Sex, Crime und 'richtige Männer'*.
46. Künkel, *Sex, Crime und 'richtige Männer'*, 274.
47. Ibid., 273.
48. Meeting of the preparation group, participation of Susanne Kimm.
49. LEFÖ, *Lust auf Emotionen*, 2.
50. http://www.lustaufrechte.at/lustauf.htm (accessed May 15, 2008).
51. Österreichische Volkspartei, Austrian People's Party.
52. http://www.socialistgroup.mobi/gpes/public/detail.htm;jsessionid=233CD4A102917D01DF5739667C045BA0?id=83089&section=NER&category=NDPR&mobi=1 (accessed July 27, 2009).
53. Ban Ying, *Wo sind die 40.000.*
54. Künkel, *Sex, Crime und 'richtige Männer'*, 280–1.
55. Christian Social Union.
56. Künkel, *Sex, Crime und 'richtige Männer'*, 275.
57. Schuster and Sülzle, *Zwangsprostitution*, 5.
58. Ibid., 5–6.

References

Andrijašević, R. 'Trafficking in Women and the Politics of Mobility in Europe'. PhD dissertation, University of Utrecht, 2004.

Ban Y. 'Wo sind die 40.000?', press release, July 11, 2006.

Beer-Odebrecht, C. 'Sex in Boxen bei EM: Frauen laufen Sturm', *Kleine Zeitung,* April 16, 2007.

Deutscher Frauenrat. 'abpfiff. Schluss mit Zwangsprostitution. Dokumentation zur Kampagne anlässlich der Fußball-WM 2006', 2006.

Deutscher Frauenrat. 'Frage- und Antwortkatalog für die Stände Fanmeile', 2006.

De Vries, P. 'An Image of Sexual Danger: Prostitution, the White Slave and the Political Campaign Against Woman Trafficking in Historical Perspective'. In *Women and Trafficking,* ed. S. Zavratnik Zimic, 21–8. Ljubljana: Peace Institute, 2004.

Diketmüller, R. 'SportMachtFrauen(Bewegung)Raum. Ein feministischer Streifzug durch die "letzte" Männerdomäne'. *Frauensolidarität* 30 (2000): 2–4.

Grenz, S. 'Prostitution, eine Verhinderung oder Ermöglichung sexueller Gewalt? Spannungen in kulturellen Konstruktionen von männlicher und weiblicher Sexualität'. In *Verhandlungen im Zwielicht. Momente der Prostitution in Geschichte und Gegenwart,* ed. S. Grenz and M. Lücke, 319–42. Bielefeld: transcript, 2006.

Ihme, L. '"Zu Gast bei Freundinnen". (Re)Konstruktion von Nation, Geschlecht und Sexualität in Narrativen über die Fußball-WM und die Prostitution'. In *Verhandlungen im Zwielicht. Momente der Prostitution in Geschichte und Gegenwart,* ed. S. Grenz and M. Lücke, 247–65. Bielefeld: transcript, 2006.

Künkel, J. 'Sex, Crime und "richtige Männer": Frauenhandelsmythen zur WM 2006'. In *Kontrollierte Urbanität. Zur Neoliberalisierung städtischer Sicherheitspolitik,* ed. V. Eick, J. Sambale, and E. Töpfer, 261–84. Bielefeld: transcript, 2007.

LEFÖ. 'Lust auf Emotionen? Lust auf Rechte!. Grobkonzept', 2007.

Lindberg, K. 'The man who traced 442 soccer slaves', *Play the Game Magazine 2006,* http://www.playthegame.org/upload/Magazine%202005/themanwhotraced442slaves.pdf (accessed August 21, 2009).

Mehler, A., and E. Tchouamou Njoya. 'Fußball in Afrika: Mehr als ein Spiel', *GIGA Focus* 6, 2006, http://www.giga-hamburg.de/dlcounter/download.php?d=/content/publikationen/pdf/gf_afrika_0606.pdf (accessed August 21, 2009).

Milborn, C., and M. Kreutzer. *Ware Frau – Auf den Spuren moderner Sklaverei von Afrika nach Europa.* Salzburg: Ecowin, 2008.

Mitrovic, E. 'Der gesellschaftliche Umgang mit Prostitution in Deutschland'. In *Von den Kinderschuhen der Gemeinwesenarbeit zur sozialen Stadt* (pre-print), ed. S. Odierna and U. Berendt. Neu-Ulm: AG-SPAK, 2004, http://besondere-dienste.hamburg.verdi.de/

arbeitsplatz_prostitution/download/data/aufsatz_gesellschaft-licher-umgang-deutschland.pdf (accessed April 25, 2009).

Munk, V. 'Migration und Sexarbeit. Dilemmata der Illegalität'. *Osteuropa. Mythos Europa: Prostitution, Migration, Frauenhandel.* (2006): 55–65.

Patulova, R., and R.M. Blum. 'Das NAG(t)' (April 29, 2006), http://no-racism.net/article/1652/ (accessed April 25, 2009).

Poli, R. 'Africans' Status in the European Football Players' Labour Market'. *Soccer & Society* 2–3 (2006): 278–91.

Poli, R. 'Migrations and Trade of African Football Players: Historic, Geographical and Cultural Aspects'. *Afrika-Spektrum* 3 (2006): 393–414.

Renzikowski, J. 'Reglementierung von Prostitution: Ziele und Probleme – eine kritische Betrachtung des Prostitutionsgesetzes'. Berlin: Bundesministerium für Familie, Senioren, Frauen und Jugend, 2007.

Sauer, B. 'Taxes, Rights and Regimentation. Discourses on Prostitution in Austria'. In *The Politics of Prostitution. Women's Movements and the State,* ed. J. Outshoorn, 41–61. Cambridge: Cambridge University Press, 2004.

Sauer, B. 'An der Front des westlichen Patriarchats. Sexarbeit, Frauenhandel und politische Regulierung in Wien'. In *Frauenhandel. Diskurse und Praktiken,* ed. J. Nautz and B. Sauer, 81–96. Göttingen: V&R Unipress, 2008.

Schewe-Gerigk, I. '"Das deutsche Prostitutionsgesetz" – Entstehung, Hintergründe, Erfahrungen und Perspektiven'. Speech given at the 19th Green Ladies' Lunch: Feministisches Institut der Heinrich-Böll-Stiftung, Berlin, Germany, March 16, 2005, http://www.glow-boell.de/media/de/txt_rubrik_2/160305_LL_Vortrag_ScheweGerigk.pdf (accessed April 25, 2009).

Schuster, M., and A. Sülzle. 'Zwangsprostitution, Sexarbeit, Menschenhandel. Kampagnen zur WM 2006'. Vienna, 2006.

Winkler, S. 'Für den Frauenhandel gibt's die Rote Karte', *Kleine Zeitung,* May 6, 2008, http://www.kleinezeitung.at/sport/fussball/euro2008/1259086/index.do (accessed April 25, 2009).

Websites

http://kaernten.gruene.at/stoppfrauenhandelfairplay/ (accessed May 8, 2008).

http://www.ban-ying.de (May 8, 2008).

http://www.diakonie.de (April 1, 2008).

http://www.frauenrat.de (April 1, 2008).

http://www.freiersein.de (July 27, 2009).

http://www.lustaufrechte.at/lustauf.htm (May 15, 2008).

http://www.noe.gv.at/Presse/Presse/Aktuelles-aus-der-Landeskorrespondenz/71713_menschenhandel.wai.html (May 8, 2008).

http://www.socialistgroup.mobi (July 27, 2009).

http://www.solwodi.de (March 27, 2008).

http://www.stoppt-zwangsprostitution.de (March 25, 2008).

EUROSCHOOLS 2008: the difficult relationship of culture, nation and anti-racism in UEFA's campaign work

Kenneth Horvath[a] and Jakob Rosenberg[b]

[a]Department of Methods in the Social Sciences, University of Vienna, Austria; [b]Department of Political Science, University of Vienna, Austria

As part of the preparatory campaign for the European Championship 2008, UEFA sponsored five 'social responsibility' campaigns. One of these projects – EUROSCHOOLS 2008 – focused on school children aged 12–17 years and ventured to combine work on three problem areas: fair play, gender equality and anti-racism. Based on the outcomes of an evaluation study, a rather negative balance has to be drawn with regard to the anti-racist part of the campaign. Examining the reasons for this obvious failure leads to a complex combination of ideological and 'practical' factors. Our article discusses some of these factors and their implications for future anti-racist work. As will be shown, one of the most important, and at the same time most complex, reasons is the ambivalence inherent to an anti-racist campaign emphasizing both cultural difference(s) and national(ist) thought patterns. The article is summed up by a cursory discussion of the possibilities and problems involved in using institutional actors such as the UEFA for anti-racist initiatives. How can the ideological background and institutional interests of UEFA & Co. be dealt with? Is a credible anti-racism-campaign coherent with UEFA's self-conception? Are campaigns such as EUROSCHOOLS 2008 bound to falter? What might viable alternatives look like?

Introduction

Racist discrimination and harassment remain among the most pressing issues in international football. UEFA has apparently acknowledged the problem – anti-racism is high on its public agenda.[1] But anti-racism can be a very complicated matter. Racism comes with a long legacy, yet the forms in which it is manifested change, reflecting its interdependency with social structures and practices, on the one hand, and the complex ideological configurations of which it is part, on the other hand. Problems on and around the pitch reflect broad social conflicts and exclusionary practices based on a complex and often contradictory mixture of perceived or constructed biological (e.g. skin colour) and cultural (e.g. religious and national identity) differences. Consequently, anti-racism is marked by a number of ambivalences and pitfalls.[2]

Using the example of EUROSCHOOLS 2008, a school project organized parallel to EURO 2008™, our article discusses how emphasizing cultural and national differences can hinder anti-racist campaigning. We start our argumentation with some theoretical issues linked to current manifestations of racism in the European context. We then present the EUROSCHOOLS 2008 campaign and examine its outcomes, using two types of material from the official evaluation of the project: quantitative survey data and essays written by the students involved. We concentrate on the latter to illustrate the consequences of the specific way in which interculturality is dealt with, pointing *inter alia* to elements of a folkloristic nationalism and essentializing constructions of cultural difference. We then turn to the negative implications this inevitably has for anti-racist campaigning, basing our argument that the identified problems are symptomatic for UEFA's approach to anti-racist campaigning on other social responsibility campaigns organized parallel to the UEFA EURO 2008™ tournament.

The many faces of racism

Assessment of UEFA's interculturality and anti-racism campaigns requires some clarity about what racism actually is. Following different authors such as Robert Miles, Collette Guillaumin and Stuart Hall, we define racism as an ideological phenomenon that is marked by the categorization of human beings into supposedly distinct groups.[3] Historically, biological notions have played a crucial role in these categorization processes, but it is important to notice that these are only relevant insofar as they are believed to be connected to (fixed) *cultural* characteristics and capabilities. And, to warrant a meaningful usage of the term, a discourse is called racist only if it is linked to social processes of exclusion and unequal allocation of resources. We cannot go into the manyfold discussions on the concept of racism in detail here, but want to point to three features characteristic of current manifestations of racism in Western European countries.

1. The focus of racism has moved from ordering people into biological hierarchies to naturalizing cultural difference

Following the Holocaust and the end of explicit colonization, outright racist argumentations have become widely banned from official discourses after World War II. This 'anti-racist consensus' was partly based on the fact that a division of human beings into 'races' is scientifically invalid – a view that was prominently expressed in a report published by UNESCO in 1950. Owing to this scientific and political de-legitimization of categorizing humans into biological groups with corresponding cultural and social capabilities, assertions claiming the superiority or inferiority of different groups due to genetic or phenotypical characteristics have almost vanished. But that is not to say that racism, although it may have been marginalized as a distinct scientific endeavour,[4] has disappeared or lost its social efficacy.[5] Apart from old-school biological arguments still reproduced by various social actors (important parts of the mass media playing a crucial role), racist thought patterns are evident in various ideological constellations, such as hostility towards foreigners or anti-Islamic agitation. Instead of vanishing, the social reality of racism has rather become more complex.

Even far-right groups have nowadays stepped back from *biological* and *inegalitarian* arguments, stressing instead *cultural* factors in a *differential* manner.[6] This 'racism without races' is referred to as new or as cultural racism, a form of racism that, by implication, no longer seeks its authorization in science but in culture.[7] By constructing culture as an immutable 'second nature', human beings can be divided into distinct groups without reference to biological factors. Once cultural traits are thus essentialized, 'difference', as Guillaumin states, inherits 'all the connotations related to the specificity of human groups which in the old days were carried by the notion of race'.[8]

That is not to say that references to cultural difference are automatically racist, the problem lies in their ambiguity. If used to point to ruptures in hegemonic identity politics, to marginalized forms of cultural expression or to the power relations behind established cultural configurations, they can play an emancipatory role and be an integral element of anti-racist campaigning. Therefore, three aspects require attention when cultural differences are stressed. First, the historical and social context has to be taken into account, because racist legacies can be inherently connected to alleged cultural differences. Second, any essentializing of cultural difference, i.e. turning cultural characteristics into pseudo-biological traits, has to be opposed. Third, the question has to be faced if cultural difference is, intentionally or not, used to subordinate and exclude 'others'.

Anti-racist argumentations and activities are thus complicated regarding both the identification of racism and the development of counter-strategies. What is to be considered a (legitimate) claim to cultural rights, what a racist statement in disguise?

2. Racism is today, as it has been historically, closely linked to nationalism and ethnicity

Concepts of cultural identity are nowadays deeply interwoven with beliefs on national belonging. Cultural difference is mainly perceived between nations, while cultural variation within nations tends to be neglected.[9] This is not a new phenomenon, in fact, the emergence of racism and the development of the capitalist nation state are historically interdependent, causing, from the nineteenth century onwards, a 'profound and complex articulation'[10] between nationalist and racist thought patterns, on the one hand, and biological and cultural arguments, on the other hand. (For this reason, the mentioned distinction between an old and a new racism is somewhat misleading.)[11] Parallel to the emergence of culturalist varieties of racism, the interdependency of nationalism and racism has regained importance, being further complicated by the emergence of discourses on 'ethnicity' following the import of labour migration after World War II.

Apart from being historically linked to racism, 'ethnicity and 'nation' are themselves troubling concepts. They are socially effective in that they are 'above all a matter of drawing boundaries around zones of belonging and non-belonging'.[12] We can make out a complex conflation of national belonging, ethnicity and racism – and these conflated concepts are used to categorize people, but in most cases not in a straightforward and bluntly racist manner. It is therefore barely possible to identify some sort of pure racist argument and, likewise, to set (harmless) national belonging against racist prejudices. Nationalism and racism interact.

3. Racism today often takes the form of institutional racism

The notion of 'institutional racism' has been widely used, but with differing and often unclear meanings. We use it in the narrow sense outlined by Robert Miles[13] to capture social structures that build on former racist discourses but 'may no longer be explicitly justified by such discourses'[14] – or even, to the contrary, may function precisely because racist categorizations are neglected. Social structures and institutional settings can have racialized effects, without any explicit racist justification. For example, labour migration to Western European countries after World War II functioned on the basis of decades of colonial and imperialist power relations tied to racist discourses, allowing for cheap and flexible labour power without need of explicit racist discrimination.

Guillaumin[15] therefore emphasizes the importance of looking at the social relations that give rise to racist ideologies and, in return, are shaped by them. This argument is closely connected to the notion of institutional racism: given a history of racist domination, social relations bound to it can prevail without the racist ideology itself becoming apparent. Despite its invisibility, it is important to examine the efficacy of racism, first, in order to tackle the problem adequately, and second, because a latent racist discourse can resurface leading to new and aggravated forms of domination and social inequality.

Anti-racists have to acknowledge that today, more often than not, racism is hard to identify due to its complex (and often institutionalized) relation to nationality, ethnicity and culture. Hence the need to adjust to the concrete forms racism takes. If anti-racist campaigns fail to take account of these points, they cannot but lose efficacy. Following this reasoning, we assess UEFA-style anti-racism on an indirect route. We first discuss, on the basis of research carried out for the evaluation of the project,[16] how the EUROSCHOOLS 2008 campaign is marked by a strong emphasis on cultural difference and national identity[17] and the consequences this has for the campaign's target of raising intercultural understanding and increasing anti-racist awareness. Because the latter was not an explicit goal (though nevertheless an important issue) of EUROSCHOOLS 2008, we dedicate the last part of our article to the argument that the problems diagnosed for the EUROSCHOOLS 2008 case can also be seen in other UEFA campaigns dealing with anti-racism.

Learning about the Other: EUROSCHOOLS 2008

EUROSCHOOLS 2008 was one of five initiatives promoted as part of UEFA's 'Respect' campaign parallel to EURO 2008™.[18] As is the case with other social responsibility activities, EUROSCHOOLS 2008 was financed by UEFA (and national state-funds linked to EURO 2008™) but not initiated or organized by UEFA itself.[19] Thus, referring to EUROSCHOOLS as an 'UEFA campaign' is actually imprecise.

Nevertheless, although it is important to keep the complex institutional and organizational structure in mind, we stick to this diction for two reasons. First, we are not interested in the role of the organizations involved and the intentions they had, but only in the concepts of interculturality and anti-racism as implemented in the campaign. We believe that the patterns we have identified are symptomatic of the way in which anti-racist initiatives are framed in the context of European Championships by UEFA, no matter what organizational structure they are built on. In this sense, 'UEFA' stands for the whole conglomerate of organizations involved. Second, we would argue that UEFA can nonetheless be considered the focal point of EUROSCHOOLS 2008 and comparable campaigns, regardless of who does the organizational work or of whether the idea for a certain campaign came from within UEFA or not. UEFA is clearly by far the most powerful player involved with regards to organizational and financial resources. The other organizations have to apply for assignments and must therefore not only sell their idea to UEFA (or respond to an initiative by UEFA), but also anticipate the desired contents and conceptualizations.[20]

EUROSCHOOLS 2008 was directed at school students aged 12–17 years from Austria, Switzerland and Liechtenstein, and had two main focuses: 'fair play'[21] and 'intercultural communication and tolerance'. Unlike high-profile campaigns such as

Unite Against Racism, the EUROSCHOOLS project rested more upon active involvement of participants than upon public visibility. School classes were meant to organize two main events: a fair play tournament in their school and a project day dedicated to one of the 53 UEFA countries (the countries were not chosen by the schools themselves but were allotted to them during a kick-off event). Furthermore, a number of regional and international activities took place.

Regarding the outcome of the campaign, a rather negative balance has to be drawn, especially concerning its interculturality dimension. The survey data collected for the evaluation of the project show neither an increase in intercultural understanding nor an increase in anti-racist awareness. Notwithstanding a number of measurement problems, two important points can be made. First, opinion patterns with an affinity to racism (to formulate it cautiously) are frighteningly widespread. Second, EUROSCHOOLS 2008 changed little or nothing about this state of affairs: no sensitization for racism-related problems can be observed.

Table 1 gives an impression of the overall picture. Seventy-four per cent of the pupils think that only Austrian or Swiss citizens should be allowed to live in Austria or Switzerland, 49% believe that Austrians (Swiss) work better than foreigners. The level of anti-foreigner attitudes after the project is almost the same, with some slight improvements on some items, although others have marginally changed for the worse – indicating random variation, but no development. Between 49 and 61% of the students who took part in both waves of the survey show the same answers per item after the project as they did before (as shown in the second group of columns in Table 1). Similar patterns can be found for items measuring 'intercultural understanding'.

Since we would argue that this outcome is partly due to problems in research design and instrument effects, we will only take it as a starting point to examine into the reasons for these results. In the following, we name two factors that we consider responsible for the lack of effect: (1) the emphasis on difference and 'otherness' in combination with a folkloristic representation of nationally defined cultures; and (2) the missing relatedness to school students' 'lebenswelt', i.e. to their personal experience realm.

We discuss these conjectures using material from the 'qualitative' part of the evaluation: essays written by the students for a contest at the end of the project. Students were asked to write about what they felt was the most significant change for themselves owing to the project; the only restriction was that the text should tell about actual experiences. Each class participating in the contest selected three essays that were then sent to the organizers who finally chose eight winning essays. Sixty-seven essays (from 16 Swiss and 4 Austrian schools) were handed in, all of which are included in our analysis.

Music, food, celebrities: folklore and the nation

Following our discussion on the many faces of racism, we focus our discussion of the students' essays on the question how culture and nation are dealt with – and how (if at all) they are connected to current patterns of racism.

Owing to its basic structure, the project's goal of 'raising awareness of the cultural diversity of Europe' is inextricably linked to questions of national belonging. Students of each school were meant to become representatives of one of the UEFA countries, as depicted on the project's homepage: 'The schools will take on the roles of

Table 1. Items measuring attitudes towards foreigners, $n = 1552$. Taking the item polarity into account, figures set in bold indicate a negative opinion towards foreigners.

	1 Level before		2 Change: before–after			3 Level after	
	Agree (%)	Do not agree (%)	Change towards agree (%)	No change (%)	Change towards do not agree (%)	Agree (%)	Do not agree (%)
Without the many foreigners our city/our town would be less vibrant	56	**44**	26	50	**24**	57	**43**
It is important to accept the foreigners who live here the way they are	45	**55**	20	56	**22**	45	**55**
Only Austrian (Swiss) citizens should live in Austria (Switzerland)	**74**	26	**25**	49	27	**73**	27
An Austrian (a Swiss) works better than a foreigner	**49**	51	**16**	61	23	**55**	45

ambassadors of the 53 countries represented in the UEFA and will deal with and learn about various aspects of intercultural dialogue'. Although this may seem conceptually reasonable in the context of the European Championships, one has to keep in mind other possible forms of interculturality that are not dealt with because of this emphasis on nationality.

Unsurprisingly, 'culture' and 'country' are strongly related in the essays, being used more or less interchangeably by the students:

> During EUROSCHOOLS I learned more about the different countries and their cultures. (Michael[22])

> Besides we now know a lot more about Portugal, its customs and habits. (Andrea)

Michael mentions 'culture' as the principal feature about a country, as does Andrea, although she sets the emphasis not on culture in general, but on 'customs and habits', thus accentuating the nation-related character of culture. 'Country' and 'culture' come to mutually define each other, 'culture' being a country's culture, and 'countries' being above all talked about in cultural terms. Culture is then, throughout most of the essays, further specified in predominantly folkloric terms:

> It was interesting to explore another culture. We sang Macedonian songs and prepared Macedonian food, which of course we also ate. (Jana)

> On 'International Day' our class performed a dance to the music of Falco's 'Vienna Calling'. (...) We also had a Viennese coffee house where some children served coffee and cake. (Marcel)

The folkloric bias to what is understood as a national culture is obvious. Music and dance figure prominently among the cultural features that seem both, noteworthy and communicable within the boundaries of a school project, being topped only by references to food and followed by language. Celebrities and sights are also repeatedly mentioned. By contrast, current political situations are only referred to in one particular case.[23]

At first sight, the folkloric accounts of nationality and culture seem harmless – they resemble notions to be found in any tourist guide. The problem is that they lead to the construction of difference along exclusively folkloric–cultural lines, blinding out political power, social, economic and military aspects, and so on. Folkloric notions serve as simple markers of national identity and come with the very problem that they hide problems. Trivial variations are reconstructed as cultural difference – as indicated in the second half of the following quotation. The other country (Macedonia) is judged positively because 'it is totally different' and it is different in the sense of having a different culture:

> I found the country we were allotted great because it had a totally different culture that we do not know here in Switzerland. (Artan)

The emphasis on folkloric and cultural imaging of countries has two interrelated consequences. First and inevitably, countries are conceived as homogeneous, with the only relevant heterogeneity occurring between countries, not within them. Second, folklore is something to be noticed not with the Self, but with the Other. Almost consistently, Austria and Switzerland do not figure in the students' essays.

Dealing with the partner countries can, of course, reduce specific stereotypes and prejudices, but that may well leave basic classifications and categorizations in place, as can be illustrated by the example of how Slovakia is talked about as a partner country:

> At that time I thought that Slovakia is a Third World country and does not belong to Europe, but I was wrong. (Nino)

> This country does not belong to those 'Balkan' countries. Slovakia is a very civilized, beautiful, cultured, interesting country. (Arian)

> At our project day we could show people: 'Hey, there are countries that do not live brutally but nevertheless are located in Eastern Europe'. (Freya)

None of these quotations shows a questioning of dominant categories (Third World, Balkan, Eastern Europe) and their negative connotations but merely a re-ordering of one country into a different category: Slovakia surprisingly belongs to Europe, not to the Third World or 'those Balkan countries' and it exemplifies that there is such a thing as 'non-brutal living' in Eastern Europe. While Slovakia is conceded the privilege of not really being Eastern, hegemonic notions of the Eastern European Other are not disputed but reproduced. The dominant Western discourse remains untouched.

The lebenswelt problem

Objects of knowledge versus self-improvement

Owing to the question the students were asked to deal with ('most significant change'), many focused their essay on questions of change and development. These stories of change are organized around two different modes of development, one behaviour centred and the other knowledge centred. Whereas the students reserved the former almost exclusively for the fair play component of the project, the latter was overwhelmingly linked to the intercultural part. Here are two typical examples of pupils referring to the fair play component:

> I also learned to play less aggressively with younger and weaker ones. It was fun to play with girls and to try to let a girl score. You learn coping with losing against younger ones. (Jason)

> Because of the fair play project in school I learned to be friendlier to others and, at home, I did so straight away. It is much more peaceful in my family. Especially my mother is glad about that. We do our work immediately and without complaining. That is FAIR! (Astrid)

The pupils frequently refer to changes in their behaviour and attitudes; they talk about how they have changed through the project, or how their outlook on different issues has developed. No such references can be found when students talk about the intercultural component of the campaign. The relevant change here is an increase in knowledge. Owing to the strong connection to the concepts of country and nation, interculturality here has no anchoring in behaviour or everyday life, it is reduced to an interesting enquiry into the peculiarities of a 'different' country. The partner countries are constructed as objects of knowledge, interculturality has no further implications for the students as social beings.

> I know much more about Latvia now. What they eat there, what the landscape looks like, what kind of climate they have. (Thomas)

> The change for me is that I know more about Portugal now. (Lukas)

Even when talking about concrete experiences, especially during the project day, students do not link their role as ambassadors to their behaviour or world outlook but only tell about interesting and fun aspects of the project day itself, the only exception being pupils who had the possibility of going to their partner country as exchange students – they tell about having found new friends.

Abstract versus concrete

The behaviour–knowledge distinction is closely connected to the difference between abstract notions and concrete stories. The pupils translate fair play into their realm of life, some of them concentrate on fair play in sports, explicitly or implicitly defining fair play as playing by the rules, avoiding fouls or team spirit. Leonie's explanation is an example:

> And because of this 'pulling yourself together' one can say that one plays fair and does not foul as much. And due to playing and sticking together in your team one is less focused on the own ego and leaves the ball to others even if they lose it, next time it may work out.

Others want to apply fair play to other areas of life, be it the family, business world or politics. Patricia writes:

> For example, thinking of different professions, let's say lawyers and housewives. Both work all day, nevertheless the lawyer gets paid more than the housewife. To be completely accurate, the housewife has, at any rate, more stress and more to do than the lawyer. So why does he get more money? I don't think that that is 'fair play'. Or let's say men and women. Why do men get more for the same work?

Frequently, students assess their personality with a view to the standards set by the fair play idea, either emphasizing that they see no need to change or with a more self-critical stance. Students thereby define fair play concretely, giving examples and typical cases – such as hassling, fouling or integrating others. Fair play acquires an everyday relevance for the students.

For our discussion, it is not important whether the changes reported by students really occurred (as it is equally irrelevant whether they really found learning about their partner country interesting). The important point here is the different mode the two project parts are dealt with and the different kinds of relevance the components had for them. Corresponding to the knowledge character discussed, no comparable lifeworld interpretation can be found regarding interculturality. Here, the definitional work done by students is mostly abstract and implicit by naming the dimensions by which the country is established as an object of knowledge, for example, geography, history or language.

Hardly any references are made to cultural diversity, multiculturalism, problems of intolerance or any other form of 'cultural' problem in the students' own country. That is surprising not least because moral arguments abound in the essays. Accordingly, there is no reporting of racist incidents in everyday life, regardless of whether students have a migration background.

The abstract construction of partner countries as objects of knowledge is connected to the lack of anchoring in students' lebenswelt, as well as to the construction of difference along national–cultural lines. Nationality and ethnicity are what Benedict Anderson[24] famously called imagined communities – their 'imagined' character implying that they do not reflect 'real' social relations in a straightforward manner. They are inherently *abstract* notions of belonging. Thus the naturalizing constructions of cultural difference and the abstract construction of objects of knowledge are intertwined.

The blocked road from 'interculturality' to anti-racism

Although EUROSCHOOLS focused on interculturality, anti-racism was considered a closely related issue that was prominently dealt with not only in the evaluation questionnaire, but also in the material accompanying the project. Building on our analysis, we can now turn to the question of why no positive effect could be detected regarding anti-racist awareness. In face of the forms in which racism manifests itself nowadays, two crucial and interrelated factors are obvious. (1) The strong focus on cultural differences defined along national lines does not allow for tackling instances of racism that are complexly linked to ideas on cultural and national belonging; quite the contrary. Essential elements of current racist discourses are strengthened, not weakened. (2) The institutionalized character of racism requires that the *concrete* configurations of cultural factors and different forms of discrimination are enquired into, an objective incompatible with the abstract and knowledge-centred character with which interculturality was dealt.

All of the mentioned features are, of course, immanently connected with the whole idea of organizing a project on interculturality around 'partner countries' and the role of 'ambassadors'. Given this approach, it is hard to conceive of any outcome other than the one sketched out. But this approach itself is anything but unavoidable. We would argue that focusing the interculturality component not on partner countries, but on the interplay of social inequality and perceived cultural conflicts in the students' own realm of experience and thus not on folkloric representations of nations but on, for example, racist prejudices manifest in school life, in neighbourhoods, in the media or – fittingly – in football contexts would go a long way in this direction.

Questioning seemingly homogeneous national identities, starting with the countries pupils live in, is another possibility. It can hardly be considered a coincidence that the only students who refer to racism and current social problems when talking about the interculturality part of the campaign (and the only ones mentioning in their essay the evaluation questionnaire asking about these aspects!) come from one and the same school – and tell about how they started the project by 'asking ourselves what our relation to Switzerland is and who we are' (Stefan). In a very simple manner, nationality is made an object in question – something that is not straightforward but a problem that requires discussion. On such a basis, references to cultural difference can be used to question nationalist thought patterns and thus develop anti-racist potential instead of being used for constructing the national Other.

Interestingly enough, the recommendation to start the campaign with a critical reflection on the own (national) identity is given in the official instructions for teachers involved in the EUROSCHOOLS campaign. But, judging from what students and teachers tell, this aspect was completely overshadowed by the far more obvious emphasis on partner countries and cultural differences. We would argue that these two approaches of focusing the campaign are incompatible rather than complementary – and the more prominent of them inevitably holds the upper hand.

Is the EUROSCHOOLS campaign symptomatic for UEFA's anti-racism?

Our findings for the EUROSCHOOLS 2008 campaign point to general problems with the way in which UEFA frames its interculturality and anti-racism initiatives in the context of the European Championships,[25] rendering them unsuitable to confront racism in its current manifestations. A strong emphasis on 'cultural difference' can be found throughout UEFA's public anti-racism campaigns. The first recommendation of the 'Braga declaration', initiated by the EUMC[26] and signed by UEFA prior to the 2004 European Championships in Portugal, names as its aim to 'celebrate cultural and ethnic diversity in and through sport'.[27] Culture is, similar to the students' essays, associated with difference. And both, culture and difference, are intimately linked to national belonging, as can be highlighted using the example of an anti-racist advertising spot shown, among others, before every match of EURO 2008™ on the stadiums' video-walls. The video clip, named 'different languages, one goal', features fans of different gender, skin colour and, obviously, ethnic backgrounds who are united around one common aim: the fortune of their national teams. Nationality, here, is the difference that matters – even if presented in a positive, festival-like atmosphere.

Of course, both examples seem harmless and may have positive as well as more troubling implications, but they illustrate the strong and anything other than self-evident linkage made between culture, difference and nationality – and how these three elements come to define a very specific 'culturalist–nationalist' form of anti-racism, virtually ignoring the complex interplay of nationalism and racism. Social relations and practices bound to racist discourses or, even, forms of institutional racism are conceptually bypassed. Anti-racism becomes an abstract affair.

The tension between abstract anti-racist avowals and the avoidance of confronting concrete racist incidents became evident during the 'Unite Against Racism' campaign. On the one hand, an enormous audience was reached via TV when the captains of the semi-final teams read out anti-racist messages before kick-off.[28] On the other hand, this message loses credibility when presented by players like Rüştü Reçber, then captain of the Turkish national team and a known nationalist, coached by managers with likewise dubious political views: the Turkish coach, Fatih Terim, is well-known for his nationalism and his Spanish colleague, Luis Aragones, caused some turmoil in 2004, trying to motivate his striker Jose Reyes by making racist remarks on Reyes' club team mate Thierry Henry ('Show that nigger that you're better than him!'). UEFA ignored this inconsistency and did not speak up against such or similar incidences, for example, when the Croat team played songs written by the known neofascist Marko Perković ('Thompson').

As these examples show, the observed ambivalences are not just isolated cases resulting from poor planning of a particular project. They have to be understood against the background of UEFA's institutional setting. UEFA 'as a quasi European IGO'[29] has to serve the dual purpose of maintaining its hegemonic position within the field of sports politics while avoiding conflicts with the different actors involved. Proposing and enforcing anti-racist efforts helps UEFA protect and strengthen its claim for leadership on sport policy topics, the predominantly abstract manner of this anti-racism allows to avoid possible manifest conflicts with the different stakeholders – the EU, national governments, ministries of sport, national football federations, clubs, fans and NGOs. In this context, it is telling that UEFA's anti-racist work is concentrated in its 'communications division' and thus part of UEFA's public relations work, contributing to the branding of its trademark and immanently linked to corporate strategic considerations.

Acknowledgements

We would like to thank Wolfram Manzenreiter, Martin Rossbacher, Georg Spitaler and Juliane Zeiser for their support and feedback.

Notes

1. The starting point to UEFA's highly visible commitment to anti-racism was when its Charity Award 2001 went to the anti-racist network FARE (the network 'Football Against Racism in Europe', founded in 1999 in Vienna, links anti-racist non-governmental organizations [NGOs] working around Europe). In 2002, a 10-point-plan to fight racism and discrimination was passed – predominantly a public condemnation of racism accompanied by steps towards sanctioning racist behaviour. The plan recommends that national football federations and clubs adopt and spread anti-racist statements, sanction racist behaviour by fans or players and guarantee equal job opportunities. The promotion and funding of anti-racist initiatives peak in the run-up to mega-events. Among the more long-term activities are the triennial anti-racism conferences (2003/London, 2006/Barcelona and 2009/Warsaw) bringing together representatives of federations, clubs and NGOs. Furthermore, UEFA has published two guides on anti-racism that can be downloaded from the Internet (http://www.uefa.com/newsfiles/82716.pdf, http://www.uefa.com/MultimediaFiles/Download/uefa/KeyTopics/448328_DOWNLOAD.pdf).
2. See Back, Crabbe, and Solomos, *Changing Face of Football*, for an analysis of various aspects of racism in English football (including a classification of various forms of racism and actors, highlighting the behaviour of fans); Garland and Rowe, *Racism and Antiracism*, for a study on racism and anti-racism in English football (including a distinguished definition of racism and the construction of national identities); Fanizadeh and Pinter, 'Rassismus und Antirassismus', for a short overview on racism and anti-racism in football (with emphases on the situation in Austria and the formation of FARE); Van Sterkenburg, Janssens, and Rijnen, *Football and Racism*, for an outline on current racist incidents and anti-racist initiatives in eight European countries (including UK, France, Germany and Italy).
3. cf. Miles, *Racism*, 42–50; Guillaumin, 'Characteristics of Racist Ideology'; Hall, 'Rassismus als ideologischer Diskurs'.
4. Nonetheless racist ideas have survived in scientific contexts – for examples in debates on 'IQ' and genetics.
5. Rattansi, *Racism*, 69–85.
6. Taguieff, *La Force de Préjugé*; Silverman, *Deconstructing the Nation*, 7–9.
7. Barker, *The New Racism*; Wieviorka, 'Development of Racism', 473.
8. Guillaumin, 'Changing Face of Race', 104.
9. Wieviorka, 'Development of Racism', 462; Silverman, *Deconstructing the Nation*, 17.
10. Ibid., 24.
11. See Guillaumin, 'Characteristics of Racist Ideology', 33–54 for an interesting discussion of the emergence and development of racist ideology.
12. Rattansi, *Racism*, 88.
13. Miles, *Racism*, 84–7.
14. Ibid., 84.
15. Guillaumin, 'Changing Face of Race'.
16. We were involved in the evaluation carried out by a team of Swiss and Austrian researchers. We would like to thank our project partners for their support and the possibility to use both the qualitative and the quantitative data for further analyses.
17. Schwery *et al.*, 'Evaluation Social Responsibility Projects', 16–26.
18. The other campaigns were: Unite Against Racism (aiming for broad perceptibility), Fan Embassies (a fan initiative offering local support to incoming fans), Football for All

(supporting players with special needs), and Score for the Red Cross (a fundraising campaign for the International Red Cross).
19. EUROSCHOOLS 2008 was a cooperative project by Streetfootballworld, the Swiss Academy for Development and the Vienna Institute for Development and Cooperation.
20. We are aware that this focus means that we cannot take the motives and roles of other (institutional) actors into account (e.g. the possible influence of the involved organizations on UEFA's policies; the individual commitment and expertise of participating schools and teachers; etc.).
21. Fair play means a kind of behaviour in sport that is characterized by respect for the other players and an emphasis not on winning, but on playing. It is commonly linked to other aims, such as the promotion of gender equality by emphasis on the participation of girls in the game.
22. For reasons of anonymity, we changed the names of the pupils.
23. The class dealing with Israel enacted a play about the Israel–Palestine conflict.
24. Anderson, *Imagined Communities*.
25. Our observations regard only the context of European Championships and its focus on interculturality and nationality. We do not take into account the various fields in which UEFA and their local partners operate on a more continuous basis and might also address other forms of racism (e.g. more concrete forms of racism, institutional racism, etc.).
26. The 'European Monitoring Centre on Racism and Xenophobia' was located in Vienna and renamed to 'European Union Agency for Fundamental Rights' (FRA) in 2007.
27. EUMC, 'Fighting Racism'.
28. Regarding the lack of 'lebenswelt' anchoring, it is noteworthy that the wording was not left to the players but provided by the organizer: 'I and my team-mates wish to make clear that we stand against all forms of discrimination. We have seen over the last three weeks how football can bring people together to enjoy our common passion whatever our religion, nationality or skin colour. Please join us to Unite Against Racism.'
29. Groll, Gütt, and Mittag, 'Political Aspects of Sport', 10.

References

Anderson, B. *Imagined Communities. Reflections on the Origin and Spread of Nationalism.* London: Verso, 1983.

Back, L., T. Crabbe, and J. Solomos. *The Changing Face of Football. Racism, Identity and Multiculture in the English Game.* Oxford: Berg 2001.

Barker, M. *The New Racism.* London: Junction Books, 1981.

EUMC. 'Fighting Racism and Xenophobia through Sport'. EUMC. http://www.eumc.eu.int/eumc/index.php?fuseaction=content.dsp_cat_content&catid=3e6c61340870c&contentid=40b7232a2838b (accessed April 1, 2009).

Fanizadeh, M., and M. Pinter. 'Rassismus und Antirassismus im goldenen Zeitalter des Fußballs'. In *Global Players. Kultur, Ökonomie und Politik des Fußballs,* ed. M. Fanizadeh, G. Hödl, and W. Manzenreiter, 257–74. Frankfurt: Brandes & Apsel 2002.

Garland, J., and M. Rowe. *Racism and Anti-Racism in Football.* Basingstoke: Palgrave Macmillan 2001.

Groll, M., M. Gütt, and J. Mittag. 'Political Aspects of Sport in the European Union. Status Report within the Framework of the Project "Sport in Europe – Social, Political Organisational, Legal Transparency in Europe"'. Sport in Europe, http://www.sport-in-europe.eu/images/stories/PDFFiles/politische%20aspekte_final_end_1201.pdf. (accessed April 1, 2009).

Guillaumin, C. '"I Know It's Not Nice, But …": The Changing Face of "Race"'. In *Racism, Sexism, Power and Ideology,* ed. C. Guillaumin, 99–107. London: Routledge, 1995.

Guillaumin, C. 'The Specific Characteristics of Racist Ideology'. In *Racism, Sexism, Power and Ideology,* ed. C. Guillaumin, 29–60. London: Routledge, 1995.

Hall, S. 'Rassismus als ideologischer Diskurs'. In *Theorien über Rassismus,* ed. N. Räthzel, 7–16. Hamburg: Argument Verlag, 2000.

Miles, R. *Racism.* London: Routledge, 1989.

Rattansi, A. *Racism – A Very Short Introduction.* Oxford: Oxford University Press, 2007.

Schwery, R., D. Cade, R. Horak, L. Greco, K. Horvath, B. Nann, J. Rosenberg, N. Schneider, R. Seiler, and G. Spitaler. *An Evaluation of the UEFA EURO 2008™ Football and Social Responsibility Projects.* Biel/Bienne: Schwery Consulting, 2008.

Silverman, M. *Deconstructing the Nation. Immigration, Racism and Citizenship in Modern France.* London: Routledge, 1992.

Taguieff, P.-A. *La Force de Préjugé: Essai sur le Racisme es ses Doubles.* Paris: La Découverte, 1988.

Van Sterkenburg, J., J. Janssens, and B. Rijnen, ed. *Football and Racism. An Inventory of the Problems and Solutions in Eight West European Countries in the Framework of the Stand UP Speak Up Campaign.* Brussels: King Baudouin Foundation 2005.

Wieviorka, M. 'The Development of Racism in Europe'. In *A Companion to Racial and Ethnic Studies,* ed. D.T. Goldberg and J. Solomos, 460–74. Oxford: Blackwell, 2002.

The EURO 2008 bonanza: mega-events, economic pretensions and the sports–media business alliance

Bernhard Hachleitner[a] and Wolfram Manzenreiter[b]

[a]*Department of Contemporary History, University of Vienna, Austria;* [b]*Department of East Asian Studies, University of Vienna, Austria*

Public reports in the media prior to EURO 2008 hailed the economic impact of hosting the event on the national economy. Whereas in the USA spectator sports have been frequently used as a device for drawing public expenditures and subsidies over the greater half of the past century, in the regional context of Europe and the focus of football such argumentations have a much shorter history, dating back to the recent football mega-events of the twenty-first century. Sports mega-events such as as the Olympic Games and the football World Cup have grown over the years and have thereby changed into commercial events, dominated by the power of satellite television and corporate interests. In comparison, the European Football Championships are much more limited in scope, yet we argue that their recent growth is based on the same socio-economic changes. Why economic issues have become so important for contemporary sports mega-events is a central question of this article. In an attempt to answer it, we take a critical look at several economic forecast studies and compare their assertions with the appreciation of the football event after its ending in Austria. We argue that the media, crucial actors of the 'sports–media–business alliance', played a leading role in the construction of the event's bonanza image.

Introduction

On May 19, 2008, Federal Chancellor of Austria Alfred Gusenbauer proudly presented the promising results of a study examining the impact of the UEFA Championships (hereafter referred to as EURO 2008) on the Austrian economy. The Austrian media closely followed the press conference of this study, which had been commissioned by the federal government itself. Press coverage particularly highlighted the key numbers published in the press release of the Federal Chancellery: it was asserted that EURO 2008 would bring some 641 million of value added, and 13,400 new jobs.[1] The outlook for Switzerland was similarly optimistic. A study conducted on behalf of the Swiss Federal Office for Sport (BASPRO) forecast that the events would produce a gross value added of CHF640–860 million (approximately 421–565 million).[2] Critical voices questioning the macro-economic effects remained comparatively unheard, even those close to the government such as Jäggi and Michal who warned that 'even the impact of a large event like the Euro 2008 is – when measured in economic scales – too small to distinguish it from other macroeconomic events'.[3] Although most sports economists and mega-event researchers agree that hosting mega-events does not yield significant economic benefits, public discourse is dominated by the opposite view. In general, expectations that hosting EURO 2008 would provide an economic windfall for the host countries were running high.

This was not the first time that economic impact and the hosting of a sports mega-event have been explicitly linked. In the USA, spectator sports have been used as a basis for receiving public monies and subsidies for more than half a century. In the regional context of Europe and the focus of football, such argumentations have a much shorter history, dating back to the recent football mega-events of the twenty-first century. An historical review of the Olympic Games and the football World Cup from the 1970s up to Germany 2006 or Beijing 2008 would demonstrate how sports mega-events have grown over the years and how they have changed into commercial events, dominated by the power of satellite television and corporate interests. European Football Championships are much more limited in scope than Olympic Games, yet we would argue that their development has been shaped by the same socio-economic changes. Why economic issues have become so important for contemporary sports mega-events is a central question of this article. In an attempt to answer it, we take a critical look at several EURO 2008 economic forecast studies and compare their assertions with the appreciation of the football event after its ending in Austria. We argue that the media, crucial actors of the 'sports–media–business alliance', played a leading role in the construction of the event's bonanza image.

The background of the economic discourse on EURO 2008

Compared with the summer Olympic Games and the men's football World Cup, the dimensions of EURO 2008 appear relatively small. For example, UEFA membership is limited to Europe, whereas the World Cup and the Olympic Games are attended by national delegations from all over the world. In terms of live participation, many more millions of fans followed the Olympic events in Beijing's stadiums or the World Cup finals in German football arenas in 2006 than the mere 1.2 million people that attended the 31 games of the EURO finals in Austria and Switzerland. However, the European Championship has shown extraordinarily dynamic growth over the last two decades. Overall, international football has gained on the Olympic multi-sports event, and hardly any tournament has benefited more from the global demand for football entertainment than the European Championship. According to Horne and Manzenreiter, major developments in mass communication technologies, the formation of a sports–media–business alliance, and the promotional value of sports mega-events are the three inter-twined processes at the core of the growing significance of sports mega-events in general and are also relevant to EURO 2008.[4]

Satellite television and live Internet streaming are the technological backbone of this global marketing of local events. The official website of the event, www.euro2008.com, tallied 105 million visitors producing 1.3 billion page views. The highest number of users on a single day was 4.9 million. Most users came from the UK (15%), which had failed to qualify for the tournament, followed by Germany (8%), Canada (6%) and Finland (3%).[5] It drew the largest continental European TV audiences of any regional tournament, in particular those from the host countries and the finalists, which in 2008 recorded some of the largest audiences in their respective television history. Apparently, every match was watched by at least 155 million people worldwide. Viewing naturally drops in other parts of the world, yet this event, broadcast live into 231 countries and territories in 2008, undeniably has some global significance.[6] TV markets outside Europe have become an important source of revenue, constituting 11% of total broadcast revenues.[7] ESPN, which broadcast EURO 2008 in the USA, reported that the group and quarter-final matches were each watched by an average of 629,000 viewers, and the most watched game was the quarter-final between Spain and Italy with 1.9 million viewers. The Spanish language channel ESPN Deportes reached a 10.1 Hispanic household coverage rating (357,000 households with 647,000 Hispanic viewers).[8]

Growing television audiences are an established means of demonstrating the importance of an event that relies heavily on media exposure. Another standard argument is a comparison of economic gains with previous revenues. According to UEFA, its income from EURO 2008 totalled 1.3 billion, about twice as much as gained from the previous EURO in Portugal. A look back at revenue streams from preceding events shows the rising economic potential of European football: in 2000 (Belgium/Netherlands) UEFA's income was 230 million, in 1996 (England) 147 million, and in Sweden 1992 it was just 41 million, or 3% of present-day turnover. The overall turnover generated by EURO 2008 can be broken down into four main sources: media rights (60%), commercial rights (21%), hospitality (12%) and ticketing (7%).[9] Media rights are the most important single source of revenue. In 2008, television rights were sold country-by-country for the first time, replacing the former European Broadcasting Union agreement. In turn, UEFA was able to increase income from broadcasting rights for the EURO by 43%. Secondary sales of naming rights to merchandisers and sponsors are also quite huge and continue to rise (37% increase). In economic terms, hospitality has shown the strongest growth rate with income increasing by 417%. UEFA sold ~ 80,000 VIP packages comprised of category-one seating, first-class catering, entertainment and gifts. This indicates that selling stadium seats as part of a package is a more lucrative business than regular ticket sales (20% increase), which account for a mere 7% of turnover.[10] Only one third of tickets were directly available to football fans, with the remainder going either to national associations or corporate sponsors.[11]

As a highly commercial event with a very limited number of tickets, the nature of the EURO has changed. The huge interest in live attendance combined with limited ticket contingencies made it possible, and economically desirable, to follow the example the FIFA set at the World Cup 2006 of occupying large spaces in the host cities for 'fan zones' and public viewing areas. In turn, the event gained visibility in urban space, providing another opportunity for official event sponsors to present themselves. Last, but not least, the consumerization of the event also left its mark on ex-ante studies about the economic effects of the tournament, which prognosticated strong positive effects spilling over from the fan zones to the macro-economies of Austria and Switzerland, as we show later.

In terms of forming a global sports–media–business alliance that has propelled the growth of sports mega-events over the past two decades, EURO 2008 reached a new level. National broadcasters and newspapers were actively involved in promoting the UEFA event: public broadcasters in the host countries obtained broadcasting rights for the domestic market, and Austria's most widely distributed newspaper, the *Kronen Zeitung*, appeared as a local sponsor. For the first time in the history of European football, the TV signal of matches was not produced by a host broadcaster but by UEFA's subsidiary UMET (UEFA Media Technologies, SA), a nominally independent company created by UEFA to provide all technology and content solutions and to guarantee full control over the images delivered to audiences. The way this power was exerted caused frequent irritation. The director of the Swiss national broadcasting company accused UMET of censorship when the broadcast feed cut out Bengal fire on the stands, and fans invading the pitch.[12] Even more unease was evoked by a sudden power breakdown in the UEFA International Broadcast Centre, Vienna, which caused an 18-minute broadcast interruption during the second half of the semi-final match between Germany and Turkey. The editor-in-chief of German broadcaster ZDF lamented that the blackout caused his network to miss attaining a national viewing record high.[13] This type of mishap is particularly apt to garner criticism from broadcasters, who see their investment values dwindling.

The sports press has been dubbed 'the world's best advertising agency'.[14] According to Dante Chinni from the Center for Excellence in Journalism, the sports press is one of society's biggest myth-makers and 'functionally speaking there is little doubt that sports journalists act as PR agents'.[15] These myths help sell sports as a product and contribute to the growth of sports events. The International Sports Press Survey, which analysed 100,000 sports articles in newspapers from throughout the developed world, found that football is the most covered sport in national sports pages, reaching 50% of all coverage, followed by cycling (6.3 %) and tennis (5.8 %) trailing well behind.[16]

Sponsoring companies, the so-called 'partners' of the governing body, promote their investments within and beyond television advertisement. McDonald's recruitment of 'Official Player Escorts' and the Coca-Cola EURO roadshow are both characteristic examples of how corporate partners promote the event itself as well as their own products among their staff, business clients, customers and the general public. Host cities and countries have adopted very similar promotional strategies. The Vienna Tourist Board touted the capital city with the slogan 'Vienna: Where the European Championship will be decided'.[17] Austrian Chancellor Gusenbauer called the EURO, 'a unique chance for Austria to present itself globally as a tourism and sports destination. [...] It would be fine to send inspiring pictures of Austria around the world, given that sports and tourism are both important economic factors in Austria.'[18] The idea of boosting tourism through mega-events is not entirely new, at least in a place like Vienna. The idea of implementing mega-events to attract tourism above and beyond the occasion of the event and thereby improve a city's global image is of relatively recent origin – and would not work without cooperation with global television. In terms of marketing locations, cities and regions are seen as labels in need of unique selling propositions, and mega sport-events are seen as an essential tool for this objective.

Macroeconomic dreams: forecasting the effects of the EURO

The commercialization and consumerization of football mega-events provide the background against which governments increasingly tend to legitimate public funding of such events by referring to short- and long-term paybacks. The discourse on the economic impact of hosting the EURO, which was conspicuously absent during failed bids for the finals of 1996 and 2004, gained increasing prominence during and after the successful bid for EURO 2008. Minutes from Austrian parliament meetings reveal that by 2002, national politics had been infiltrated by the standard argumentations of mega-event promoters, 'sports mega-events within the country produce a positive image for sports and the country alike; they encourage athletic participation and stimulate respective economic sectors, particularly tourism and construction. Sports generate jobs and economic incentives.'[19] Concrete numbers fleshed out this general assertion. A case study delivered by the Institute for Advanced Studies anticipated the creation of value of up to 290 million and 6600 new jobs, mainly from construction projects and spending by about one million visitors during the month of the tournament. These figures were replicated and disseminated by national television, local newspapers, publications by national sports federations, and the Austrian Federal Economic Chamber.

The same pattern of shaping public discourse occurred in 2007, after the national government had commissioned SportsEconAustria to conduct an update of the study. This think tank for the study of the economics of sports was founded and directed by one of the authors of the first study assessing the macroeconomic value of hosting EURO 2008, who in the meantime had also been appointed chief economist of the Federation of Austrian Industries. The new study forecast a slightly higher total value added, 321 million, with lower contributions from the construction sector and higher expectations for tourism expenditure and spending by event organizers. This shift partly explains why the forecasted impact on the labour market shrank to 5400 jobs. Nonetheless, the study's authors repeated their former conclusion that 'the economic impact of UEFA Euro 2008 signifies a huge impetus for the Austrian economy as a whole'.[20] As in the past, representatives from national and local governments, business and industrial federations, and event organizers echoed the figures for anticipated effects in their press statements. Media coverage of these statements played a substantial role in shaping public awareness.

Fifteen months later, SportsEconAustria upped its prediction again, all the way to 641 million.[21] It was explained that this 100% increase was the result of observations of fan spending during the World Cup 2006 in Germany. 'Differences within the results can be traced to the fact that the present update not only includes the demand effects caused by stadium guests, but for the first time also the crowding-in effects and effects of public viewing events. Crowding-out effects have been included in this study as well, so that the present study displays the total, EC-determined, tourist net effect.'[22] Yet as the expectations of financial gains increased, overall appreciation appeared to have cooled down: 'an economic boom, triggered by the European Championship, cannot be expected in the year of the event'.[23]

This remarkable shift aligned the Austrian study with updated findings of its Swiss counterpart, Rütter+Partner. This agency had conducted an initial study of the economic effects of the EURO on behalf of the Swiss Federal Office for Sport in 2004 and likewise increased the predicted gross value added in 2008.[24] However, as the maximum gains of CHR860 million would amount to less than 0.2% of the Swiss gross domestic product, they were quite conservative about the potential impact the event could have on the 336 billion economy. This cautious stance was substantiated by the findings of a comparatively rare ex-post impact study conducted by German economists.[25] They demonstrated that the World Cup impact on the German economy was quite negligible, contradicting the over-optimistic expectations that had flourished prior to the event in 2006, despite the huge success of the football World Cup and the additional sources of revenue generated by fan zones. Even though such studies hardly gained the same attention as the bold claims of ex-ante studies, they are taken into serious consideration by researchers and they also occasionally manage to sow seeds of unease, doubt and critical questioning among media representatives.

In November 2007, the renowned *Neue Zürcher Zeitung* identified five main problems characteristic of ex-ante studies. First, assigning effects to a specific source or single country is not an easy task to accomplish. Second, it is difficult to distinguish between gross and net effects. Third, it is problematic to deduce the secondary impact on investments and employment from the immediate net effect. The fourth main problem is how to quantify effects that are not easy to measure, like those of image and public health. Fifth and finally, such effect analyses should, but generally do not, examine the effects that alternative measures would produce.[26] Some weeks before this article, the independent Austrian football magazine *ballesterer* published a similar assessment of classic fallacies, which was reproduced by the national newspaper *Kurier*. This assessment also pointed out the vested interests of researchers, who are much more likely to obtain funding and a forum for forecasts than for ex-post impact studies.[27]

Microeconomic realities: tourists, sustainable infrastructures, and public expenditure in Austria

This section identifies some of the shortcomings of ex-ante studies that became evident during and after the EURO in Austria. The tourism sector, the largest single source of economic impact, was predicted to benefit from 2.2 million up to 3.2 million additional overnight stays, depending on the success of the German team and other neighbouring football powerhouses. The difference in the numbers of visitors predicted by the 2002 study was due to the anticipated attraction of the new fan zones, which did not appear in the forecast models prior to 2006. However, there is hardly any evidence that these special event zones did indeed create significant value-added. Spending by locals is unlikely to produce extra profits for the Austrian economy and there is evidence that visitor turnout in fan zones correlated closely with the appearance of national teams representing either the host nation or the national background of ethnic minorities. In Vienna, the Austrian national team as well as Turkey, Germany and Croatia drew the largest audiences into fan zones.[28]

According to the official final report, more than 3 million people attended games and live screenings in Austria; 2.2 million were counted in the fan zones and other public viewing areas.[29] Such numbers from the official pamphlets most likely disregarded the number of repeaters and overestimated foreign visitors. A survey of economic effects and visitor satisfaction conducted in the host cities revealed that 65% of stadium visitors and 47% of fan zone attendance comprised foreign travellers. Spending per head and day ranged between €256 for overnight visitors and €176 for day-trippers, contributing to a primary net effect of €287 million.[30] At the time of writing, Austria's Institute of Economic Research was using these numbers to investigate secondary and fiscal effects. Results are unlikely to exceed an additional €150 million, if survey methods are used that yield results matching the input–output analysis usually applied for forecast studies.

In terms of total visitors to Vienna, June 2008 showed a slight increase over June 2007, and 2008 finished with a plus of 5.8%, followed by a sharp decline.[31] Although these figures indicate a positive short-term and negative mid-term effect, it is impossible to distinguish between the effects of the football event and the overall economic environment switching from boom to crisis after overheated financial markets collapsed later that year. Hence, neither net gains nor net losses are easily quantified or allocated. Tourism experts who were aware of crowding-out effects warned against the negative impact on cultural or convention tourism during the month of the event. Visitor figures from cultural institutions and Vienna's most popular tourist spots, such as Schönbrunn Palace, the Hofburg museums or the Staatsoper, recorded quite dramatic declines in comparison with the same month in 2007.[32] Vienna's main theatre, the Burgtheater, was closed during the tournament and rented out to one of the event's local sponsors as an 'exclusive viewing zone'.

After tourism, infrastructure projects and the construction sector provided the second most important source of economic effects. Construction projects for the event architecture were estimated to total €173 million, including 30 million for resizing the stadia after the event to match standard demand. All funding came from the federal government and municipal or regional governments. The city of Vienna renovated the Ernst Happel Stadium, Austria's largest sports facility dating back to the prime days of the socialist city government of the interwar years. Innsbruck and Salzburg adjusted their comparatively new stadia to UEFA requirements of at least 30,000 seats, and Klagenfurt built a completely new stadium.

However, after the event it became evident that construction expenses had been underestimated and that the premises on which funding had been granted were no longer valid. The renovation of the Ernst Happel Stadium required nearly €20 million more than forecast by the SportsEconAustria study,[33] and construction expenses for the Klagenfurt arena increased from €53 million to €72 million.[34] Only the Innsbruck stadium was downsized according to the original plan for subsequent use. Salzburg and Klagenfurt insisted on maintaining the larger capacities which clearly exceeded the range permitted by the legally required assessment studies on environmental impact. because home teams pay only a nominal fee to the public owners of the facilities, the subsidizing of private sport entrepreneurs with public money has become an additional source of criticism.[35]

The examples of Klagenfurt and Salzburg indicate the attraction of mega-events for local governments to apply for federal subsidies that are channelled into the acquisition of prestigious edifices. Because capacities far exceed average demand, daily business operations inevitably generate losses and the maintenance of such event architecture alone requires long-term additional spending of public funds. Forecast studies generally downplay issues of sustainability or ignore the negative effects of concepts for subsequent usage being deliberately changed. Since public spending for sports infrastructure initiates a chain reaction of additional financial support measurements, stadium construction should be called public consumption rather than public investment.

The third largest source of economic impact was from the budget of the event organizers. Austria's federal government spent €133 million on stadiums, traffic management, tourism promotion, sustainability and other support programmes.[36] The comprehensive security concept involving 27,000 police officers, army personnel and private security guards consumed €44 million but apparently was not included as part of the event budget.[37] Local governments spent equally on infrastructure projects, municipal image marketing, security and support programmes. During the event, criticism focused on the opening of underused fan zone facilities and the use of public subsidies for private enterprises that transformed swathes of the urban landscape into commercial venues. In particular, the high costs of an additional public viewing zone in Vienna's Hanappi Stadium were heavily criticized. This public viewing area was funded by the city government at a cost of €3.98 million but opened only four times and was visited by a mere 17,760 people. The overblown expectations of tourist spending sparked a heated debate between the agency in charge of managing the primary fan zone in Vienna's city centre, its clients and the city government mediating between the parties. Caterers complained loudest about the non-appearance of the foreshadowed visitor masses. Particularly during the day and on days without matches, most fan zones were deserted. The caterers saw their prospective revenue dwindling due to excessive rental fees, restrictive UEFA rules on sales and a strict pricing policy imposed by the primary contractor, who bankrupted later that year. After a week of open conflict, contracts were renegotiated with lower rental fees for caterers and more sensible beverage pricing.

Once EURO 2008 was over, the economics of the event largely vanished from public discourse. Occasional reports on additional expenses, unveiled only after the books had been closed, often stirred up criticism by local opposition parties and the liberal media. In Innsbruck, where regional government auditors uncovered that fan zone operators had generated a deficit of €930,000, the deputy mayor in charge of managing the event was forced to resign from his position. In contrast to this single instance of taking political responsibility for obvious mismanagement, all other cities presented an unreservedly positive position on the event and its management. A comprehensive ex-post survey was never conducted, since public funding for this purpose was not available.[38] SportsEconAustria produced a study on selected aspects of the economic impact on behalf of the Federal Economic Chamber, but its results were not released.[39]

The media reflected the general consensus: the hosting was successful, the organization perfect and Austria delivered a great impression to visitors and spectators alike. Instead of concrete target numbers, economic effects were vaguely referred to in terms of marketing expenses and prospective investments for the promotion of the tourist destination Austria.[40] In Switzerland, Rütter+Partner conducted an ex-post study of economic impact on behalf of the national government. Compared with the forecasts, the impact study highlighted the significantly higher spending by event organizers and the increased number of visitors, which exceeded the predicted maximum scenario by 20%. According to this study, which included crowding-out effects, the event generated a net effect of 135,000 overnight stays in Switzerland, a total value-added of CHF870 million (approximately €567 million) and employment effects of 7100 jobs.[41] To some degree, these numbers seemed to exceed the forecasts, which were delivered by the same study authors, but still represented a diminishingly small contribution to the Swiss economy as a whole.

Conclusions

This article attempted to provide insights into the fabrication of the public discourse on EURO 2008 by emphasizing the economic aspects of the mega-event. This particular panoramic view has acquired central status in connection with the growth of sports mega-events and considerable social and economic changes of their environment. As we have shown, the media and public discourse focused upon economic issues much more than in earlier years. While it is reasonably safe to state that hosting EURO 2008 had no significant effects on the national economies of Austria and Switzerland, the sports mega-event merged well with the dynamics and processes of an event-driven service society. As sports have become an integral part of the global entertainment industry, their economic dimensions have captured the public imagination. This process is neither a natural consequence nor a random coincidence. Our analysis identified a number of key actors that actively contributed to the crafting of an image of the sports tournament as an economic windfall for the hosting society. The community of boosters includes public administration representatives, private enterprises, semi-independent think tanks and the mass media.

Local politicians using sports events to garner prestige or to forge large urban redevelopment projects refer to prospective economic gains in order to legitimate the deliberate spending of the taxpayers' money. Similarly, private enterprises use forecast studies to attract public subsidies and private investments. Data analysis and interpretation are conducted by research institutes which often depend on public contracts. Political decisions are based on the ex-ante economic impact studies of these institutions although said studies are often methodologically flawed or underdeveloped. Some common shortcomings, such as underestimating public expenses and crowding-out effects or replacing one source of income with another, have been discussed in greater detail. Funding for ex-post analysis is extremely difficult to obtain. Demand for accurate information about costs and benefits is low for two reasons: on the one hand, most sports mega-events are a once-in-a-lifetime experience meaning that because of their rare occurrence there is no need to legitimate similar hosting politics in the foreseeable future. On the other hand, as auditing reports of the host city administration have demonstrated, there is a definite danger of unveiling spectacular cases of corruption and mismanagement.

The mass media, including national newspapers and broadcasters, which also benefit from positive coverage of the event, because they generate revenues from the sports event as media content and occasionally serve as official sponsors, multiply the problems of ex-ante studies. Without critical investigation, the media are apt to reproduce key figures from executive summaries, press releases and public announcements that accompany the presentation of such studies. While these highlighted numbers of revenue streams, induced expenditure, gross value-added and jobs created look impressive in isolation, they are rarely put into context with the national economy as a whole or compared with alternative types of public investment. As the media become part of the entertainment industry, or more specifically the sports–media–business alliance, they become prone to neglect their traditional role of critical observer and whistle-blower.

Notes

1. SPÖ Bundespressedienst, 'Gusenbauer: Studie belegt erhebliche wirtschaftliche Bedeutung der EURO 2008', Austrian Press Agency, May 19, 2008. One job equals one year of full-time employment.
2. Rütter+Partner, 'Wirtschaftliche Wirkungen der UEFA EURO 2008', 4.
3. Jäggi and Michal, 'Entdecke das Plus', 67; see also Manzenreiter, 'Falsche Hoffnungen'.
4. Horne and Manzenreiter, 'Sociology of Sports Mega-Events'.
5. UEFA EURO 2008 Review, July 29, 2008, 4.
6. Ibid.
7. UEFA, *Financial Report*, 48.
8. ESPN, Press release, June 26, 2008.
9. UEFA, EURO 2008 Review, July 29, 2008, 2
10. UEFA, *Financial Report*, 46–7.
11. Media report from UEFA, May 29, 2008, http://www.uefa.com/newsfiles/634586.pdf. Online registration was required to obtain tickets. 10.4 million bids by 589,000 applicants from 142 countries went into a draw for ~ 350,000 tickets.
12. 'TV-Sender beklagen Zensur der Uefa bei EM', *Focus Online*, June 15, 2008.
13. Sports Business Daily, 'UEFA Apologizes for Botched Feed during Germany–Turkey Game'. http://www.sportsbusinessdaily.com/article/121951. An average of 29.4 million viewers watched the ZDF coverage of the semi-final, half a million less than the record 29.7 million for the Italy–Germany FIFA World Cup semi-final in 2006.

14. 'The World's Best Advertising Agency: The Sports Press', *Mandag morgen*, October 31, 2005.
15. Ibid., 2.
16. Ibid., 4.
17. Vienna Tourist Board, 'Vienna: Where the European Championship will be Decided'. b2b.wien.info/data/artikel-db/e/Euro2008-en.doc.
18. ASKÖ. 'Dienstag, SPÖ-Sport-Enquete zur EURO 2008 am 6.3.2007 im Parlament', http://www.askoe.at/de/menu_main/marketarchivshow-thema-der-woche-----spoe-sport-enquete-euro-2008
19. http://www.parlinkom.gv.at/pd/pm/XXI/I/texte/012/I01241__614.html.
20. Helmenstein, Kleissner, and Moder, *Makroökonomische und sektorale Effekte*, 81.
21. Helmenstein and Kleissner, *Volkswirtschaftliche Effekte*, 14.
22. Ibid., 124.
23. Ibid., 15.
24. Rütter+Partner, *Wirtschaftliche Wirkungen der UEFA EURO 2008*, 2007.
25. Brenke and Wagner, *Zum volkswirtschaftlichen Wert der Fußball-Weltmeisterschaft*.
26. Franck and Helmut, 'Keine gesamtwirtschaftlichen Effekte', *Neue Zürcher Zeitung*, November 1, 2007.
27. Manzenreiter, 'Falsche Hoffnungen'.
28. Steinert, *Über das Fassungsvermögen*. This article presents data and an analysis of this issue.
29. Koordination Bundesregierung, *Endbericht*, 17.
30. Ibid., 94–5; cf. Preuss, *Wirtschaftliche Wirkungen*.
31. Vienna Tourist Board, http://b2b.wien.info/article.asp?IDArticle=1056). The number of overnight stays in Vienna 2008 was higher than in 2007: June +0.4%, July +7.7%, August –0.2%, September +3.9%, October +6.5%, November 0.0%, December+0.2%.
32. Nina Haslinger, 'Fußballfans ließen Schönbrunn und Hofburg links liegen', *Wirtschaftsblatt* July 8, 2008. In contrast to the month of the EURO, these institutions had an increase in visitors over the whole year.
33. Koordination Bundesregierung, *Endbericht*, 35.
34. *Der Standard*, June 6, 2009.
35. 'Fußball: Salzburger Stadion wird nicht rückgebaut', *DiePresse*, February 18, 2009.
36. Federal Coordination Office. 'Uefa Euro 2008 Football Unites. Final Report by the Federal Coordination Office on the Uefa Euro 2008 in Austria', http://www.oesterreich-am-ball.at/DocView.axd?CobId=33711, 29.
37. *Der Standard*, June 4, 2009.
38. E-mail from Christian Helmenstein of SportsEconAustria on May 25, 2009. According to Helmenstein, SportsEconAustria would have liked to do such a study but it was impossible to get funding for the necessary research during the European Championship.
39. SportsEconAustria Institut für Sportökonomie. 'Ex-post-Evaluierung von Effekten der UEFA EURO 2008 in Österreich' (April 2009) im Auftrag der Wirtschaftskammer Wien. Wien
40. That is, Sommerbauer, '844 TV-Teams', *Die Presse*, June 27, 2008, 18; 'Turnier der Gastfreundschaft'. *Salzburger Nachrichten*, June 28, 2008, 16; Mayr, 'Es ist ein wunderbares Fußball-Fest', *Wiener eitung*, June 27, and many other newspaper articles on the last days of the event and the week after it.
41. Rütter+Partner, *Wirtschaftliche Wirkungen. Ex-post Analyse*.

References

Brenke, K., and G.G. Wagner. *Zum volkswirtschaftlichen Wert der Fußball-Weltmeisterschaft 2006 in Deutschland* [On the macroeconomic value of the Footbal World Cup 2006 in Germany]. Berlin: Deutsches Institut für Wirtschaftsforschung, DIW Berlin Research Note 19/2007.

Helmenstein, C., and A. Kleissner. *Volkswirtschaftliche Effekte der UEFA EURO 2008 in Österreich. Rahmenstudie im Auftrag des Bundeskanzleramts/Sektion Sport und der Wirtschaftskammer Österreich unter Einbeziehung von Teilstudien des Bundesministeriums für Wirtschaft und Arbeit und der Wirtschaftskammer Wien* [Macroeconomic effects of EURO 2008 in Austria]. Wien: SportsEconAustria Institut für Sportökonomie, 2008.

Helmenstein, C., A. Kleissner, and B. Moder. *Makroökonomische und sektorale Effekte der UEFA EURO 2008 in Österreich. Studie im Auftrag der Wirtschaftskammer Österreich.* [Macroeconomic and sectoral effects of EURO 2008 in Austria]. Wien: SportsEcon-Austria Institut für Sportökonomie, 2007.

Horne, J. and W. Manzenreiter, 'An Introduction to the Sociology of Sports Mega-Events'. *Sociological Review* 54, s2 (2006): 1–24.

Jäggi, S., and S. Michal. 'Entdecke das Plus. Was die Euro 2008 volkswirtschaftlich bewirkt' [Discover the Surplus. Macroeconomics effects of the EURO 2008]. *Die Volkswirtschaft. Magazin für Wirtschaftspolitik* 11 (2007): 67–70.

Koordination Bundesregierung, ed. *Endbericht Koordination BUND zur UEFA EURO 2008TM in Österreich* [Final report UEFA EURO 2008 by the federal coordination group] Wien: BM.I – Abteilung IV/4 – Digitalprintcenter, 2008.

Manzenreiter, W. 'Falsche Hoffnungen' [False pretences]. *ballesterer* 27 (2008): 32–4.

Preuss, H. *Wirtschaftliche Wirkungen und Zufriedenheit der UEFA EURO 2008TM in Österreich [Economic effects and satisfaction during the EURO 2008 in Austria].* Mainz: Johannes Gutenberg-Universität, 2008.

Rütter+Partner. *Wirtschaftliche Wirkungen der UEFA EURO 2008TM in der Schweiz. Aktualisierung der Studie von 2004* [Economic effects of EURO 2008 in Switzerland. Update of the 2004 study]. Magglingen: Bundesamt für Sport (BASPO), 2007.

Rütter+Partner. *Wirtschaftliche Wirkungen der UEFA EURO 2008 TM in der Schweiz. Ex-post Analyse (provisorische Ergebnisse)* [Economic effects of EURO 2008 in Switzerland. Ex-post analysis (preliminary results)]. Magglingen: Bundesamt für Sport (BASPO), 2008.

Steinert, H. *Über das Fassungsvermögen* [On fan zone capacities]. www.folks-uni.org/index.php?id=180 (accessed August 3, 2009).

UEFA. *UEFA EURO™ 2008 Review.* Nyon: UEFA, 2008.

UEFA. *UEFA Financial Report 2007/08.* Nyon: UEFA, 2008.

Material and representational legacies of sports mega-events: the case of the UEFA EURO™ football championships from 1996 to 2008

John Horne

School of Sport, Tourism and the Outdoors, University of Central Lancashire, UK

Major sports events (MSE) include the well-known sports mega-events (SME), the summer Olympic Games and the FIFA football World Cup Finals, as well as other, lower order, though major international, sports events such as the Winter Olympics, the UEFA football championships, the Commonwealth Games and Track and Field World Championships. In addition, major events such as the World Cups for rugby union and cricket, and the annual Six Nations Championships in rugby, are also thought to contribute in varying degrees to social and economic well-being and development in Europe. The main objective of this article is to critically reflect on the legacies for the imagined community of Europe associated with MSE/SME, and in particular the UEFA football championships. Although consideration will be given to material legacies the article focuses mainly on the representational legacies – how Europe as a whole is represented and how participant football nations are represented – in connection with the second largest football spectacle in the world. The article thus seeks to engage with debates about the idea of Europe and European culture via consideration of European football.

Introduction

Just as modern competitive sport and large-scale sport events were developed in line with the logic of capitalist modernity, sports mega-events and global sport culture are central to late modern capitalist societies. They provide cultural resources for reflecting upon identity and enacting agency, and more generally, for the construction of 'a meaningful social life in relation to a changing societal environment that has the potential to destabilze and threaten these things'.[1] Sports mega-events are important elements in the orientation of nations to international or global society. Hence sport, here in its mega-event form, comes to be an increasingly central, rather than peripheral, element of urban (post-) modernity.

One of the most powerful discursive resources utilized to frame sports mega-events in the past two decades has been that of 'legacy'. As concerns have persisted over the material consequences and impacts of hosting large-scale sports events, what might be called 'legacy talk' has been increasingly incorporated into the validation of the sports mega-event by organizers. Legacies – both material and symbolic – have thus become the battlefield on which boosters and sceptics engage in semiotic struggle. As issues such as the environmental consequences of sports mega-events have emerged to challenge mega-event proponents, legacy has mutated from a concern with more material outcomes into a quest for more representational and sustainable results. The UEFA Football Championship is no exception to this shift as we will see. In addition the development of the European Championship in football parallels the development of a European economic 'common market' and political union over the past 45 years and as such also has representational implications for European identities.

In reflecting on these developments, this article has three main objectives. First, it outlines the social (economic, political and cultural) significance of the Union of European Football Associations (UEFA) European Football Championships (EURO™, but hereafter 'Euro') as one of the most significant sports mega-events.[2] Second, it details recent developments in the Euro football competition from 1996 to 2008 as part of what Anthony King refers to as the 'European ritual'. Third, it suggests that even in the midst of the changes that have occurred, such as the increased commercialization and global media presence of the tournament, the phenomenological dimensions of the Euro remain in need of consideration. Before this we briefly discuss the growth of the attraction, and discourse about the legacies, of sports mega-events, especially in Europe.

The legacies of sports mega-events

The aftermath or repercussions of sports mega-events today are often discussed in terms of their 'legacies'. Yet legacy is a warm word, sounding positive, whereas if we consider the word 'outcomes' it is a more neutral word, permitting the discovery of both negative and positive outcomes. In addition, outcomes can be tangible and material or intangible and symbolic. Economists and urban planners have tended to focus their research attention on the former, whereas sociologists, political scientists and social geographers have been more interested in the intangible, symbolic and representational outcomes.[3] In the case of the Euro competition, some of these are the representation of the hosts, the competing football teams and the overall idea of Europe as an imagined community that is produced. As the largest European-wide sports competition, the focus here then is on the social constructedness of social solidarities, the possibilities for promotion and resistance, uniting and dividing people, in the space and symbolic realm of football in Europe.

In this respect, it is useful to draw on the ideas of social geographers such as McNeill who focuses on Europeanization as a social construction and in flow. Like Appadurai,[4] he recognizes that there are economic, technological, financial, ethnic and image mobilities that help construct the contemporary social 'scape'. As a movement in process it can be pushed forward and also resisted. Europe is invented symbolically through flags and anthems, educational policies, the issuing of passports, the currency, food and different forms of popular culture, such as sport and music.[5]

While this mobility is occurring, however, 'the national' continues to operate at the everyday level according to socially recognized routines. These include popular competences, embodied habits and synchronized enactions; everyday ways of living and assumptions that become embodied and part of people's habitus.[6] For many (mostly, but not exclusively, men) the European football ritual fits in with this routinization of everyday life.

Through this, and the mediation of football, there is stereotyping, the confusion of bodily performances with physical traits, and the comparing of styles of play in sport with national economic performance. Because football is where an organic European identity both exists and where rivalries among near neighbours are heightened, it unites and divides. As McNeill states: 'national identity becomes more focused at times when collective European activity takes place'.[7] European integration thus enhances the symbolic identity of the nation-state, although it is in cities, especially capital cities (of regions and provinces as well as nations), with leading football club teams, that much of this takes place.

The European ritual: football in the new Europe

At the simplest level, the answer to the question 'what is European about the Euro football competition?' is that the Euro is European because it is only intended for football associations that are members of UEFA, the international non-governmental organization (INGO) that regulates football in Europe. This means that, by definition, only European football associations can enter. Regulations also dictate that only member associations of UEFA (or combinations of them) can bid to host the tournament finals. But this simple set of answers needs to be qualified. Regulations concerning which football associations can be members have altered over time. The number of member associations has expanded from just over 30 to 53 since the early 1990s with the collapse of the Soviet Union. There has also been a move in recent years to accept co-hosting bids – and three of these have been successful.[8]

A more complex answer to the question about the role of football in generating European identity leads us to refer to recent writings about the Europeanization of Europe through football and other UEFA competitions as well as the Euro. Anthony King argues that football is a public ritual in contemporary European culture through which emergent social solidarities and new economic networks can come about. The sport dominates the lives of many Europeans. This change has happened since the 1990s as the dominance of the free market has changed European society from an international order of nation-states to a transnational regime in which cities and regions can become more prominent.[9]

The growing significance of big city football clubs in Europe has not yet 'undermined the relevance of international football' in people's lives. Transnationalism has strengthened rather than weakened the national team, and led to improved international experience for players and the acceptance of foreign managers as coaches of club sides and national teams. But King suggests that in the future as the 'transnational regime becomes more established, club football, ...will become relatively more important in relation to the international game than it has been in the past'.[10] In this context, we can now turn to a brief examination of the material and representational legacies of the four championships held between 1996 and 2008.

From Euro '96 to EURO 2008™

As we have suggested, there have broadly been two types of analysis of 'legacies'. One has tended to focus on the impacts or outcomes of the event for *material* development (economic, technological, urban infrastructure) and taken a managerial, marketing or administrative and policy approach. The other has tended to look at the *ideologies* represented by media representations of the locations and actors involved – especially the fans, athletes or teams – and the relationship of these to national identities. There are close connections between the two foci, for example, forging points of identification with media audiences assists in the reach, retention, response and thus overall expansion of audience involvement. The role of the mass media in varied forms is central to making sport and any sports event matter significantly. Hence there is a cultural economy of sports mega-events that deals with the materiality of representational images and the representations of material spaces. In this section, brief consideration is given to studies of both material and representational legacies – how Europe as a whole has been represented and how participant football nations have been represented – in connection with the past four editions of second largest football spectacle in the world.

Euro '96 was the first major tournament held in the United Kingdom since the 1966 Football World Cup and the first European Championships to use the 'Euro' abbreviated name.[11] There was considerable pressure therefore to demonstrate national hosting and organizing capability, especially in a sport that had seen England club sides banned from European competitions as a result of crowd disorder in the previous decade. Marketed as the tournament when 'Football Comes Home', Euro '96 was assisted by renewed public appreciation for the sport and investment including stadium rebuilding that followed the launch of the English Premier League in 1992. Boosted by a doubling of teams in the finals, previously held in Sweden in 1992, from 8 to 16, financially it was the most successful European championships tournament to date. From a two-week event in compact stadiums, the 1996 edition featured 31 matches across three weeks in some of Europe's most well-known, largest and most recently refurbished stadiums. Ticket sales, television and sponsorship revenues all added to a significant boost to the British economy according to a survey. Eleven official tournament sponsors – including Coca-Cola, McDonald's and Carlsberg, Canon, MasterCard and Vauxhall (GM) – paid an estimated £3.5 million each to UEFA. UEFA obtained a record profit of £69 million, and dispersed £49 million in prize money.[12]

Euro '96 contributed to the shift in perception among corporations, politicians and policy makers away from viewing sports mega-events as loss making. Public money was being spent to stimulate consumption and generate externalities – or spillover economic effects – and civic boosters argued that the positives outweighed any negatives when it came to the reckoning of opportunity costs and benefits. Dobson *et al.* used an expenditure-based multiplier approach to calculate estimates of the economic impact of Euro '96 in the host cities and other parts of England. Their report lent support to the idea that the event provided a significant economic stimulus – through both increased sales of snack food (pizzas, lager) and casual clothing and footwear during the three week event and also through tax revenues – VAT, betting taxes and corporation taxes. The television audience was estimated at 445 million across 192 countries with a cumulative audience of 6.7 billion. Outside Europe, Asia was the next biggest audience with a cumulative total of 1.89 billion viewers. There was a 65% world-wide audience increase on the 1992 European championships.[13] Although such estimates have to be treated with caution, the event attracted considerable interest in the countries of those involved in the closing stages – half the population of England and one-third of the German population watched the semi-final encounter live on television.

The framing of the competition by the host countries' mass media – and especially the England–Germany match – has been analysed by several authors.[14] The broad conclusion, at least as far as the British print media were concerned, was that coverage of the tournament served more to divide than to unite Europe.[15] These authors suggest that the specific local or national context is important for shaping the mediation of any event. In this case, concerns about national decline, fragmentation and moves toward greater European integration perceived as a threat were uppermost in the coverage of the event in most British national daily newspapers. In relationship to televised coverage of Euro '96 it was also found that match commentary and pre- and post-match comment tended toward the establishment of English identity over British/European identity. Sports media discourses thus reinforced both invented traditions and encouraged the affirmation of particular national identities. This conclusion has also been reached in cross-national studies of football writing in other European countries.[16] What happened when an event was co-hosted, as was the case with the next European Championship in 2000?

For Euro 2000, held between June 10 and July 2, 2000, Belgium and the Netherlands, two of the 'low countries', acted as co-hosts for the 'party' for the first time. On the back of the growth of global interest in the event, sponsorship rights doubled in value and 12 corporations paid £7 million each for official status.[17] Television rights were sold for £1.6 billion in Europe alone, and it provided eight European countries with their highest television viewing audiences of the year.[18] With such an increased televisual presence and interest in the tournament it is perhaps not surprising that image-making and awareness generation were fundamental aspects of the co-hosts' marketing strategies. In the Netherlands, for example, the four host cities – Amsterdam, Arnhem, Eindhoven and Rotterdam – all sought to increase knowledge of their location among viewers and visiting fans alike. According to Oldenboom, however, who undertook a survey of awareness in five other European countries – France, Germany, the UK, Italy and Spain – such attempts to promote awareness tended to be short-lived, especially if the national teams were no longer involved in the tournament.[19]

Once again England played Germany – with England winning on this occasion – and this produced further academic analysis of the meaning of the event in the UK. Following close textual analysis of the match held in Charleroi, Belgium on June 17, 2000, Bishop and Jaworski concluded that the nation was treated as a 'monolith' in commentary and media discourse generally.[20] The match was also framed by conflict between English and German supporters in Charleroi and Brussels in the build up to the game. Material legacies may be more long-lasting than representational ones, but they also have to contend with the maintenance of images of nations through stereotyping and prevailing media discourses.

For the next championships, Euro 2004™, held in Portugal, there were ten new or refurbished venues built in eight cities at a cost of over €600 million. Security costs reached €40 million with €16.5 million spent on new equipment for the Portuguese police forces. In total, the Portuguese government estimate for running the tournament was €4 billion, only a small fraction of which they planned to get back in return.[21] The tournament presented a great challenge to the host nation's physical and human resources, its logistics and infrastructure. It also placed Portugal at the centre of the world's media stage for over a month in June and July 2004. As Boyle and Monteiro showed in their analysis of print media coverage of Euro 2004™, for Portugal, as for other smaller European countries, media discourses both within and outside the country often equate sporting success with political and economic status. Hence the 'tournament becomes a discursive vehicle for a display of performance. Not simply the national team's performance, but also that of the nation'. National media can thus inflect and represent international media events through national frames of reference.[22] In so doing, the 'global game' of football can become an ideological vehicle for the retelling of national narratives about contemporary societies.

Commercially, Euro 2004™ marked the most overt use of the trademark symbol in association with the event. The number of sponsors was reduced to eight – JVC, Canon, Hyundai, T-Mobile, alongside Coca-Cola, Carlsberg, MasterCard and McDonald's – but each paid an estimated £15 million for the rights – twice the amount for Euro 2000. Hence in three successive editions of the competition total official sponsorship revenues had risen from less than £40 million to £84 million and then £120 million. Coca-Cola sponsored its fifth consecutive European Football Championship as it sought to retain its close relationship with the game and fend off the interests of rival Pepsi-Cola, that had signed up several football superstars, such as David Beckham, to appear in global advertisements endorsing its product.[23] For the first time, UEFA also secured an agreement in 2002 with sponsors Carlsberg and McDonald's for two championships in advance (2004 and 2008). Under the terms of its deal, Coca-Cola would have perimeter fence advertisements for all 31 matches, broadcast sponsorship, commercial airtime rights and the ability to run consumer ticket promotions. The commercialization of football as a global 'cash cow' was most noticeable in this tournament.

The most recent tournament, EURO 2008™, staged between June 7 and 27, saw Austria and Switzerland attempt to produce the first 'green' football mega-event based on sustainable practices. Euro 2008 SA, a 100% subsidiary of UEFA, was in charge of the overall organization of the finals. The total costs involved amounted to €600 million – including €184 million to participants, €2.2 million support for non-profit projects and a €234 million operating budget. According to the *Sustainability Report* total revenues were €1.3 billion and so the residue will be used to develop European football in its 53 member associations over the years up to 2012. The federal government in Austria spent €133 million, before security costs, to build the stadium infrastructure, transportation and other associated projects including cultural and art events. Initial studies of expenditure suggest that the finals generated €286 million from visitors. In Switzerland, €113.8 million was budgeted for the staging of EURO 2008™, including security, by federal government, cantons and host cities.[24] At the time of writing, analysis of the economic effects of the tournament is still being conducted.

In line with the European Union (EU) and the domestic policies of the two host countries, it was the first European Football Championships to incorporate a sustainability strategy from the outset. Initiatives such as the 'kombi-ticket' – a match ticket functioning also as a free ticket for travelling to and from matches anywhere between Geneva and Vienna on public transport, that was partly funded with €5 million from the operating budget – the use of returnable cups in stadiums, the use of green-sourced electricity and the introduction of an Eco-Management and Audit Scheme (EMAS) all added up to producing one of the most environmentally friendly mega-events ever staged.

Similar to the co-hosts of Euro 2000, a major consideration of Austria and Switzerland in 2008 was to produce an event that, although it might only have short-term positive economic impacts, via tourism and the creation of a few new jobs for example, would have intangible effects on awareness and imagery of the host cities and countries. As the *Final Report* of the Swiss Tourism Agency noted, 'Switzerland: Discover the Plus', the national marketing sub-project associated with EURO™ 2008 aimed 'To present Switzerland as a pleasant, safe, modern country, open to the world. To strengthen the Swiss brand and the development and awareness of, and sympathy for Switzerland, its people and products. To ensure that Switzerland is considered as THE event-venue country'.[25] According to a study of the likely economic impact of the event conducted for UEFA and the Swiss football association in 2004 'Much more important and decisive is the end effect of *contented visitors* recommending Swiss vacations to their friends'.[26] Hence the material gains of co-hosting were mainly being assessed in terms of the representational legacies.

Sport signifiers: from place to consumer identity

As we noted earlier, the growth of the Euro tournament from 1996 to 2008 has taken place against a changing economic, political, social and cultural context. Sport was long believed to be a vehicle for the creation and maintenance of collective identities, especially around the local (city or town), the region (county, province or state) and the national (nation-state).[27] When the nation-state as the main form of collective identity is challenged globally and locally – by supra- and sub-national forces – the role of sport changes. David Whitson has outlined the way in which consumer identities, rather than place identities, have been naturalized through association with sport in late twentieth-century capitalist consumer culture. Sport contributes through its transnational appeal and creates the basis for strong consumer identities.[28] The mass media creates more cosmopolitan forms of belonging by projecting sport and elite athletes as commodities.[29] The Euro and UEFA's club-based tournament, the UEFA Champions League (UCL), are at the forefront of this globalizing process.

Levermore and Millward have investigated how this process might be impacting on regional, European, identities. They suggest we should distinguish between 'identity' – an official or at least formal sense of collective belonging based on territory – and clusters of 'belonging' – a more informal, multilayered 'transversal' identification. They ask to what extent might a sense of identity and/or belonging to Europe be developing through sport?[30] A pan-European identity might develop that replaces national identity or at least complements national identity as a significant collective identity. They argue that whereas football offers regionalist challenges to the nation-state territorialized collective, identity is challenged by other 'transversal interactions'. People can share belongingness across regions. The manufacture of European identity has been seen as a requirement since the formation of the EU and sport might play a role in unifying identities, through transversal networks and informal interactions of European peoples.

Official, institutional, attempts to create a European identity have stemmed from organizations such as the EU, the Council of Europe and sports organizations such as UEFA and the European Olympic Committees. Delanty suggests that four main symbols of European identity have been produced by the EU: the € (euro) common currency; cultural policies; scientific and educational policies; and flags, anthems and other collective devices. Sport figures in the last three of these especially – in statements, declarations, articles, documents and workshops held; in the education policy of the EU; and the 'flagging' of Europe at certain sports events.[31] In addition, the 'Europeanization' of elite European football has been stimulated through intervention into the economics of the sport – over competition (especially broadcasting rights) and employment (the famous 'Bosman' case) – and social affairs concerning such matters as crowd disorder (football hooliganism).

Yet deliberate, official, attempts to produce European identities generate scepticism and potential resistance. Hence unofficial, informal and transnational interactions (sometimes mediated via the Internet) may be in a better position to shape transversal dimensions of 'belonging' to Europe. Following Castells' theory of network society, cities may act as the key nodes in this.[32] In football, the G14, an interest group for 14, then 18, elite professional football clubs, played a role as one of the key nodes in the formation of European society from 1998/2000 until 2008, when it was disbanded to be replaced by the European Club Association, ECA. Of course, the G14 only applied to clubs in a small number of the 53 football associations in UEFA – England, France, Germany, Italy, the Netherlands, Portugal and Spain – but these included the big five leagues in club football (the Netherlands and Portugal being the exceptions). Although a European consciousness may exist here, among the fans of these elite clubs, it might be considered that the consciousness is lessened in other countries and among fans in these countries that are not part of the 'elite'.[33] Events such as the European Football Championship may show that 'whilst many supporters applaud players with different European nationalities when playing for "their" club, when the same players put on a national shirt, our everyday heroes are suddenly enemies again'.[34]

From a survey of web-based comments made by supporters of two G14 clubs – Liverpool and Arsenal fans – at the time of Euro 2004 Levermore and Millward noted that 'leanings toward a European consciousness continued'. In addition, fans exhibited 'intra-national xenophobia' – especially against players with elite clubs of the same nation. Levermore and Millward suggest that although football does not create a standard, tangible, European identity, UEFA competitions do create 'identification or consciousness which transcend national boundaries'.[35] How far can this go? Sport is effectively subject to the principle of subsidiarity in the EU – it is a matter for member states. Hence at present without the ratification of the Lisbon Treaty, the EU can only contribute to debates about sport and offer statements of encouragement, rather than direct it.[36] Concerns over the possible creation of an EU superstate emerge when it appears that deliberate attempts are being made to forge identities. European consciousness is different from European identity. Sport provides the basis for both reinforcing senses of belonging and also undermining, through eroding or resisting, collective identification. The relationship between the EU and sport therefore is seen as an ongoing and incomplete project.[37]

Questioning the sustainability of the Euro competition

Arguably the UCL now overshadows all other club competitions in Europe. This competition enriches the wealthy clubs and hands them more resources (direct and indirect via enhanced sponsorship and promotional opportunities) with which to dominate domestic leagues. Western European teams tend to dominate the final stages of the competition. National team football thus takes second place to club football, and although this may not have always been the case, elite athlete mobility in Europe has impacted on football playing styles, standards and the leagues, and arguably also on national team performance. Satellite TV, the changed format of the UCL and the effects of the Bosman ruling in 1995 on domestic competitions have also contributed to football's changing environment not just in Europe, but also around the world. These developments have tended to assist in the concentration of football and economic power and wealth with a handful of clubs in the main European national leagues – the big 5 and the 'G14'. In this context, has the Euro competition, from 1996 to 2008, been (and looking forward to 2012 and beyond, is it likely to be) a success for the host countries and cities, the people of the host countries and cities, or mainly economic and cultural elites? It is possible to respond in the negative to this question at the economic level. The overestimation of benefits and the underestimation of (opportunity) costs underpin the rhetoric of sports and other cultural mega-events. But might it be possible to think at other levels – the social and representational – that legacies can be positive, and not just for elites?

It may be suggested that sports and other international competitions and the proximity they encourage do not simply produce automatic unified national subjectivities via stereotyping, although these are widely conveyed in the print and broadcast media. Instead, there may be more interpretive and imaginative readings that can be made. Football is an attraction valued highly by men, even if some women will respond to the events, but so too will social class, 'race', ethnicity and generation impact on the readings that people take from the events in Austria and Switzerland in 2008. Despite widely promoted mythologies, especially in the case of sport and football in particular, of war and conflict, other readings are possible. As we have seen in a series of articles focusing on the media representations of England, Germany and other European nations during the Euro '96 tournament, it has been suggested that European integration at the political level is outpacing European integration at the emotional level. Anti-Europeanism in the British press, in particular, was based upon two features: nostalgia (for a golden age, in terms of political and economic as well as sporting power); and an ethnic assertiveness and/or defensiveness with respect to other European countries. As Whannel suggests, however, it is possible to analyse the same data with a reading allowing for a greater degree of ambiguity, contradiction and potentially more positive conclusions about competitions such as the Euro.[38]

There are three ways, Whannel suggests, that this can be understood. First, constructions of nationalisms – particularly in the British press about Germany – depict similarities as well as differences. There are some desirable qualities about the stereotypes – for example, what is wrong with German efficiency? Second, if we accept that much of the media – print tabloids especially – operate according to certain postmodern conventions that forefront irony, it is possible to read playfulness into the stereotyping. This often takes the form of teasing, for example, about particular styles of dress and music, and teasing suggests greater closeness than distance. Third, and related, the print press articulates a particular humour which forges at least masculine solidarities.

This is not to deny that the construction of national sporting contests as the pinnacle of the sports landscape has been weakened – the growth of sport in consumer culture has ensured that sports stars enjoy enormous symbolic value and economic power, as do the most successful club sides. In their commodified and branded form, sports competitions and associations, clubs and individual athletes may undermine the primacy of the nation in (inter-)national sports competitions. Global mobility, the circulation of media images, often associated with commercial endorsements, has assisted in the commodification of sport as a lifestyle. The growth of the 'global sport–media–tourism complex' as John Nauright refers to it, also leads in some respect to greater secrecy and lack of transparency on the part of the organizations involved.[39]

The use of the phrase 'Expect Emotions' as the slogan for UEFA EURO 2008™ reminds us 'the systematic engineering of affect has become central to the political life of Euro-American cities'.[40] As Bennett, with respect to Australian cities, and more recently Whitson, with respect to Canada, have suggested staging (sports mega-) events is as much about engineering the emotions of the local populations as welcoming foreign visitors.[41] I agree with Thrift that although there has been some attempt to develop a sociology of emotions in recent years, as an analytic device 'affect' is undeveloped. Elsewhere Thrift suggests that cities can be considered as 'emotional knots'. Fear sells and there is a market in anxiety over many urban circumstances. Rather than focusing on the risks (hooliganism, street crowd disorder, petty criminality, etc.) associated with sports mega-events, we should recognize as Thrift suggests that a certain amount of dislike of one's fellow citizens is inescapable. Sociality is not the same as liking others, but it can be based on a certain amount of conviviality.[42]

Conclusion

Mega-events are short-life events with long-life pre- and post-event social dimensions, not least because of their scale, their occupation and maintenance of a time cycle and their impacts (whether conceived of as positive or negative). As sports mega-events have become global media events they have taken priority over World's Fairs or Expos as a result. In the past, much attention has been focused on the structural impacts of sports mega-events. Following improvements in global mediation, corporations use sports mega-events to leverage business opportunities more than ever before, and this neatly sums up some major criticisms of them. Consumer identities and consumer spaces are produced by these trademarked events. At the same time, European-wide involvement in football, sport, culture and (pop) music events runs across north–south, old–new–aspirant divisions in European nations. There are flows and mobilities of people and non-human entities. Of course, there are risks – of civil order/disorder, internal/outward image projection, as well as the costs/benefits. But in the midst of this new European social identities – interlinked through social class, gender, ethnic, religious and national differences – may be produced, resisted and sustained. Roche draws attention to these phenomenological dimensions of mega-events. In particular, he looks at the role of 'megas' in providing time-structuring resources – both interpersonal and public – and suggests that this is one of the main reasons for their popularity, at least among those who live in the cities and places that host them – the 'once in a lifetime' opportunity.[43] Roche argues that mega-events are memorable and popular because they mark time between generations and thus link the everyday life world (micro) with the meso and macro social spheres. They are 'a special kind of time-structuring institution in modernity'.[44]

Cashman suggests that memory regarding sports mega-events can take three forms – individual or private memory, spontaneous collective memory and cultivated public memory. This begs questions about who does the sustaining of memory – at the grass-roots, citizens, the media or politicians – and for what ends? There can be a tendency when recalling events toward what he calls sports mega-event 'reductionism'. Here memories are reduced to the highlights – 'a few events which are repeatedly mentioned in public discourse' – and usually only the official achievements.[45] Is it possible that UEFA also reduces the Euro tournament to these key events or will it be possible to go beyond these official accounts?

This article has outlined the social significance of the UEFA Football Championships as one of the most significant sports mega-events. In particular, it has detailed developments in the Euro competition from 1996 to 2008 in terms of material and representational legacies. It has suggested that even in the midst of the vastly increased commercialization and global media presence of the tournament, the representational dimensions of the Euro remain an important consideration. 'Legacy talk' has been increasingly incorporated into the validation of the event by organizers, as it has by organizers of all other sports mega-events. Legacies have thus become the battlefield on which boosters and sceptics engage in semiotic struggle. Future research will therefore need to examine the discursive resources utilized in more detail.

Notes

1. Roche, *Mega-Events and Modernity*, 225.
2. Some suggest that it is the third biggest sports event in the world. This claim is made for several other events and the debate about this is not discussed here in detail.
3. cf. Horne and Manzenreiter, 'Introduction to the Sociology of Sports Mega-Events'.
4. cf. Appadurai, *Modernity at Large*.
5. McNeill, *New Europe*, 41–3.
6. cf. Edensor, *National Identity*.
7. McNeill, *New Europe*, 43.
8. A joint 'Celtic' bid by the Republic of Ireland and Scotland failed to get beyond the first round of voting in 2002 when the hosts for the 2008 competition were decided; the same happened to Hungary and Croatia in 2007 when the decision was made about 2012. A joint Scotland–Wales bid to host the finals tournament in 2016 was withdrawn in 2008 owing to the credit crunch and the increasing number of stadiums required following UEFA's announcement of its expansion to 24 teams.
9. cf. King, *European Ritual*.
10. King, *European Ritual*, 246, 247.
11. cf. Dobson, Holliday, and Gratton, *Football Came Home*.
12. Gratton, Dobson, and Shibli, 'Economic Importance of Major Sports Events', 21.
13. Dobson, Holliday, and Gratton, *Football Came Home*, 10.
14. For example, Garland and Rowe, 'War Minus the Shooting?'; Maguire and Poulton, 'European Identity Politics in EURO 96'; Poulton, 'Mediated Patriot Games'.
15. Maguire and Poulton 'European Identity Politics in EURO 96', 27.
16. Crolley and Hand, *Football, Europe and the Press*, 161.
17. 'Costs Spiral as Sponsors Go Football Crazy', *The Guardian*, June 9, 2000.
18. 'Sponsors Will Win Euro 2004', *The Guardian*, June 7, 2004, 9.
19. cf. Oldenboom, 'Impact of the Broadcasting of Sports Events on the Image'.
20. cf. Bishop and Jaworski, '"We beat 'em"'.
21. 'Portugal May Win Euro 2004 But How Much Does It Stand to Lose?', *The Business*, June 13/14, 2004, 7.
22. Boyle and Monteiro, 'A Small Country with a Big Ambition', 225, 239.
23. 'Coca-Cola Invests in Euro 2004', *The Guardian*, May 20, 2002.
24. Federal Ministry, *UEFA EURO 2008™ Sustainability Report*, 24–6.
25. EURO 2008 *National Promotion, Final Report*, 8.
26. Rutter+Partner, *Economic Impact* , 11.
27. cf. Blain, Boyle, and O'Donnell, *Sport and National Identity*.
28. Whitson, 'Circuits of Promotion', 57–72; see also Whitson and Gruneau, 'The (Real) Integrated Circus'.
29. Whannel, *Media Sport Stars*; Maguire, *Global Sport*.
30. Levermore and Millward, 'Official Policies and Informal Transversal Networks', 147.
31. Delanty, 'Is There a European Identity?'
32. cf. Castells, *Network Society*.
33. Levermore and Millward, 'Official Policies and Informal Transversal Networks', 158.
34. Peter Preston, *The Guardian*, June 19, 2000, quoted in Levermore and Millward, 'Official Policies and Informal Transversal Networks', 162.
35. Levermore and Millward, 'Official Policies and Informal Transversal Networks', 153, 155.
36. For example, in the European Council's four-sentence 'Declaration on Sport' adopted in December 2008, which begins: 'The European Council recognises the importance of the values attached to sport, which are essential to European society' available online at http://ec.europa.eu/sport/news/news692_en.htm (accessed March 30, 2009).
37. cf. Henry, 'Sport, the Role of the EU and the Decline of the Nation-State?'.
38. Whannel, *Sport, Culture and Politics*, 175–85.
39. Nauright, 'Global Games', 1334.
40. Thrift, 'Intensities of Feeling', 1.
41. cf. Bennett, 'Shaping of Things to Come'; Whitson, 'Bringing the World to Canada'.

42. Thrift, 'But Malice Aforethought', 138, 145.
43. 'Innsbruck deputy mayor Christoph Platzgummer is hoping the Austrian city can make the most of a "once-in-a-lifetime" opportunity as it gears up to hosting three group games at UEFA EURO 2008™', 'Innsbruck aims to grab chance', uefa.com (accessed 15 February 2007).
44. Roche, 'Mega-Events, Time and Modernity', 102.
45. Cashman, *Bitter–Sweet Awakening*, 21–2, 25.

References

Appadurai, A. *Modernity at Large.* Minneapolis: University of Minnesota Press, 1996.

Bennett, T. 'The Shaping of Things to Come: Expo'88'. *Cultural Studies* 5 (1991): 30–51.

Bishop, H., and A. Jaworski. '"We beat 'em": Nationalism and the Hegemony of Homogeneity in the British Press Reportage of Germany versus England during Euro 2000'. *Discourse & Society* 14, 3 (2003): 243–71.

Blain, N., R. Boyle, and H. O'Donnell. *Sport and National Identity in the European Media.* Leicester: Leicester University Press, 1993.

Boyle, R., and C. Monteiro. 'A Small Country with a Big Ambition'. Representations of Portugal and England in Euro 2004 British and Portuguese Newspaper Coverage'. *European Journal of Communication* 20, 2 (2005): 223–44.

Cashman, R. *The Bitter–Sweet Awakening: The Legacy of the Sydney 2000 Olympic Games.* Petersham: Walla Walla Press, 2006.

Castells, M. *The Rise of the Network Society.* Oxford: Blackwell, 1996.

Crolley, L., and D. Hand. *Football, Europe and the Press.* London: Frank Cass, 2002.

Delanty, G. 'Is There a European Identity?' *Global Dialogue* 5 (2004): 76–86.

Dobson, N., S. Holliday and C. Gratton. *Football Came Home: The Economic Impact of Euro '96.* Sheffield: LIRC, 1997.

Edensor, T. *National Identity, Popular Culture and Everyday Life.* Oxford: Berg, 2002.

EURO 2008 National Promotion. *Final Report /Subproject 03. Location Marketing.* Zurich/Berne: EURO 2008 National Promotion, 2008.

Federal Ministry of Agriculture, Forestry, Environment and Water Management, Austria, and Federal Office for Spatial Development, Federal Office for the Environment, Federal Office of Sport, Switzerland. *UEFA EURO 2008™ Sustainability Report.* Berne and Vienna: Author, 2008.

Garland, J., and M. Rowe. 'War Minus the Shooting? Jingoism, the English Press, and Euro 96'. *Journal of Sport & Social Issues* 32, 1 (1999): 80–95.

Gratton, C., N. Dobson, and S. Shibli. 'The Economic Importance of Major Sports Events: a Case Study of Six Events'. *Managing Leisure* 5, 1 (2000): 17–28.

Henry, I. 'Sport, the Role of the EU and the Decline of the Nation-State?'. In *Sport and Society,* ed. B. Houlihan, 513–31. London: Sage, 2008.

Horne, J., and W. Manzenreiter. 'An Introduction to the Sociology of Sports Mega-Events'. *Sociological Review* 54, s2 (2006): 1–24.

King, A. *The European Ritual: Football in the New Europe.* Aldershot: Ashgate, 2003.

Levermore, R., and P. Millward. 'Official Policies and Informal Transversal Networks: Creating "Pan-European Identification" through Sport. *Sociological Review* 55, 1 (2007): 144–64.

McNeill, D. *New Europe: Imagined Spaces.* London: Arnold, 2004.

Maguire, J. *Global Sport.* Cambridge: Polity, 1999.

Maguire, J., and E. Poulton. 'European Identity Politics in EURO 96: Invented Traditions and National Habitus Codes'. *International Review for the Sociology of Sport* 34, 1 (1999): 17–29.

Nauright, J. 'Global Games'. *Third World Quarterly* 25, 7 (2004): 1325–36.

Oldenboom, E. 'The Impact of the Broadcasting of Sports Events on the Image and Awareness of Host Cities Abroad.' *Belgeo ZDB-Info* 2 (2008): 167–80.

Poulton, E. 'Mediated Patriot Games. The Construction and Representation of National Identities in the British Television Production of Euro '96'. *International Review for the Sociology of Sport* 39, 4 (2004): 437–55.

Roche, M. *Mega-Events and Modernity.* London: Routledge, 2000.

Roche, M. 'Mega-Events, Time and Modernity: On Time Structures in Global Society'. *Time & Society* 12, 1 (2003): 96–126.
Rutter+Partner. *Economic Impact of the UEFA EURO 2008™ in Switzerland.* Ruchlikon Magglingen: Bundesamt für Sport (BASPO), 2004.
Thrift, N. 'Intensities of Feeling: Towards a Spatial Politics of Affect'. *Geografiska Annaler Series B* 86, 1 (2004): 57–78.
Thrift, N. 'But Malice Aforethought: Cities and the Natural History of Hatred'. *Transactions of the Institute of British Geographers* 30 (2005): 133–50.
Whannel, G. *Media Sports Stars. Masculinities and Moralities.* London: Routledge, 2002.
Whannel, G. *Culture, Politics and Sport.* London: Routledge, 2008.
Whitson, D. 'Circuits of Promotion: Media, Marketing and the Globalization of Sport'. In *MediaSport,* ed. L. Wenner, 57–72. London: Routledge, 1998.
Whitson, D. 'Bringing the World to Canada: "The Periphery of the Centre"'. *Third World Quarterly* 25, 7 (2004): 1215–32.
Whitson, D., and R. Gruneau. 'The (Real) Integrated Circus: Political Economy, Popular Culture, and 'Major League' Sport'. In *Understanding Canada: Building on the New Canadian Political Economy,* ed. W. Clement, 359–85. Montreal: McGill-Queen's University Press, 1997.

The European stage for next-generation stars and fans: the Under-17 Championship 2009 in Germany

Christian Tagsold

Department of Japanese Studies, Heinrich Heine University Dusseldorf, Germany

UEFA's EURO is one of the biggest sport's mega-events in terms of media interest, numbers of spectators and economical impact. Since European championships for women's football, futsal or youth teams are standing in the shadow of EURO, they tend to be neglected when speaking about the influence of UEFA's competitions in shaping European identities and the future of sport's mega-events. Yet these tournaments can be surprisingly large and influential. Based on participant observation as a member of the Local Organizing Committee I describe how the UEFA U17 tried to instill a sense of 'Europeaness' in a region riddled by unemployment and a bad reputation for lingering xenophobia. UEFA's educational measures targeted the public as well as the youth players. But the players' hopes of starting a professional football career and the interference of clubs and scouts who want to built future human capital often lead to competing views of what education in this context could mean and achieve. Stage and backstage seem to contradict each other to a certain level. Both were in a sense reconciled by the attempts of German FA to use the tournament not only to attract new young football fans but to balance the budget. Economical logic overruled tensions between lofty ideals and down-to-earth efforts to create talent for the future.

Introduction

The UEFA European Football Championship is one of the world's largest sports mega-events in terms of media interest, audience size and economic impact, but this is not the only championship hosted by UEFA (the Union of European Football Associations). In addition, UEFA organizes European championships for women's and youth football, as well as for futsal (a variant of association football played indoors). Because of the immense shadow cast by the European Championship, these other events tend to be neglected in discussions of UEFA competitions in shaping European identities and the future of sports mega-events. Despite this lack of interest, these tournaments can actually be remarkably large and influential. Their impact is dependent on variables like the success of a championship's hosting nation in a tournament, the presence of famous players on the field, and the willingness of the hosting nation's football association to invest time and money in generating interest; but if these stars align, significant crowds are drawn, sponsors' interest is attracted, and television stations begin broadcasting games live.

UEFA's Under-17 Championship 2009 is a good example of an event that is both easily ignored and significant at the same time. Held that year in eastern Germany, the tournament drew over 70,000 spectators and was broadcast live by Eurosport, with the final between Germany and the Netherlands broadcast by German state-owned broadcaster ARD, as well. This tournament is contested every year due to the fact that most teams consist only of their country's best 16-year-old players – it is very rare that a highly talented younger player makes it onto a national squad. The DFB (the German football association) is often the host of the various youth championships because German football is relatively well off in financial terms and because, as one of the world's football powerhouses, it has a vested interest in developing younger players. This year's tournament cost 1.8 million euros, a small sum compared to a mega-event like the European Championship or the World Cup, but a major investment nonetheless. With Germany defeating the Netherlands in the final, however, and securing the top position among the eight competing national teams, the DFB's money was surely well invested.

This paper is based on my experience as a member of the Organizing Committee of the UEFA Under-17 Championship, where I was a team liaison officer (TLO) for the English team. This experience allowed me to analyze internal workings of the tournament not normally accessible to participant observation. The role of TLO is one I have previously filled for the Japanese team at the 2006 FIFA World Cup as well as on other occasions.[1] I was therefore able to compare the organization of the U17 and the delegations' expectations, as well as journalist' focus, and work on location with those of full-scale sports mega-events.

In this sense, this paper follows the ethnographic imperative as defined by John MacAloon over two decades ago but still not often adhered to.[2] Or to quote Guilanotti who transferred MacAloon's imperative from Olympic studies to football: 'Too often social researchers on football leave themselves open to the accusation of "armchair theorizing". They draw upon newspaper reports or other poor secondary sources rather than assemble data through empirical research.'[3] Participant observation, the major method of ethnographic fieldwork, is excellently suited to avoid 'armchair theorizing'. However, because the Under-17 Championship was a rather small tournament with a very limited scope of time, ethnographic research connected to it was also necessarily limited and had to be enhanced by an analysis of media surrounding the event. This media analysis was also enriched by my field research – without an understanding of the context in which media reports of an event are generated, a great deal of meaning can be lost. In this case, an important fact that became clear to me was that there was only a very limited number of journalists present at the tournament, meaning that all news stories about the event were based on the reports of only these few observers.

Though the tournament was unquestionably a success for the DFB, I will address questions that nonetheless remain regarding the event's intended meaning. Because of the relatively small size of the Under-17 Championship, it is interesting to ask what sort of narrative it produces. There are two such narratives that stand out, and a third that is significant in its absence. The first such was the UEFA's campaign against racism, joined by the DFB and the *Bundeszentrale für Politische Bildung* (National Center for Political Education).[4] Although this campaign was very successful overall, it was met with a certain amount of ambivalence from the spectators of the tournament. This was in part due to the difficulty of translating the term 'anti-racism' into German – which points to underlying problems of nationhood and multi-culturalism in Germany.[5] The second narrative was the presentation of the Under-17 Championship by the media, UEFA, the DFB and participants as a stage for talents or great stars of the future. This is not surprising given that many of the young players are expected to become professional football players at some point. However, the fact that not all players – not even the majority of Under-17 competitors – will actually play at the highest level in the future resulted in an ambivalent reaction to this narrative on the part of players and delegation members. The third narrative, the one made conspicuous by its absence, was a message of European identity. The reasons for this absence become clearer once the background of the tournament's financing is examined. I will therefore discuss how the DFB, as the tournament's organizing body, balanced the event's costs and benefits.

Anti-racism and the East

The organizers of the UEFA Under-17 Championship attempted to use this tournament to convey educational messages even more so than typical football mega-events. The European Championship and the UEFA Champions League also frequently feature campaigns promoting fairness, anti-racism, or to other similar ends. However, these are often eclipsed by advertising, giving the impression that the campaigns are only minor afterthoughts employed to camouflage the events' commercial nature. Because the Under-17 Championship is primarily a tournament for young players and spectators (dedicated fans make up only a small part of these), there is a much stronger focus on education. In 2009, the main message was anti-racism. For many years, racism has disturbed the atmosphere of football all over Europe; but as Michael Fanizadeh and Markus Pinter have pointed out, it is only in the last decade that the sport's governing associations have come to see it as their responsibility to fight this phenomenon.[6] Pressured by NGOs and other diverse grassroots campaigns, various programs have been created by FIFA, UEFA and national FAs to fight racism on and off the pitch. In the case of the Under-17 Championship, UEFA's efforts were supported extensively by the DFB and the Bundeszentrale. Since most of the fans were of school age, the Under-17 Championship offered a good opportunity for these institutions to connect to the youth.

The tournament was held in former East Germany, in the three states of Saxony, Saxony-Anhalt and Thuringia. They have been plagued by unemployment and economic troubles in the two decades since the German reunification. The region has a strong tradition of football, but a lack of funds has resulted in the relegation of local clubs to lower leagues. Additionally, former Eastern Germany seems to have had many more problems with neo-Nazism in the last two decades than the better-off former Western states, with the ultra-right wing NPD (German National Party) gaining ground in recent elections and especially increasing its support among the youth. This has had a significant impact on football in the region. The city of Jena, where the tournament's organization was based and where two of the preliminary matches were held, is the home of Carl-Zeiss Jena, a football team that is regularly affected by racist sentiments. Like Tottenham Hotspur, Carl-Zeiss Jena – a very successful club before reunification – is dispraised as a Jewish team by rival fans, and 'Juden Jena' (Jews Jena) is often chanted at its matches.[7] Such problems made the anti-racism campaign seem tailor-made for the region, and the Bundeszentrale and the DFB were as happy to utilize the platform offered by the Under-17 Championship as regional football officials were to have the support of the national and international institutions in combating the problem.

One full year in advance of the tournament and with the help of the Bundeszentrale, the DFB started a campaign in which schools were offered materials to teach their pupils about football and anti-racism, and were invited to take part in various competitions. The campaign was a success in that many regional schools took part. Equally important to the DFB, the campaign helped to create an environment in which schools would see Under-17 Championship matches as a worthwhile destination for school sponsored excursions. This resulted in the tournament stadiums generally being well filled – something that have been expected at the German team's matches in any case, but even other matches had crowds reaching into the thousands. To make the events as attractive as possible to youth, some kick-offs were scheduled for mornings at 11 o'clock to coordinate with the school day, which in Germany generally does not extend past lunchtime. Additionally, schools were offered free or discounted tickets and many took the chance to combine seeing the next generation of professional football players with lessons on anti-racism. The success of this promotion can be seen in the example of the first match between England and the Netherlands, at which approximately 50 of the 5,000 spectators had purchased their tickets at the normal price. Attracting large numbers of the area's youth was not only important in order to make the educational campaigns a success, but also to put crowds in the stands in order to create a festive atmosphere for Eurosport, which broadcast nine of the sixteen matches.

UEFA's campaign against racism caused interesting problems and ambivalences. The German word for 'anti-racism', 'Antirassismus', has long been mainly used by the left. The German Ministry of the Interior has even officially advanced the view that the concept of 'Antirassismus' is one of the main focuses of extreme leftists.[8] Though the term 'Rassismus' (racism) is in general use, official and mainstream political language uses the terms 'Integration' and 'Fremdenfeindlichkeit' (xenophobia) when discussing problems related to racism. 'Fremdenfeindlichkeit' has especially problematic undertones in this context, since its use in German implies that it is foreigners (Fremde) who are targeted by racists. This semantically excludes black Germans from their status as being German. Through anti-racist programs sponsored by the EU, FIFA and UEFA, the word 'anti-racism' has been in wider use in recent years. In assessing the FIFA World Cup's campaign against racism, however, the German Minister of the Interior, Wolfgang Schäuble, preferred to use the words 'Integration' and 'Fremdenfeindlichkeit'.[9]

This use of words has even deeper implications. A study of PMP in cooperation with the Institute of Sport and Leisure University Loughborough commissioned by the EU has shown that there is an assumption of national homogeneity in Germany favoring measures of integration for migrants instead of promoting cultural diversity. For a long time, in fact, even integration was not on the agenda – the Germans were seen as ethnically homogenous. But today there is no way denying that migrants are entitled to be valid part of society. Sport in this context is seen as 'vehicle for tackling problems of general social exclusion'.[10] Programs are set up to pave the way for migrants into German society but not to underline the value of diversity. This analysis fits very well in relation to observations of the Under-17 Championship.

The Under-17 Championship was an example of the increased acceptance of the term 'anti-racism' due to its connection with international sports-associations. Prior to matches, school children carried large flags bearing anti-racist messages into the stadium, and such messages were broadcast via the public address system as well; in these cases the German 'Antirassismus' was used rather than 'Fremdenfeindlichkeit' or 'Integration'. The Bundeszentrale used the term 'Antirassismus' in its own campaign as well, including a message from the agency's president in materials it and the DFB distributed to schools. In the same brochure however, the Minister of Families, Ursula von der Leyen, avoided using this term in the same context and spoke only of football's 'appeal uniting people'. Nevertheless, sport could very well help to change opinion on diversity in Germany from the obsession to integrate and assimilate.

Doubts within the tournament

While the anti-racism campaign was met with some ambivalence from without, the status of the Under-17 Championship as a stage for new talent was not questioned. From within the event, though, partially contradictory stakes were negotiated between players, UEFA, national federations and delegation staffs. For the players, the tournament was first and foremost an opportunity to improve their chances at a career in professional football – something that is still uncertain for all but a very few players at the age of sixteen. A few have already taken their first successful steps into professional football. England's captain, John Bostock, for example, has played in the UEFA Cup and is alleged to have cost Tottenham Hotspur one million pounds when he transferred to them from Crystal Palace. Another English player, Jonjo Shelvey, was a regular player with Charlton Athletic in England's second division. The vast majority of players, however, are playing in the youth squads of major European clubs, many of them for prestigious English powerhouses like FC Chelsea.

Former Under-17 Championships have produced stars like England's Wayne Rooney, Spain's Iker Casillas and Germany's Clemens Fritz, examples often emphasized by UEFA and the DFB during the event. Only a minority of players, though, will actually have highly successful professional careers, while most will either remain in the lower ranks of professional play or fail to establish a professional career altogether. Johann Harscoët has very vividly described how recruitment centers for young players set up by French professional football clubs work in this respect.[11] He comes to a much bleaker conclusion than Richard Guilianotti, who has concluded that similar centers set up by English clubs are driven by a holistic approach to developing social identities.[12] The English system of football-apprenticeship indeed educates young players on relevant topics for future careers, one example being in the area of nutrition. But it has been criticized for not fulfilling basic educational tasks.[13] For example an outlook on alternative career paths is rarely offered but would be extremely helpful, especially in light of the percentages of young players who are able to start a professional football career. According to Harscoët, only 3% to 10% of the young men who pass through recruitment centers in France establish a professional career, while the rest are left with insufficient education and often shattered dreams. In other words, even playing for the farm team of a powerhouse like Olympique Lyon, FC Liverpool or Chelsea, is far from being a guarantee for a professional career. Most young players will not make it into men's teams or even into lower-level professional teams. In some ways this situation resembles the observations of Andrew Zimbalist on college sports in the USA.[14] Young men are drawn into the realm of professional sports with the hope of achieving stardom, but most will not and only end up without the education they could have had if their career-planning had been more realistic and balanced.[15]

It seems that having made it into a national team by the age of 16 should surely be an indicator of better chances than one in ten. But even a player like Michael

Zepek – seen as one of the most promising talents ever and having played a record number of 58 matches for German national teams at the youth level – barely made it into the second league as an adult and is now, at his prime age of 29, playing in Germany's fourth league. Out of the 18 players who played for the German team at the 2002 Under-17 Championship in Sweden (now aged 24 or 25), only three have made it to the top German league – incidentally, all three play for the national team. In contrast, seven of the players no longer play professional football, defined in Germany as being in Leagues 1 to 3.[16] Of course, such statistics are not emphasized by UEFA, whose website focuses instead on 'golden players' of the past and the 'ten future stars from the 2009 finals.'

Because the players at the Under-17 Championship have such an uncertain future, the impression they make on club delegates and scouts is very important. To most of the young men, the rather wealthy atmosphere of such a tournament is also a new experience. A very impressed English player told me that he had never slept in such a nice hotel as the one he stayed in while in Jena, though the hotel's four stars would have been nothing special for a professional football player. In this respect the 16-year-olds are not different from other young men, a fact that is easily forgotten. Especially live broadcasts of the matches tend to distort impressions. Many within the tournament shared their impression with me that the players look much older and more professional when shown on the screen. The tournament created an atmosphere that led the players to feel that this tournament was very significant and might be an important step in their careers.

The downside of this atmosphere was the high pressure the players felt, causing some of them to occasionally stumble. I observed two cases of players suffering the effects of this pressure, with one player so angered at being replaced that he refused to speak to anyone for days and had to be treated by hastily summoned psychologists. The other player put his career chances into question after being slightly injured. Though the teams were relatively relaxed in general, there were moments of great tension.

The question of players' future careers had more twists to offer those accompanying the players. Despite efforts to form the young men by means of educational activities and rules of behavior, team staff members were not optimistic. One experienced delegation member told me that only a few of his former players would greet him after they had become successful. Most would simply ignore him and ask themselves, to quote one of my contacts, 'Who is this old asshole and what does he want here?' This made his efforts and those of the UEFA pedagogic seem ineffectual. He was not alone in harboring doubts. While not all delegation members had such a bleak outlook, some of those to whom I spoke questioned the entire event to some extent. Given that only two or three players of the 18 on their squad would ever be great successes, keeping them out of school and nourishing their ultimately unrealistic dreams seemed to them to be a high price to pay. When analyzed this way by delegation members, the whole tournament seems to create a lose-lose-situation: Either the players will not live up to the great expectations and lose the chance for a better life, since they spent too much of their youth pursuing football, or players will achieve their goals and start a professional career but turn into problematic characters. While both alternatives might be overstated by delegation members, one can see the basic dilemma. Neither option is fully satisfying for delegation members as educators.

There is another issue especially emphasized by English delegation members: They suspect that most clubs are not in favor of sending their players to the Under-17 national teams, due to inconvenient scheduling which interferes with team planning and/or the risk of players being injured or scouted by rival squads. FA staff believe the cause of this to be that clubs no longer care about national teams, or nations in general. Arsène Wenger of Arsenal London has been cited often by the FA staff as being an example of this problem. They feel that he withheld English players from the national team while allowing players from his native France to compete in the Under-17 Championship. This undermines the work of the FA, but also caused the delegation members to question national identity itself. By assuming that Wenger was treating their players differently from his own countrymen, FA staff tried to reconcile their knowledge of football as a market with the idea of national teams. This was after all the legitimation of FA's actions.

On the UEFA's side, everything seemed to run smoothly. The internal governance of the tournament seemed to be a simple reflection of its external appearance. One focus was on the education of respectful and fair future professional players. Each team was required to attend an anti-doping class given by two UEFA officials, warning players about food supplements and drugs and emphasizing each player's responsibility for anything found in their bodies. The issue of anti-doping measures at youth tournaments is a very complex one, made particularly difficult by the fact that though UEFA implies otherwise in such classes, youth players are not adults and thus cannot always be held legally responsible for their actions.

UEFA's lack of concern for ambivalences concerning the future hopes of the young players stood in contrast to the focus it brought to its anti-racism campaign, but the two attitudes are opposite faces of the same coin. Since the UEFA's official position is that all of the players have the chance to become future stars, there is no room for racism. The very concept of sport presupposes the 'equality of opportunity to compete', as pointed out by Allen Guttmann in his classic study *From Ritual to Record.*[17] Under such equality, talent will prevail and any doubts would only be a disturbance. The connection of anti-racism and talent was very present in Reinhold Yabo, the captain of the German Under-17 team and one of the team's three black players. The Under-17 Championship's advertising focused strongly on him and he was depicted on the tournament's official poster as a symbolic link between the two messages of anti-racism and talent.

European Championship between region and Europe

While anti-racism and the stage for talent were well promoted at the Under-17 Championship, there was noticeably less focus on the European Community. Though the Under-17 is a European tournament, its scope is much harder to assess than in the case of sports mega-events such as the UEFA European Football Championship. This seems to be in contradiction of the clear fact that the Under-17 Championship is a European tournament, as it is governed by UEFA, played by European teams and broadcast by Eurosport. The analysis of the event's range as well as the stakes of various institutions such as regional FAs, the DFB or UEFA, however, shows a more complicated picture. The European, national and regional scope less resembles the high-profile EURO than a large regional event. Persons regionally involved here easily outnumber those involved nationally or in Europe, a reverse situation to EURO. But the regional event does draw the interest of highly specialized and important persons in the field of football, such as club officials, FA officials and scouts – even if their absolute number is small. The Under-17 Championship is quite important to and for the functional elite of football.

The most intense coverage of the tournament came from local and regional newspapers. Journalists at press conferences were mainly from the states of former East Germany and interpreted the tournament in regional terms. The main focuses of these journalists were on issues of regional interest, such as the tournament's impact on football in eastern Germany, preparations and renovations at local stadiums, and the attitude of the area's inhabitants toward the competition. Another important focus was on the performance of the German team, especially on the role of Florian Trinks, a recent recruit to powerhouse Werder Bremen. He played a crucial role in the final, scoring the decisive goal against the Netherlands. Since he is from the region and has played for Carl Zeiss Jena, regional media were very interested in his performance.

National newspapers only made occasional reports of game results, and as the tournament approached its end they commented on the multi-ethnic German team, which was seen as a blueprint for future men's national squads and for the successful integration of diasporic groups in Germany. The influence of the English Premier League and its ability to draft young players from all over Europe was also discussed in some detail. This was due to the fact that Christopher Buchtmann, one of the stars of the German team, plays for FC Liverpool, and that Shkodran Mustafi announced that he would be leaving Hamburg SV and joining FC Everton. This transfer was reported at the national level and was even taken up by the *Bild Zeitung*, Germany's most widely read tabloid. The victory of the German team in the finals did get more recognition in national newspapers than youth tournaments normally get. The Internet played only a marginal role at the tournament, as only UEFA and the FAs published detailed reports online, and the intensity of coverage by other Internet sites was low compared to larger events. This was largely because the tournament coincided with the Champions League final and the final matches of major European leagues.

Stadium attendance consisted mostly of students from local schools. Only players' parents, scouts, and club and FA officials lent a European dimension to the crowds. Despite the largely local crowds, each team attracted supporters. England, for example, had about 50 fans from the area who cheered for the team even when it played against Germany. The area's small Turkish diaspora cheered for its team as well. After their final victory against England, members of the Turkish diaspora even organized a parade of cars through the town of Gotha, where the match was played. To this extent the tournament was a European phenomenon, even if it was simultaneously regional.

Media coverage on television was more complex and balanced. The regional state broadcaster MDR was most active in covering the event, starting at the draw in Leipzig. Eurosport broadcast nine of the sixteen matches live and thus turned the tournament into a truly European event, though audience rates were low – especially for matches starting at 11 o'clock. Despite this, such a widely accessible broadcast was surely a success for a youth tournament. National television jumped in when the German team proved to be highly competitive, and interviews with key German players were conducted, focusing again on the multi-ethnic character of the team and especially on Reinhold Yabo. The final in Magdeburg, a near sell-out with about 24,000 spectators, was broadcast live not only on Eurosport but also on German state television. As this match also started at 11 o'clock, it was no great sacrifice for the ARD to spend about two hours on a match of 16-year-olds. Even still, such media-interest proves that the tournament was of some national or even European interest but not a focus beyond the region it was hosted in.

While the nature of the attention paid to the tournament by the public and media characterizes it as a mostly regional event, other perspectives can also be considered. Aside from the matches between young European players, the tournament was very European in one important respect. FAs use events such as the Under-17 Championship to meet and communicate on all levels, both formally and informally, and while it is clear that team delegations came into contact with each other – especially the preliminary groups, which shared single hotels – interactions of higher ranking officials merit a closer look. Heads of delegations, in charge of a group of 18 players and eight or more officials, were less concerned with the daily routines of their teams than with communicating with other high-ranking officials. The best opportunities for this were at official dinners like the Under-17 Championship tournament dinner. This took place in a rustic old castle and hosted over 60 official guests with high-class catering brought in from Munich. As one of the DFB's vice-presidents put it at the official U17-dinner, 'Whenever I see well-dressed men who have brought lots of gifts with them I know it is a gathering of football officials.' Both the hosts as well as all of the guests had brought along expensive gifts for each other, the most valuable being of course reserved for top members of UEFA, DFB and head of delegations. Exchanging the gifts after the dinner gave ample opportunity to communicate matters of football. These symbolical gift exchanges – very much resembling those described in Marcel Mauss's classical study[18] – and the accompanying conversations concern the governance of European football. The importance of such meetings is clearly underlined by the high status of some of those acting as delegation heads or accompanying officials. The Swiss federation was headed by the president of that country's FA. The hosting German FA sent two of its vice-presidents and many other top officials. Additionally, UEFA was represented by Jim Boyce, chairman of the UEFA Youth and Amateur Football Committee and former head of the Northern Irish FA. Looking at such gatherings from the perspective of Sugden and Tomlinson's analysis of FIFA, they can be seen as part of the inner circles of football governance which undermine rational democratic and bureaucratic processes.[19] On the other hand, they constitute the basis for the exchange and mutual trust so important in international governance.

In another sense the tournament is much larger than European and expands into global realms. The UEFA campaign promoting anti-racism contains no specifically European messages. It rather addresses a global concern of soccer, one also reflected in FIFA campaigns. Additionally, the question of anti-racism is only on the agenda because Europe has been globally entangled for centuries. It is mainly black football players who are victims of racist attacks, though racism of course can and has turned against different minorities. In the case of Germany, Turkish, Eastern European, and Jewish players have also been among those most often attacked. Nevertheless, through focusing on players such as Reinhold Yabo, even the Under-17 Championship campaigns used blacks as symbols of the necessity of anti-racism. Since the phenomenon of blacks in Europe is mainly linked to colonialism, anti-racist campaigns are a symbol of awareness of global history and its consequences. Coming to terms with post-colonialism through sporting event campaigns for awareness is probably a rather European tradition.

Financing the tournament

Examining the finances of the Under-17 Championship makes it quite obvious that such a tournament cannot be classified as a sports mega-event. Similar to interest shown by the media, the investments demonstrate that the tournament was more regional than national or European. The Under-17 Championship had an impressive official start with the drawing for the two preliminary groups in Leipzig in the spring of 2009. Though an official informed me that drawings for other European youth championships are generally staged in hotel halls and accompanied by a PowerPoint presentation, the DFB used a professional stage with high-tech equipment in the town hall in Leipzig for this spectacle. After organizing the 2006 FIFA World Cup, the DFB's expectations for international tournaments had been set to a high standard. Some of the attending DFB officials complained that money was wasted by this and asked themselves whether a low-budget approach was not much more fitting for a youth tournament. After all, even the DFB had to restrict itself in spending money on the tournament; even for a relatively wealthy FA, the 1.8 million euros spent on the tournament is a sum that begs for cost-cutting. But the speech of Wolfgang Niersbach, DFB General Secretary, answered this criticism. Niersbach clearly pointed out that the tournament served as a measure to strengthen east German football and to make up for not having hosted more FIFA World Cup 2006 matches in the region. Only Leipzig had served as a venue at that point. The investment by the DFB can therefore be seen as more proof of the regional character of the tournament.

The venues for the Under-17 Championship made relatively high investments to host matches. Notwithstanding the fact that most stadiums saw only one game, some cities went to great length to be included in the match schedule. They added new roofs to the stands and brushed up changing rooms and functional spaces for media. Even if investments were not very high overall, they were substantial for a region that has been plagued by unemployment and low tax revenue for communalities. The three regional FAs of Saxony, Saxony-Anhalt and Thuringia also shared parts of the financial burden.

Ticket sales, typically a major source for financing the expenses of organizing committees at sports mega-events, were an insignificant factor due to the fact that most tickets were given away or sold to school children for two euros. Filling stadiums and educating new fans was deemed to be more important than trying to finance the tournament by ticket sales, as is usually the case. Selling tickets at a higher price would have probably not raised more money, since many spectators would have stayed away in an economically struggling region. In addition, offering the youth of the region a chance to see future stars and learn about anti-racism was deemed to be most important. Scouting tickets for club officials were free in any case. UEFA wanted to avoid mixed seating of scouts and official guests by handing out tickets for other sections of the stadium.

The organization of an UEFA tournament brings along with it many duties, including payment for hotels, transportation, etc. But compared to the FIFA World Cup 2006, UEFA's governance of the tournament was relatively unobtrusive. Yet this also proved less helpful in easing overall organization. The Local Organizing Committee, functioning as a temporary branch of the DFB, had more freedom than in the case of a sports mega-event. A basic framework of rules was applied, but UEFA sent only limited staff to eastern Germany, consisting mostly of freelance media specialists and administration staff. With the exception of Tim Boyce and three or four other officials, most of the staff were in their 20s and, like the players themselves, still in an educational process regarding major tournaments. Of the older members, two technical advisors stood out, including Holger Osieck, who has served technical advisors for the FIFA World Cup 2006 and is a standing member of the FIFA Technical Study Group. This clearly shows that though the tournament had only a slight European focus, it was important in scouting for the functional elites of UEFA.

The Ambivalences of the U17

In conclusion, to what extent can we characterize the Under-17 Championship as a truly European event? There was a strong framework integrating all activities, with the whole tournament placed in an educational context stressing UEFA's anti-racist goals. This in turn links to a strong European policy focus on non-discriminatory measures over the last years. In this sense, the Under-17 Championship is in line with many of the recommendations formulated in a report for the EU co-edited by PMP and the Institute of Sport and Leisure Policy Loughborough University. In transforming the tournament into an event for promoting anti-racism among students and thereby also among their teachers, a 'celebration of diversity'[20] was clearly enhanced. The German FA along with the Bundeszentrale used team captain Reinhold Yabo as the campaign's face and role model for the students. Additionally, 'anti-racism' – a term deemed problematic by German politicians but in line with EU policies – was widely used in the context of the tournament. The focus on young talent helped to promote the tournament and characterize it as well as football in general as an inclusive arena rewarding the best – regardless of personal background. The catch is that the slim chances of young players building a professional career due to fierce competition are simply ignored by the UEFA for its Under-17 Championship. It is only internally that worries are articulated and exceptional tension can be felt in some cases. Football is part of a neo-liberal world which does not care for losers but rewards winners disproportionally. Again this might be a reminder of EU policies reaching out even beyond EU borders to the rest of Europe.

While some of the underlying messages and values of the tournament were strongly European, the event itself unfolded mostly on the regional level. It spans between regional awareness and involvement of European functional elites but sparks only low interest nationally or in Europe as a whole. This is reflected in the stakes invested in the tournament. The DFB sponsored the Under-17 Championship as a means of education as well as a method of subsidizing the struggling sport of East German football. Comparisons to the EURO are therefore invalid since the Under-17 Championship is not a sports mega-event. It is nevertheless European, because of its name, its meaning in the world of sports and for a limited albeit important group of people. There are after all many other similar tournaments organized by UEFA below the all-attention-drawing EURO.

Notes

1. Tagsold, Spiel-Feld; Tagsold, 'Was wir jetzt noch'.
2. MacAloon, The Ethnographic Imperative.
3. Giulianotti, Football, 170.
4. The National Center for Political Education was founded in 1952 and has since published popular books and brochures on political topics free or at a low price. Additionally, it has launched educational programs and organized educational events.

5. PMP, Studies on Education and Sport, 6.
6. Fanizadeh and Pinter, Rassismus und Antirassismus im goldenen Zeitalter, 268f.
7. The most severe incidence of anti-Semitic chanting against Jena took place in the opening match of the third league's 2008 season against Erfurt, the main regional rival. See Glindmeier, '"Juden Jena"-Rufe'.
8. Ceylanoglu, Linksextremismus in Deutschland heute, 143.
9. The homepage of the ministry gives 85 hits for 'Fremdenfeindlichkeit' while mentioning 'Antirassismus' only 19 times, usually described as a term used by extreme leftists.
10. PMP, Studies on Education and Sport, 8.
11. Harscoët, '"Tu Seras Pelé, Maradona, Zidane"'.
12. Giulianotti, Football, 114f.
13. Parker, 'Training for Glory'.
14. Zimbalist, Unpaid Professionals.
15. The situation of the young football players in Europe is probably better than those of their colleagues in the USA. Football is most likely not the only chance to earn a decent living, as suspected by the black male youth of inner city high schools; see Zimbalist, Unpaid Professionals, 31. On the other hand, college players can get real compensation for their efforts in earning a bachelor degree – at least if they work very hard and are not impeded by coaches who see learning as a obstacle to the success of their team. Such possible compensation for pursuing a professional career can hardly be seen in Europe if players fail to step into professionalism.
16. Finding and developing talent is a complex task for FAs. A study conducted in Germany pointed out some of the related stereotypes proving that youth recruitment is highly volatile. Since January 1st is used as the date demarcating age cohorts in youth football, date of birth does matter. Young players born in autumn or winter have considerable lower chances of making it onto national teams because their growth is a bit behind that of their peers. After adolescence, these differences equal out and just as many players born in the second half of the year become professional football players as in the first half. See Lamek et al. Der "Relative Age Effect" (Rae).
17. Guttmann, From Ritual to Record, 16.
18. Following Bronislaw Malinowski's description of the Kula exchange, Mauss in The Gift described how gift and reciprocal gifts help to knit tight webs of communication between those involved. The gifts in this context are not judged according to their intrinsic value but for their symbolic meaning. The concept has often been used to describe the goings-on in modern western societies.
19. Sugden and Tomlinson, FIFA and the Contest for World Football,7.
20. PMP, Studies on Education and Sport, 86.

References

Bromberger, C. *Football: La bagatelle la plus sérieuse du monde.* Paris: Bayard Éditions, 1998.

Ceylanoglu, S. 'Linksextremismus in Deutschland heute'. In *Extremismus in Deutschland: Erscheinungsformen und aktuelle Bestandsaufnahme,* ed. by Bundesministerium des Inneren, 136–62. Berlin: Bundesministerium des Inneren 2004.

Fanizadeh, M., and M. Pinter. 'Rassismus und Antirassismus im goldenen Zeitalter des Fußballs'. In *Global Players. Kultur, Ökonomie und Politik des Fußballs,* ed. by M. Fanizadeh, G. Hödl, and W. Manzenreiter, 258–74. Frankfurt: Brandes & Apsel/ Südwind, 2002.

Giulianotti, R. *Football: A Sociology of the Global Game.* Cambridge: Polity Press, 1999.

Glindmeier, M. '"Juden Jena"-Rufe überschatten Thüringen-Derby'. *Spiegel Online.* http://www.spiegel.de/sport/fussball/0,1518,572535,00.html.

Guttmann, A. *From Ritual to Record: the Nature of Modern Sports.* New York: Columbia University Press, 1978.

Harscoët, J. '"Tu seras Pelé, Maradona, Zidane" ou. rien: L'industrie de football et ses centres de formation.' *Le Monde diplomtique,* 2006, June, 24–5.

Lamek, M., C. Dreckmann, K. Görsdorf, and Karsten M. Schimanski. 'Der "Relative Age Effect" (RAE): Neue Hausaufgaben für den Sport'. *Leistungssport* 38 (2008): 4–9.

MacAloon, John J. 'The Ethnographic Imperative in Comparative Olympic Research'. *Sociology of Sport* 9 (1992): 104–32.

Mauss, M. *The Gift: Forms and Functions of Exchange in Archaic Societies.* Glencoe, IL: Free Press, 1954.

Parker, A. 'Training for "Glory", Schooling for "Failure"?: English Professional Football, Traineeship and Educational Provision'. *Journal of Education and Work* 13 (2000): 61–76.

PMB, and Institute of Sport and Leisure Policy, Loughborough University. *Studies on Education and Sport: Sport and Multiculturalism (Lot 3): Final Report.* ed. European Commission DG Education & Culture, 2004.

Sugden, J., and A. Tomlinson. *FIFA and the Contest for World Football: Who Rules the People's Game.* Cambridge: Polity Press, 1998.

Tagsold, C. '"Was wir jetzt noch tun können, ist an sie zu glauben": Ethnographische Skizzen zu den Anhängern der japanischen Nationalmannschaft während der Weltmeisterschaft 2006'. In *Kopfball, Einwurf, Nachspielzeit: Gespräche und Beiträge zur Aktualität und Geschichte des Fußballs,* ed. U. Baumann and D. Dahlmann, 405–14. Essen: Klartext, 2008.

Tagsold, C. *Spiel-Feld: Ethnografie der Fußball-WM 2006.* Konstanz: UVK, 2008.

Zimbalist, A.S. *Unpaid Professionals: Commercialism and Conflict in Big-Time College Sports.* Princeton, NJ: Princeton University Press, 1999.

After the crunch: a new era for the beautiful game in Europe?

Anthony King

Department of Sociology and Philosophy, University of Exeter, UK

In the last two years, the global economy has suffered a major financial crisis which has precipitated a world-wide recession. The 'credit crunch' has been widely seen as the end of the neo-liberal regulatory regime introduced in the 1980s by Ronald Reagan and Margaret Thatcher and a return to the Keynesian management of the immediate post-War period. There is a wide consensus among scholars writing on football that the organization of the professional game has paralleled wider regulatory regimes. Accordingly, during the 1990s, professional football in Europe was organized on a neo-liberal, transnational basis in which economic and playing power congregated among a group of super clubs. Following the credit crunch, it seems likely that a new regulatory regime will appear in football. On the basis of current debates and trends, this article explores the character of the emergent political economy of football. Against the sometimes self-interested claims of administrators like Michel Platini or Sepp Blatter, it is proposed that football is not re-entering an era of Keynesian management by national and international federations. Super-clubs will remain a dominant force in European football. Rather, the new era might be characterized as one of 'regulated transnationalism'. The major clubs and their transnational interconnections will remain central features of the new era but their activities will be monitored and controlled by a regulatory complex consisting of national and international federations, European institutions, national governments and the clubs themselves. Finally, the article explores how fan cultures are likely to change in the coming decade in the light of the new regulatory regime.

Introduction: football and the credit crunch

In a speech to the European Parliament on 17 February 2009, Michel Platini drew a pessimistic parallel between football and the current financial crisis; 'European clubs are telling [UEFA] that our system is in danger of financially imploding in the medium term'.[1] Platini's concerns have been demonstrated by recent events at Manchester United. In 2008 AIG, the financial security company, recorded the greatest losses in financial history, \$61.7bn (£44.1bn), in the last quarter of that year. In February 2009, AIG announced its collapse and was put into receivership; it was, up to this date, the most serious casualty of the credit crisis and had an immediate impact on football. In 2005, Manchester United signed a record four-year shirt-sponsorship deal with AIG worth £56.6m but, on 21 January 2009, AIG confirmed that it would not be renewing its contract with the club. Indeed, the Serious Fraud Office is currently investigating the contract with further potential damage for the club.

The collapse of AIG has serious implications for Manchester United. The club had wage bills of £92m and, following the Glazer takeover in 2005, has debts of ~ £605m. It does not seem unlikely that the decline in shirt-sponsorship will be matched by declining merchandising, gate and television revenue in the near-term future. At this point, Manchester United's wage bill and debt begin to look potentially dangerous for the club. Like the financial institutions that precipitated the crisis, in the near future, Manchester United might find itself trading on the basis of credit which it does not have. Its wage bills and debt may vastly exceed its capital. If creditors demand repayment, Manchester United would be in serious difficulty and would have to release many of it players in order to reduce wage costs. Manchester United is not alone. Other major clubs in Europe seem equally exposed and the kind of implosion which Platini has envisaged seems entirely conceivably. Indeed, in the 2007 season, Leeds United collapsed financially when it was unable to pay the interest on its loans and went into receivership. Southampton is currently in the process of a financial collapse. It seems clear that, at the end of the first decade of the twenty-first century, football was entering a period of crisis out of which a new era of regulation is likely to emerge.

The regulation of football in the twentieth century

There is general consensus within the sociology of football today on the development of European football.[2] European football has gone through three regulatory phases since the end of World War II. From the 1950s to the early 1970s, competition between European football clubs was organized by sovereign national federations controlling, for the most part, autonomous national player markets, coordinated internationally by UEFA. This system coincided with the success of the initial phase of European integration after the Treaty of Rome in 1957 and, based on national leagues whose interactions were administered by a supranational authority, was compatible with the international political structure of Europe at this time. This was the era of affluent, Fordist football under a Keynesian paradigm of national control and limited markets. In 1970, the early optimism of the international era began to collapse in the face of declining playing standards, corruption, foul play and hooliganism; football suffered its own Eurosclerosis. This crisis reached its nadir in 1985 with the deaths of 39 Juventus fans in the European Cup Final in the Heysel Stadium in Brussels.

After the crisis of the 1970s and 1980s, football has been transformed in the last two decades into a post-Fordist, deregulated and transnational ritual. The process of marketization, primarily in the form of the influx of television revenue and the Bosman ruling, has precipitated the concentration of economic and playing power in a network of European 'super' clubs which now compromise the authority and autonomy of national leagues, federations and UEFA. In the early part of this decade, this transnational regime, represented most clearly in the Champions League, seemed to have stabilized. A political settlement was broadly agreed between the national federations, UEFA, the 'super' clubs, television and sponsoring interests and the European Commission about the status of the major clubs and the format of competitions. The credit crunch seems to signify the end of this transnational regime. It is possible that in the immediate future, financial instability will demand a reform of European football and, in particular, a new system of regulation. It seems likely that in the near future a new hierarchy may appear in European football.

The new regulation of football

The current financial crisis has been widely interpreted by commentators as the definitive end of the free-market period of globalized capitalism, originally promoted by Ronald Reagan and Margaret Thatcher in the 1980s. Accordingly, the collapse of the financial system has encouraged a renewed interest in the mid-twentieth century system of economic regulation. After almost three decades of disfavour, Keynesianism has once again become extremely attractive to governments, commentators and bankers themselves. As Joseph Stiglitz has declared:

> We are all Keynesians now. Even the right in the United States has joined the Keynesian camp with unbridled enthusiasm and on a scale that at one time would have been truly unimaginable. For those of us who claimed some connection to the Keynesian tradition, this is a moment of triumph, after having been left in the wilderness, almost shunned, for more than three decades. At one level, what is happening now is a triumph of reason and evidence over ideology and interests.[3]

Today, governments have created rescue packages for banks and mortgage lenders; they have recognized that they must protect the commanding heights of finance-led service-oriented economies. The nationalization of prominent financial institutions has followed. Close state control of relatively discrete national economies seems to be becoming the norm once again.

In football, a similar move to Keynesianism seems to be evident. UEFA President Michel Platini has been a decisive figure here, explicitly demanding new forms of regulation: 'In football, as in the economy in general, the market is incapable of correcting its own excesses, and it was not the UEFA president who said so, it was Barack Obama …'[4] Platini has been particularly critical of English clubs, especially Manchester United, Liverpool and Chelsea which have all posted large debts. Platini wants to curb the rapaciousness of clubs through the authority of UEFA and the national federations;[5] 'We are looking at the idea of limiting a club's expenditure on staff – salary and transfer fees combined – to an as yet undecided percentage of its direct and indirect sporting revenue'. Platini wants to introduce a system of regulation in which club finances and debts are monitored centrally, while wages and spending are limited in proportion to club income. Platini's calls for a managed, restricted economy in football recall both current reforms in the financial sector, but also reference back to the managed 'Keynesian' system of football administration which predominated in Europe in the 1950s and 1960s. At that time, the economic and playing activities of clubs, including the transfer and retention systems, were controlled by the federations. In March 2009, Platini renewed his calls for regulation, proposing that the major clubs are taxed, and their excess revenue redistributed to poorer clubs. For UEFA, this policy has a number of advantages. Decisively, it would potentially equalize disparities in play which have now become extreme in most European leagues. Olympique Lyonnais won France's Ligue 1 seven times successively from 2002 to 2008, while Porto has won Portugal's Liga six times in the same period.[6] The English Premier League is now dominated by four clubs who have consistently monopolized Champions League places over the last decade. In addition, it would introduce financial discipline into the sport and limit the spending of major clubs. UEFA officers have visited Major League Baseball in the USA to investigate how redistributive models operate in those competitions.

Since 2008, FIFA's president, Joseph Blatter, has also made several interventions into the question of regulation in the light of the current crisis. His appeal for some form of regulation of the clubs has focused on a different issue to Platini; the restriction of foreign players. In December 1995, the European Court of Justice made its now famous decision on Bosman. Although primarily focused on the transfer system, the most important element of the Bosman decision was its elimination of internal borders within the EU player market. In a single stroke, a unified EU player market was created. It has transformed the geography of European football.

Blatter has identified the borderless post-Bosman EU as a fundamental problem in world football. It has accentuated long-standing European domination and the promotion of club football, especially the Champions League, to the detriment national teams, international football and the World Cup. In place of a free market for EU players, Blatter proposed a 6+5 rule. In any club side, six players must be native with a restriction of a further five foreigners, from either EU or non-EU countries. Blatter referenced the Premier League's quarter-final Champions League ties in February 2009 when Liverpool, Chelsea, Manchester United and Arsenal fielded only nine English players in total, winning three of their games and drawing the other: 'Do you think that is the right thing? We are at a crossroads in FIFA. We have to intervene in football to make sure that club football is identified if not locally then nationally, that you have the majority of players from the same country in a team'. Blatter commissioned a report from the Institute for European Affairs (INEA). The Düsseldorf-based think tank claimed that there was no conflict with European law, the 6+5 rule was, it claimed, 'legally not directly linked to the nationality of the footballer but applies to the qualification for the national team'.[7] As the president of FIFA, whose prime competition is the World Cup, Blatter's advocacy of the international football is understandable. Indeed, Platini has himself expressed similar concerns.[8] He too wants to limit economic investment in football, restricting the ownership market, in order to protect the connection between clubs, national leagues and the nation. In effect, both UEFA and FIFA want minimally to reaffirm the validity of national borders in European football, separating markets and reversing the process of radical transnationalization which followed the Bosman decision. For them, against the liberal transnational regime of the last decade, regulation with a re-emphasis on the nation as a fundamental organizing principle is a means of stabilizing football financially. (UEFA's own '2+2' home player ruling are much less restrictive and are favoured by the clubs; see below.)

Twenty-first century regulation: the enduring influence of the big clubs

The proposed return to Keynesian management in football would seem to suggest a rebalancing of authorities and, decisively, a re-subordination of the clubs. Indeed, this is precisely what Platini's proposal of a wage cap and restricted spending implies: he wants UEFA and national federations to control clubs by restricting the transfer market and their participation in it. It is obvious from his comments that Platini's main objective is the 'super' clubs, whose power and influence he wants to curb. He is correct. A significant revision of the regime of regulation and, certainly, any return to the kind of international, regulated system of the post-War era would require a fundamental alteration in the current status of professional football clubs and especially the 'super' clubs.

There seems to be some evidence that the decline in the authority of clubs, which Platini would desire, has indeed occurred. In debates about a proposed European Superleague, a nascent lobby group of major clubs called the 'G14' crystallized in

November 1998 and established itself on a legal basis with offices in Brussels. It eventually expanded to 18 clubs and played a role in influencing a number of UEFA decisions. In 2007, the G14 were considering expanding yet again, adding a further 16 clubs to their complement. At this point, the G14 engaged in a long-standing debate with UEFA and the national federations over compensation for the release of players for national duties. International players had always congregated at the biggest clubs in Europe but since Bosman this concentration of international talent in 15 or, at most, 20 super clubs was particularly evident. Consequently, because almost the entire squad of the post-Bosman super clubs were internationals (before the 1990s, major clubs typically had three to five international players), the pressure of national duty was significant. Not only did it take numerous key players away from training, but national games always involved the risk of injury. In January 2008, the dispute was finally resolved. Federations would compensate the clubs for using their players.[9]

The deal was not without its costs for the major clubs. In return for this payment, the G14 agreed to disband itself as an autonomous body outside of UEFA. A new European Clubs Association (ECA), consisting of 103 clubs representing all the leagues in UEFA, was instituted. Blatter celebrated the new accord because he assumed that the incorporation of the clubs into UEFA denoted their final subordination; 'Something very special has happened today. The clubs, which are the basic cells of our game and fundamental to its thriving, are at last to become a part of the pyramidal football organisation'.[10] For him, the clubs were safely incorporated into (and subordinated by) a hierarchy. The disbanding of the G14 seemed to provide clear evidence of the emergence of the neo-Keynesian regime in football when the international federations, UEFA and FIFA, have reasserted the primacy they had enjoyed over clubs in the mid-twentieth century.

In reality, this nascent regime may involve no such return. Although the disbanding of the G14 and the incorporation of the biggest clubs into a larger UEFA association has been represented as a victory for Platini, in particular, the development of the European Club Association cannot be so easily viewed as the elimination of clubs from European football politics. On the contrary, the absorption into UEFA offers several benefits for the members of the G14. The G14 had worked very effectively for the major clubs in disputes about the Champions League in 1998. However, since that time, it had become a less useful vehicle for mobilization. Although the G14 were able to lobby at the European level as a transnational interest groups, their elite membership was disadvantageous to them at certain points. Necessarily, they excluded many important clubs of national and indeed international stature. This exclusiveness undermined the legitimacy of the G14 as the self-proclaimed representative of club football. It was easy for UEFA to portray the G14 as an arrogant and greedy elite. Indeed, the G14 recognized their vulnerability in this area, which seems to have become the reason why the group planned to expand so far beyond its original constitution to include 32 clubs. However, once at the unwieldy proposed size of 32, the organizational advantages of elitism – the easy coordination of interests – were gone. Yet the G14 still suffered from a lack of legitimacy; it remained exclusive. Consequently, although apparently a loss of authority, the willingness of the G14 to disband may reflect not their obeisance to UEFA, but the fact that these clubs now see the ECA as a better vehicle for advancing their distinctive interests.

It is notable that G14 clubs are over-represented on the ECA. The ECA consists of a group of 17 clubs, defined as founding members, and a further 86 clubs. The founding members include eight of the original G14 clubs (Manchester United, Bayern

Munich, Juventus, AC Milan, Ajax, Porto, Real Madrid and Barcelona) and a further two clubs from the expanded group (Olympique Lyonnais and Valencia). All the other G14 clubs, except for the always less-influential Marseille and Paris St Germain, are normal members of the ECA. In addition to the founding members, the ECA consists of a transitional board, on which there is heavy G14 representation. It is chaired by Karl-Heinz Rummenige (Bayern Munich), Joan Laporta (Barcelona), John McClelland (Rangers), Umberto Gandini (Milan), Peter Kenyon (Chelsea), Maarten Fontein (Ajax) and Jean-Michel Aulas (Olympique Lyonnais); five of seven members represent major, former G14 clubs. It seems almost certain, given the over-representation of the G14, especially at the upper levels of the ECA, that the super clubs will have a disproportionate impact over policy decisions and the regulation of the game. Illustrating the enduring authority of the G14, at its first meeting in 2009, the ECA rejected FIFA's 6+5 rule in favour of UEFA's proposed quota system. When it started – as the so-called 2+2 or 'home-grown-players' rule – clubs' 25-man squads needed to include at least two players trained by that club for at least three years between the age of 15 and 21, plus two more trained within the same national association. By 2008/09, UEFA's rule for UEFA competitions will be 4+4. Crucially, however, these rules are not based on nationality. If Arsenal, for example, recruit Spanish youngsters and train them, they are 'home-reared' for UEFA purposes. Because the European Commission has already declared their objection to the proposal as inconsistent with EU Law, it seems almost certain that the major clubs on the ECA will defeat Blatter on this issue. The change is important. Neither Blatter's predecessors at FIFA nor Platini's at UEFA would have considered deferring to clubs. Yet, for Blatter, this representation at UEFA itself, independently of the national federations, is now normalized. He accepts that the clubs have an unignorable place in the administration of the European game.

Even more strikingly, Blatter and UEFA officials have had to accept that the directors and managers of major European clubs are now free to criticize them publicly. In the summer of 2008, Cristiano Ronaldo, still under contract with Manchester United, was approached – illegally – by Real Madrid. Manchester United complained but Real Madrid continued to pursue him. Eventually, Ronaldo was obliged to abide by his contract at Manchester United, where he remained until end of the 2008/09 season. Intervening in this dispute, Blatter declared that he thought that Ronaldo should be free to go to Real Madrid and that holding him at Manchester United against his wishes was tantamount to 'slavery'. This claim engendered a furious reaction from many notables including Alex Ferguson. Comparing Blatter with an African despot, Ferguson stated that: 'I think that Sepp Blatter is in danger or has reached a point now where he is being mocked within the game … from a position of great power, he has uttered so many ridiculous statements that he is in danger of seriously damaging his credibility'.[11] Ferguson's comments are a typical example of his acerbic Glaswegian character, but they demonstrate a wider point: the unignorable status and influence of the clubs at the international level. Ferguson was able to command sufficient media interest that he could broadcast his condemnation of Blatter globally and, just as significantly, receive no censure for it. He displayed quite openly the power of the biggest clubs over FIFA. The contrast with Ferguson's predecessor in the 1950s and 1960s, Matt Busby, who had taken Manchester United into Europe against the Football League's ruling, was instructive. Busby defied the English Football League once, taking Manchester United into the European Cup against their advice, but neither he nor his peers engaged in the consistent and *ad hominem* critique of football authorities which has now become normal. The enduring power of the major clubs is likely to have a decisive influence of the regulatory regime which is currently emerging.

The financial power of the biggest clubs

There are a number of reasons for the enduring prominence of the major clubs in the new regulatory era. As the concentration of playing and economic power has demonstrated, the biggest European clubs have been relatively advantaged – or alternatively least disadvantaged – by increasing economic competition in the game. These clubs were best able to cope with increased wages in the 1990s. It seems plausible to suggest that their relative advantage due to their size will continue into and beyond the recession. The credit crunch may indeed affect football very badly in 2010 and 2011 but it is likely that the biggest clubs will be best positioned to endure the current problems. They remain the most attractive clubs for fans, television and sponsors alike. Consequently, the absolutely larger debts of the big clubs are likely to be relatively smaller in relation to their turnover than the debts of small clubs. The AIG episode at Manchester United seems to suggest this relative advantage. With the collapse of AIG, Manchester United lost a record shirt-sponsorship deal. Manchester United were confident that they would be able to find new sponsors since a number of companies, including an Indian corporation, Sahara, were offering attractive terms. In the event, on 3 June 2009, Manchester United confirmed a new four year sponsorship deal with AON, the American financial giant, worth £80m. The deal is the largest in global football and represents an improved financial package for the club. With a recorded turnover of €250m in 2008, Manchester United has very substantial assets to mitigate against the current financial crisis. By contrast, it seems certain that other smaller and less globally popular clubs, as equally exposed financially, will suffer even more in the coming recession. Declines in sponsorship, television and gate receipt revenue are likely to be proportionately worse at the small clubs. As Dan Jones of Deloitte Touche Tohmatsu noted: 'It's a paradox that the top 20 includes a couple of clubs that are having some financial difficulty – but their income is amongst the highest in the world, so the source of any financial difficulty doesn't lie with the revenues they earn."[12] In fact, the situation is not paradoxical. Precisely because they are the richest clubs with the largest turnover, the super clubs are able and allowed to sustain the highest levels of debt. They are relatively advantaged simply by their scale and importance to the game; much like the major banks whose collapse has had to be prevented by governments.

Current patterns of ownership seem to further benefit the major clubs. In the 1990s, a number of English clubs issued shares and floated themselves on the stock market as a means of increasing their capitalization in order, in many cases, to rebuild their stadiums. Manchester United was the most successful club to adopt this strategy. Until the early 2000s, European clubs were interested by the English experiment and were exploring the possibility of going public themselves. In the end, outside England, only a few major European clubs, including Borussia Dortmund, Porto and Ajax floated. More significantly, what in the early part of the decade appeared to be a business strategy that would be widely adopted, in fact, turned out to be a very short-term phase in England and Scotland. In the last five years, all the major English clubs which had gone public have been re-privatized as the value of their shares declined. Buying up majority stakes in the clubs from existing directors, Roman Abramovich bought Chelsea in 2003, Malcolm Glazer took control of Manchester United in 2005, George Gillett and

Tom Hicks bought Liverpool in 2007 (and there have been further ownership discussions with Kuwaiti business groups and other interested parties) and Arsenal is now part-owned by Alisher Usmanov. Many of these takeovers were controversial. There was some intense dispute about the Glazer takeover with elements within Manchester United's fan base fundamentally opposed to the purchase. They rightly saw the takeover as a loss of control over the club which, to a small degree, they had been able to exercise through their ownership of shares. However, in terms of the financial stability of the clubs, these takeovers may have been timely. As in the admittedly distinctive case of Chelsea, the takeovers have injected new levels of capital into the club, raising their status. Abramovich's money elevated Chelsea from an important national club into an international player. More specifically, they removed clubs from the volatility of the financial markets before the credit crunch and the subsequence share crashes in 2009. They have protected the clubs from the economic crisis.

In effect, the provincial businessmen who were typically the patrons of European football throughout the nineteenth and twentieth centuries have been replaced by global entrepreneurs. Only English football has been open to genuinely foreign investors but, across Europe, entrepreneurs of international stature have invested in clubs. Like their forebears, economic motives are not irrelevant (and often they are important), but in many cases, profit-making has not been the primary motivation for club ownership. The new owners seek status, publicity, political legitimization or business connections to further their activities in other areas. Of course, the entrepreneurs who are becoming a more important feature of European football have themselves been attracted not necessarily to the objectively most profitable clubs, but to those with the highest status; the super clubs. Consequently, since it is in their interests to sustain the clubs, it is likely that they will accept the liability for debts which may accrue during the current recession at the major clubs. Malcolm Glazer's takeover of Manchester United is a case in point. Opponents of Glazer argued that, in order to service the debt he had accrued to buy Manchester United, he would asset-strip the club, selling its best players. This was a manifestly irrational policy, whose likelihood was always remote. Unsurprisingly, no such policy has unfolded. On the contrary, the Glazers have invested in the club and have presided over one of its most successful periods, culminating in Champions League and Premier League victories in 2008 and a near 'quadruple'[13] in 2009. A similar pattern of investment, protection and patronage is observable elsewhere not only in England, but especially in Spain and Italy, where the arrangement is one of long-standing. Smaller clubs have also found entrepreneurs to invest in them but, here again, the largest clubs are advantaged. Precisely because of their status they have tended to attract particularly powerful financial and political backing.

Indeed, the enduring power of the biggest clubs rests not just on money, but on reputation. In 2009, Manchester City's attempt to hire the Milan player Kaka unraveled at the last moment, apparently when Kaka realized the relatively low status of the club. The failed bid for Kaka demonstrates the advantaged position of the biggest clubs, which actually transcends pure monetary value and, therefore, protects them from financial collapse. The popularity, history and success of the biggest clubs assure them an enduring place in European football, almost irrespective of their immediate economic predicament. Indeed, the deregulations of the 1990s have accentuated this situation, promoting major clubs to such a position of dominance that it would be very difficult to dislodge them. Whatever their actual economic value, and as Platini has himself emphasized even the largest clubs have a turnover of the size equivalent only to a local supermarket, this popularity acts as a gold standard attracting investors and sponsors, no matter how many other financial institutions collapse.

One of the defining features of the deregulated era of the 1990s was the concentration of economic and playing power at the biggest clubs. Relatively, the processes of concentration are likely to be exacerbated and accelerated by the credit crunch. The transnational geography which began to crystallize from 1990 is likely to be affirmed and consolidated with the largest clubs, now officially part of UEFA, in a relatively better financial and political position. These clubs are likely to continue to dominate European and domestic competitions and therefore sustain and indeed increase their popular appeal and public profile. Indeed, the recent transfer of Ronaldo to Real Madrid seems to prove precisely this point. Having failed to attract Ronaldo in 2008, Real Madrid succeeded eventually in luring him from Manchester United for a £80m transfer fee. The recording-breaking fee and the wages Ronaldo will earn at Real Madrid indicate that the super clubs, buttressed by the patronage of entrepreneurs and sponsors, are very substantially isolated from the wider economic down-turn. Indeed, even though Manchester United was relatively modest during the 2009 close season, the club spent £23m on players while making a sustained, but ultimately unsuccessful, bid for Frank Ribery for a rumoured £63m. The super clubs do not seem to have been unduly affected by the new financial austerity.

In addition, with the creation of the ECA, these major clubs are likely to play a decisive role in the regulation of the game. For example, the only plausible means by which a wage cap would be introduced into European football is if the major clubs, who are the drivers of wage levels, agree to limit their expenditure and institute ways of assuring cooperation with this rule. This regulation could not really be described as a return to the international regime of the post-War era of close control of national leagues. Transnational networks and transfers are too developed and the federations and UEFA no longer have the authority to administer the clubs from above. However, there could be limited transnational regulation of clubs. At the national level, clubs and their federations may collaborate with each other to ensure stability (as they are over television revenue and player quotas), coordinated at the transnational level by the ECA and UEFA. Major European clubs, as part of a transnational network, are likely to constitute a critical nexus in this new geography, but interactions and competition between them may be mediated by collective agreements between multiple actors; the clubs themselves, UEFA, the federations, the European Commission, national governments, all heavily influenced by the media and sponsors. Football is likely to be regulated by a multipolar arrangement of differing and convergent interest groups. Regulation is likely to be more intrusive than it has been, especially since 1995, but a return to a Keynesian international order is unlikely. It might be more accurate to argue that European football is entering an era of *regulated transnationalism*. In short, the future would not seem to be a return to the organizational regime of the 1950s in which sovereign federations controlled their own leagues and the clubs within them. Rather, the new regime is likely to involve a complex organizational structure in which UEFA coordinates the regulation of football through negotiations with complicit clubs and federations and the institutions of European Union. In this institutional complex, the clubs are no longer subordinate but at least as important a party as the federations and UEFA themselves. However, the fundamental features of the transnational geography which emerged in the 1990s will not be reversed. Borders will remain porous in football and the transnational links between the super clubs, as concentrations of playing and economic power, are likely to remain a defining feature of the new era.

Conclusion

Football has always reflected and been influenced by wider historical conditions. The credit crunch signals the end of one kind of 'disorganized' capitalism. The recession itself and the new regulatory regime, which emerges from it, are likely to have a significant impact on European football in the early twenty-first century. However, despite the frequent appeals to Keynes as the father of regulation, it is unlikely that either the wider economy or football will return to heavy nationalist economic management. Governments are likely to control the financial sector in coordination with other polities. Similarly in European football, UEFA in close cooperation with the major clubs, whose authority has now been institutionalized, is likely to introduce some relatively modest reforms around salaries and expenditure. A wage cap, of some kind, is the most likely development, not least because it is the easiest to administer and monitor. There will be no end of the EU market for players. Such regulation will be important but it will not fundamentally alter the trajectory of concentration and transnationalization which has been evident in European football since the 1990s. European club football and the network of major clubs – rather than football in European member states – are likely to develop and strengthen throughout the recession and into any future recovery.

Where does this leave the fans? *The European Ritual* described how fan solidarities have themselves reflected regulatory developments. As the power localized at a selected group of elite clubs, so did the fans begin to mobilize themselves on an increasingly localized basis at both club and national level. Urban identities often inflected with explicitly racist ideology, reflecting the new conditions in local areas, appeared among ultra groups across Europe. Concepts of national identity were similarly renegotiated and as unified nations states have fragmented in Europe since the 1990s, localized identities (English, Walloon, Belgian, Croatian, Bosnian, Serbian, Dutch and Flemish) began to be invested with increasing significance. It seems almost inevitable that the social effects of the recession will find expression in stadiums across Europe. In January 2009, there were major protests by British workers against the use of Italian IREM construction labourers who were being employed in North Killinghome, Lincolnshire, England on a short-term contract by the oil company Total to work on an oil-refinery. In the light of the recession, British unions claimed that these jobs should in the first instance go to local workers. Others were less diplomatic. Placards by some protesters read: 'British jobs for British workers'. Lazio fans have already used the stadium as a venue for protesting about local immigrants and such discontent could spread and deepen. It seems likely that these protests will be articulated at football games, as urban populations congregate to express their concerns. There were significant fears that a recent friendly between England and Spain in Madrid would be marred by racist abuse by Spanish fans. It seems highly likely that racism – not only against ethnic minorities but against migrant workers much more generally – might become a common feature of European football, especially in those areas heavily exposed to the recession. Indeed, the emphasis of Blatter and Platini on national and local autonomy may even promote this kind of xenophobia. In this, European football may be returning not to the Keynesian era of stability – the 1950s – but, on the contrary, to an era reminiscent of the collapse of that consensus in the

1970s. By the early 1970s, Gabriel Hanot, the architect of the European Cup, despaired at what he had created when he saw a noble concept perverted by bribery, foul play and violence. It is not inconceivable that European football in its immediate future will return to its ugly past. There may be increasing political protest, disorder and violence among the fans. At the end of his book, David Goldblatt, perhaps optimistically, suggests that 'We must be bold enough to think we have the guile, the heart and the wit to bring it [football/the world] under control'.[14] Perhaps with sensitive, inclusive regulation, football might be able to address and even transcend the very grievances and fears which may deface it in the coming years. The regulation of football in the twentieth century would suggest that optimism about the future would be unwise, however.

The new regulation of football in the coming decade has some potentially important implications for football but developments within the game are likely to have a much wider relevance to Europe more generally. Scholars have consistently sought to demonstrate the close connection between European football and the wider political and social order. Football is a distinctive activity. However, it represents an important area of cultural life in which millions of Europeans participate. The transformation of football is in and of itself, therefore, a transformation of Europe. Reformations of the game are *ipso facto* European reformations. The new regulatory regime which seems to be appearing in football is evidence of a new concept of Europe within this limited sphere. The free-market, liberal Europe of the 1990s is being replaced by a more-regulated space in which localized tensions are likely to be higher. However, football is not simply one sphere of activity in Europe. As a public ritual, it is embedded into wider institutional and political realities of which it is a conscious reflection and manifestation. It is an arena in which wider political forces and social understandings are condensed and magnified. It is one of the stories 'we tell ourselves about ourselves'.[15] Consequently, football may be able to provide a perspicuous view of Europe's future. It is perhaps not too implausible to suggest that this future will be characterized by complex, transnational regulation between governments, the European Council, Commission and Parliament and multinational capital as they manage social tensions within states and regions, heightened by the current crisis.

Notes

1. Nick Harris, 'Platini warns of "impending implosion"', *The Independent* February 19, 2009, 54.
2. King, *End of the Terraces*; King, *The European Ritual*; Maguire, *Global Sport*; Horne and Manzenreiter, *Sports Mega-Events*; Giulianotti, *Football*; Giulianotti and Robertson, *Globalization of Football*; Goldblatt, *The Ball is Round.*
3. Joseph Stiglitz, 'The Triumphant Return of John Maynard Keynes', Project Syndicate December 2008.
4. See Note 1.
5. David Charter,'Platini uses Kaka bid to push for wage cap', *The Times* February19, 2009, 83.
6. Roger Blitz, 'Richest football clubs could be forced to pay tax on star players' *Financial Times* March 26, 2009, 1.
7. Kevin Eason, 'Blatter steps up campaign as report says quota is legal', *The Times* February 27, 2009, 92.
8. 'How Platini is Writing UEFA's Obituary', *Daily News* October 9, 2008.
9. Cherie Getchell, 'G14 disbands as Platini records 2nd victory', *SoccerLens* January 17, 2008.

10. Martyn Ziegler, 'G14 axed after deal with FIFA and UEFA', *Birmingham Post* January 16, 2008, 31.
11. 'Ferguson rekindles feuds with Blatter and Real', *Morning Star* October 29, 2008. More significantly, Blatter openly contradicted himself. In January 2008 he had supported the Court of Arbitration for Sport's ruling on Andrew Webster's breach of contract with Heart of Midlothian, which stipulated that Webster had to pay the Scottish club £150,000 in compensation. Yet, in the Ronaldo case, he derided any suggestion that players should be made to abide by contracts which they had signed freely (cf. Brian Moore, 'Sepp Blatter, is this really slavery?', *The Daily Telegraph* July 22, 2008). Blatter's position seems to be further weakened by a focus on the Premier League's current dominance where he seems to arbitrarily favour the activities of other clubs especially in Spain and Italy over the major English clubs.
12. 'The Deloitte Rich List – the world's top football clubs', http://www.deloitte.com/dtt/press_release/0,1014,cid%253D41013,00.html
13. Manchester United won the Premier League and the League Cup, reached the final of the Champions League and were knocked out in the semi-final of the FA Cup.
14. Goldblatt, *The Ball is Round*, 911.
15. Geertz, 'Deep Play', 448.

References

Geertz, C. 'Deep play: notes on the Balinese cockfight'. In *The Interpretation of Cultures,* ed. C. Geertz, 412–53. New York: Basic Books, 1973.

Giulianotti, R. *Football: A Sociology of the Global Game.* Cambridge: Polity, 1999.

Giulianotti, R., and R. Robertson. 'The Globalization of Football: A Study in the Glocalization of the "Serious Life".' *British Journal of Sociology* 55, 4 (2004): 545–68.

Goldblatt, D. *The Ball is Round.* Harmondsworth: Penguin, 2007.

Horne, J., and W. Manzenreiter, eds. *Sports Mega-Events. Social Scientific Analyses of a Global Phenomenon.* Oxford: Blackwell, 2006.

King, A. *The End of the Terraces: The Transformation of English Football in the 1990s.* London: Leicester University Press, 1998.

King, A. *The European Ritual.* Aldershot: Ashgate, 2003.

Maguire, J. *Global Sport.* Cambridge: Polity, 1999.

Index